Social Policy and Development Studies in East Asia

Series Editors

Joshua Mok, Lingnan University, Hong Kong

Jiwei Qian, National University of Singapore, Singapore, Singapore

"Social Policy and Development Studies in East Asia" aims to provide a platform for academics, researchers and policy analysts to contribute their reflections and analysis of how rapid social, economic, cultural, political and even political economy changes would have affected the formulation, implementation and evaluation of social policy responses in handling/managing rapid changes and risk management issues confronting East Asian governments and societies.

More information about this series at
https://link.springer.com/bookseries/15726

Ka Ho Mok
Editor

Cities and Social Governance Reforms

Greater Bay Area Development Experiences

palgrave
macmillan

Editor
Ka Ho Mok
Institute of Policy Studies
Lingnan University
Hong Kong, China

Social Policy and Development Studies in East Asia
ISBN 978-981-16-9533-9 ISBN 978-981-16-9531-5 (eBook)
https://doi.org/10.1007/978-981-16-9531-5

This Palgrave Macmillan imprint is published by the registered company Springer Nature Singapore Pte Ltd.
The registered company address is: 152 Beach Road, #21-01/04 Gateway East, Singapore 189721, Singapore

Contents

1 **Cities and Social Governance Reforms: China's Greater Bay Development Experiences** 1
Ka Ho Mok

2 **Policy Background for the Greater Bay Area Development in South China** 17
Genghua Huang and Ka Wai Tam

3 **Greater Bay Area Cities on Mainland China: Perceptions of Hong Kong Residents** 31
Alex Yue Feng Zhu

4 **Competition for Premium Human Resources: Cooperation and Rivalry Between Hong Kong and Shenzhen** 51
Alex Yue Feng Zhu

5 **Understanding Migration into Greater Bay Area Cities in Mainland China as an Investment for Hong Kong Young Adults** 73
Alex Yue Feng Zhu and Ka Ho Mok

6 **Combating the COVID-19 Pandemic and Enhancing Social Integration: Health Coverage Support for Hong Kong Residents in the GBA** 95
Genghua Huang and Zhaiwen Peng

7 **Variations on Contracting Out Social Services in China's Cities: The Case of Beijing, Shanghai and Guangzhou** 109
Chak Kwan Chan and Xue Liu

8 **Contracting Out Social Services and the Development of Non-governmental Organizations in China** 123
Chak Kwan Chan and Xue Liu

9 **Cities and Social Integration: Reimagining China–Africa Relations in the Greater Bay Area** 137
Obert Hodzi and Padmore Adusei Amoah

10 **Managing the Global COVID-19 Crisis: China's Strategies and Greater Bay Area Residents' Responses** 159
Francis Arthur-Holmes and Ka Ho Mok

11 **Cities, Higher Education and GBA Development from Comparative Perspectives** 185
Ka Ho Mok

Index 197

List of Contributors

Padmore Adusei Amoah School of Graduate Studies, Lingnan University, Tuen Mun, Hong Kong SAR, China;
Institute of Policy Studies, Lingnan University, Tuen Mun, Hong Kong SAR, China;
Department of Applied Pychology, Lingnan University, Tuen Mun, Hong Kong SAR, China

Francis Arthur-Holmes Department of Sociology and Social Policy, Lingnan University, Hong Kong, China

Chak Kwan Chan Asia-Pacific Institute of Ageing Studies, Lingnan University, Hong Kong, China

Obert Hodzi Department of Politics, University of Liverpool, Liverpool, UK

Genghua Huang Institute of Policy Studies, Lingnan University, Hong Kong, Hong Kong SAR, China

Xue Liu Asia-Pacific Institute of Ageing Studies, Lingnan University, Tuen Mun, Hong Kong SAR, China

Ka Ho Mok Institute of Policy Studies, Lingnan University, Hong Kong, China

Zhaiwen Peng Research Center for Social Security, Sun Yat-Sen University, Guangzhou, China

Ka Wai Tam School of Graduate Studies, Lingnan University, Hong Kong, Hong Kong SAR, China

Alex Yue Feng Zhu Institute of Policy Studies, Lingnan University, Tuen Mun, Hong Kong SAR, China

List of Figures

Fig. 3.1	Frequency of institutional concerns about mainland GBA cities (*Note* As respondents can choose up to three options, the total frequency exceeds the sample size [N = 1033]. All frequencies reported were weighted by age and gender)	39
Fig. 3.2	Frequency of institutional motivations to migrate to mainland GBA cities listed by respondents (*Note* As respondents can choose up to three options, the total frequency exceeds the sample size [N = 1033]. All frequencies reported were weighted by age and gender)	40
Fig. 3.3	Comparing the latent means of individual concerns about mainland GBA cities of younger and older Hong Kong residents (*Note* N [younger group] = 208; N [older group] = 825. I = intercept of the item. Results are produced after constraining weights and intercepts. For all unstandardized, standardized weights [in parenthesis], and intercepts, $p < 0.001$, *** $p < 0.001$)	41

Fig. 3.4 Comparing latent means of individual concerns about mainland GBA cities of Hong Kong residents with lower and higher educational achievements (*Note* *N* [lower educational achievement] = 626; *N* [higher educational achievement] = 386. I = intercept of the item. Results are produced after constraining weights and intercepts. For all unstandardized, standardized weights [in parenthesis], and intercepts, $p < 0.001$, *** $p < 0.001$) 42
Fig. 3.5 Comparing latent means of individual concerns about mainland GBA cities of professionals and non-professionals (*Note* *N* [professionals] = 286; *N* [non-professionals] = 215. I = intercept of the item. Results are produced after constraining weights and intercepts. For all unstandardized, standardized weights [in parenthesis], and intercepts, $p < 0.001$, *** $p < 0.001$) 43
Fig. 3.6 Different interpretations of individual concerns about mainland GBA cities by professional and non-professional workers (*Note* *N* [professionals] = 286; *N* [non-professionals] = 215. I = intercept of the item. Results of unconstrained model are reported) 44
Fig. 5.1 The distribution of respondents among the four clusters (*N* = 1214) (*Note* The *K*-mean cluster analysis was performed) 86
Fig. 6.1 Number of Hong Kong residents (aged 18 and over) living in mainland China (*Source* C&SD [2009]) 97
Fig. 6.2 Distribution of Hong Kong residents (aged 18 and over) living in the mainland (December 20) (*Source* C&SD [2009]) 98
Fig. 8.1 Annual growth rate of social organizations (2010–2019) (*Source* Statistical bulletin on the development of civil affairs [China], http://www.mca.gov.cn/article/sj/tjgb/) 128
Fig. 9.1 Number of inward international students 2008–2016 (*Source* Ministry of Education [2019], China) 143
Fig. 9.2 Growth rate of inward international students, Africa and other regions (*Source* Ministry of Education [2019], China) 144

Fig. 9.3 Funding sources of international students in China including Africans (*Source* Ministry of Education [2019], China) 144
Fig. 10.1 Evaluation of governments' COVID-19 crisis management by Chinese citizens in the GBA (*Source* The authors) 170

List of Tables

Table 2.1	Major Economic Indicators of cities in the Guangdong–Hong Kong–Macau Greater Bay Area (2020)	23
Table 2.2	Designated role of each city in the GBA	24
Table 2.3	Comparison between Guangdong–Hong Kong–Macao Greater Bay Area and other major bay areas in the world (2020)	25
Table 4.1	Decision rules for comparison	59
Table 4.2	Comparing differences in subjective assessment on the city of residence between younger and older people in Hong Kong and Shenzhen	61
Table 4.3	Comparing the difference of subjective assessment on the city of residence between well-educated and less well-educated people in Hong Kong and Shenzhen	62
Table 4.4	Comparing differences in subjective assessment of the city of residence between higher-income and lower-income people in Hong Kong and in Shenzhen	63
Table 5.1	Descriptive statistics ($N = 1214$)	81
Table 5.2	Mean and standard deviations of the four clusters on the four key variables regarding the GBA	84
Table 5.3	Results of binary logistic regressions ($N = 1214$)	87
Table 6.1	Hong Kong residents in the Guangdong Province (2013–2019)	98
Table 6.2	Descriptive statistics for the variables used in this study	102

Table 6.3	Multiple and logistic models explaining the support for migrant healthcare coverage	104
Table 7.1	Similarities and differences in contracting out social services in the three studied cities	117
Table 9.1	Typologies of African students in China	149
Table 10.1	Details of China's COVID-19 assistance to reaching to Latin American and Caribbean Countries	165
Table 10.2	Details of Chinese government COVID-19 assistance to some Southeast Asian countries	167
Table 10.3	Responses from recipient countries toward China's international health aids	171
Table 11.1	Number of world-leading universities located in different bay areas	190

CHAPTER 1

Cities and Social Governance Reforms: China's Greater Bay Development Experiences

Ka Ho Mok

Introduction

This book critically examines how the Chinese government has proactively engaged the nine cities and two special administrative regions (SARs) in the Greater Bay Area (GBA) in Southern China for deeper collaborations to transform the country from a 'world factory' to become a leading world economy in innovation and entrepreneurialism. Although the majority of existing studies related to China's GBA development have offered economic and technological advancement perspectives, this book focuses on critical reflections on how the call for mega-cities development and deeper regional collaborations in GBA would affect people's livelihood, social integration and urban governance. The central theme of this

K. H. Mok (✉)
Institute of Policy Studies, Lingnan University, Hong Kong, China
e-mail: kahomok@ln.edu.hk

K. H. Mok (ed.), *Cities and Social Governance Reforms*, Social Policy and Development Studies in East Asia,
https://doi.org/10.1007/978-981-16-9531-5_1

book builds around 'cities, social Cohesion and governance'. Additionally, this book uses policy and document analysis, first-hand fieldworks and surveys and intensive interviews with major stakeholders responsible for pushing the GBA development as bases in offering regional perspectives in analyzing such a development, particularly by comparing development experiences within China's different bay economies (e.g. Shanghai and Zhejiang Bay areas and Beijing and Bohai Bay areas). The present volume also draws comparative and international insights from other well-established bay economies (e.g. Tokyo Bay, Florida Bay and New York Bay areas) in analyzing GBA development in China.

Brief Contextual Background for This Book

China's GBA Development Strategy

After realizing the strategic importance of promoting innovation-centric entrepreneurship in transforming China's economy, the Chinese government announced the *Development Plan for the Guangdong–Hong Kong–Macao Greater Bay Area* (GBA Plan, hereafter) in February 2019, outlining the guiding ideology, basic principles, strategic positioning and development objectives for making GBA a globally competitive innovation and technology hub, with a well-built and modern industrial system and quality circle for living, working and traveling (GBA Plan, 2019). The Chinese government refers to other world-leading Bay areas with successful bay economies in positioning the Southern China GBA as a major regional hub for further enhancing the 'Belt and Road Initiative' through strengthening cooperation across nine cities in Guangdong with the two SARs (i.e. Hong Kong and Macau). In going beyond economic incentives for the GBA Plan, the national government is markedly optimistic that people from the two special administrative regions, particularly the Hong Kong people, could use this opportunity to venture in GBA for work and residence (Q. W. Yu, 2019).

Note that the GBA Plan did not start from scratch, but the development blueprint has built upon a series of policy reforms targeting economic and social developments in the Pearl River Delta. In March 2015, the GBA concept was firstly proposed in *The Vision and Action for Promoting the Construction of the Silk Road Economic Belt and the 21st Century Maritime Silk Road*, which was jointly promulgated by the National Development and Reform Commission, Ministry of Foreign

Affairs and Ministry of Commerce (Ministry of Commerce of the People's Republic of China [PRC], 2015). In March 2016, GBA was highlighted in the *13th Five-Year Plan for National Economic and Social Development of the People's Republic of China* (State Council of the PRC, 2016). Since then, the GBA concept has been incorporated in major government documents, such as the *Government Work Report* presented by Premier Li Keqiang in March 2018 and during the 19th National Congress of the Communist Party of China meeting in October 2017. In February 2019, the Central Committee of the Communist Party of China and State Council formally announced the GBA Plan, offering a guide to GBA's development toward 2035 (State Council of the PRC, 2019). The publication of the GBA Plan clearly shows China's regional development approach; this plan also forms part of broad development plans with various regional development projects with strategic importance in other areas in the country (i.e. Jing-Jin-Ji Coordinated Development Initiative, Yangtze River Economic Belt and Yangtze River Delta Regional Integration Strategy) (Xie et al., 2021).[1]

Mega-Cities, Regional Development and Social Cohesion

The major findings of the Asia Mega Cities in 2030 Report suggest that rising stars lie in China, with eight Chinese cities amongst the top ten on the ranking scale adopted by Asian Insights SparX, surpassing the levels in Singapore and Hong Kong. The same report also suggests Shenzhen's wealth will match Singapore; although Hong Kong and Singapore will maintain their lead, growth potential is likely to be slower compared with China's mega-cities. One point that deserves attention is that the preceding data were reported in July 2018 (DBS, 2018). The COVID-19 pandemic since the late 2019 and early 2020 would have changed the preceding mega-city positions. With highly stringent measures, the Chinese government has relatively succeeded in combating the COVID-19 crisis and has become the first country in the world to have gradual but healthy economic recovery. Meanwhile, the Chinese central government,

[1] The author thanks Prof. Ailei Xie for sharing the historical review of the GBA development, and the materials presented in this paper draw reference from him. For other relevant references on the strategic position of GBA in China's regional and global development, see Xu et al. (2019) and Guo (2021).

realizing the strategic importance for enhancing economic competitiveness in the Greater China Region, has initiated a strategic institutional arrangement amongst Guangdong cities, Hong Kong and Macau called the Guangdong–Hong Kong–Macau Bay Area development policy (Hu, 2019). This regional development policy is expected to deepen Chinese economic reform and facilitate considerable openness to the rest of world (Hu, 2019). Hong Kong, Macau and Guangdong cities have started to cooperate in emissions and low-carbon development, tourism development, smart cities and science and technology innovation (Jiang et al., 2018; Zhou et al., 2013). To further facilitate economic partnership, the importance of physical integration characterized by cross-border work and life settlement has emerged (Govada & Rodgers, 2019). Therefore, infrastructure and transportation networks have been improved to enhance regional accessibility and integration (Govada & Rodgers, 2019).

The critical review of the international literature on urbanization and mega-cities has chosen various foci, and the prominent ones are related to infrastructure, spatial information management, planning coordination and implementation and risk assessment and management (Cheeseman & Gramont, 2017; Fuchs et al., 1994; Hui et al., 2018; Lyu et al., 2019; Marshall, 2005). Meanwhile, other research projects have opted to examine the social and human aspects affected by the emergence of mega-cities (i.e. examining well-being, health and quality of life, social and cultural integration related issues) (2022 Foundation, 2019). This volume, which is set against the previously highlighted broad international literature, critically examines how citizens living in the Southern China GBA assess and evaluate challenges/opportunities when contemplating on/engaging in the regional development project. Against the changing socio-economic and broader political economy contexts for GBA development plans, this book critically examines how different local governments in the GBA region adopt policies/measures in coping with diverse development needs and investigates how these governments have tried to manage citizens' expectations and social integration.

Given policy makers' strong conviction to promote regional collaborations and integration, they are extremely interested in how to encourage Hong Kong residents to resettle in Mainland cities for life and work, particularly in GBA cities. This type of migration is labeled 'the flow from Global North to Global South', the nature of which is migration from economically developed regions to economically developing regions. The current literature has yet to investigate this field because this type of migration contributes only a small proportion (6%) to the global trends. In analyzing China's GBA development from different waves of economic transition, namely, rural industrialization, land-centered development and urban tertiarization, such waves have facilitated the development of GBA in Guangdong toward super city regions. New policies and planning, with strong bottom-up initiatives, are needed to cope with such challenges as jurisdictional fragmentation, socio-spatial inequality and environmental externalities (Yeh & Chen, 2019). Although other research related to GBA in Southern China has focused considerably on regional economic development not only for the ongoing process of deepening reforms in the country (Cai, 2021; Li, 2021; Zhao, 2021), we could interpret that GBA Development Initiatives intend to support the national government's global development blueprint (i.e. Belt and Road Initiative) (Li & Kwok, 2019). The present book goes beyond conducting research on the economic development perspective and sets out against the international literature on mega-cities development to critically examine the emergence of city regions in Southern China, specifically analyzing social cohesion- and governance-related issues.

Major Objectives and Research Focus of the Book

This book is conceived against the GBA development context to critically examine how the Chinese government has attempted to promote people-to-people bond through work and studies across nine cities in Guangdong Province and two SARs (i.e. Hong Kong and Macau). The major objectives of this volume are to critically reflect on how rapid urbanization in Southern China's GBA has promoted people mobility across the region and its impact on social integration and people-to-people bonding. Given that the majority of previous publications examining China's GBA developments have primarily focused on economic development and innovation/technological advancements across cities in the Bay Area, this book focuses on ***social governance reforms***, particularly reflecting on policy implications when the emergence of cities in the Bay Area lead to growing complexity in social welfare and urban governance. In this volume, social governance in China refers to 'a systematic project under the leadership of the CPC Central Committee to safeguard the social harmony and stability by coordinating with all parties in the society' (Liu, 2018, p. 1). Specifically, the contributors will discuss how the Chinese government responds to changing circumstances driven by the external and domestic social, economic, political and broader political economy environments in adopting policies/strategies/measures to address the development needs of GBA.

This volume uses surveys, intensive interviews, focus discussions and fieldwork conducted in Southern China's GBA and also in the Shanghai and Zhejiang Bay area and Beijing and Tianjin Bohai Bay area as bases in offering comparative and regional perspectives when analyzing the emergence of cities and its impact on social integration, social policy and urban governance. Specifically, the following core research questions are answered in this book:

- How do Hong Kong citizens, as well as citizens in the Bay Area of South China, perceive and evaluate development opportunities conceived through the GBA Plan?
- Are Hong Kong citizens keen on working and living in GBA with strong government policy support?
- What are their concerns/worries if they plan to work and reside in GBA?
- What are the social and psychological considerations when migrating across the border?
- What are the policy implications for increasing people-to-people mobility across the region?
- How do young people evaluate their experiences when embarking on learning and work journeys in Mainland China?
- What are the major challenges for social welfare provision and urban governance?
- How would the development experience in China compare with global experiences?
- Would China offer a unique development model through its Bay Area development?

Special Features of the Proposed Book

1. *Regional Development Experiences with Comparative Perspectives*
   This book refers to the GBA development experiences in Southern China, and attempts to compare such experiences with other Bay Area developments in Mainland China, such as Shanghai and Zhejiang Bay Area and Beijing and Tianjin Bohai Bay Area, offering

comparative perspectives when analyzing regional developments in China. Additionally, in analyzing GBA in Southern China, this book will refer to other major international bay economies, such as Tokyo Bay Area, Florida Bay Area and New York Bay Area development experiences, critically reflecting on the emergence of cities and the policy implications for Bay Area developments.

2. *Policy Analysis and Empirical Studies*
This book draws from policy and documentary analysis and fieldwork conducted in GBA in China, and offers extensive empirical data generated from surveys, interviews and focus group discussions conducted by the authors in the past three years. The research findings and analyses of the present book come from a few research projects, such as the General Research Fund, which focuses on social service management reforms in China supported by the Hong Kong Research Grants Council; and projects co-supported by the Joint Research Centre for Greater Bay Area: Social Policy and Governance. From 2018 to the present, a research team led by Professor Ka Ho Mok (first author) has conducted a few surveys examining how Hong Kong citizens, particularly young people, evaluate and perceive the development opportunities and challenges in GBA in Southern China. These surveys and interviews provide extensive empirical data, thereby enabling us to conduct a critical examination of the extent to which the development strategies adopted by the Chinese government are sufficiently effective for regional development through urbanization and the emergence of cities.
3. *Interdisciplinary Approach: Cities, Social Policy and Governance*
Although current and major publications have analyzed China's Bay Area development from the economic perspective, the present book offers an interdisciplinary approach when examining GBA development from the vantage points of cities, social policy reforms and urban governance. This situation is particularly true, given that the Chinese government has called for close collaborations across the nine cities in Guangdong and Hong Kong and Macau. The announcement of the GBA Plan in February 2019 indicated economic collaboration to motivate the country to upgrade its economic structure by advancing innovation and technology and promoting innovation-centric entrepreneurship across universities and industries in the region. Moreover, the Development Plan does not lose sight of the social and human development perspectives, as

it calls for social integration and people-to-people bonding through close collaborations. Through an interdisciplinary approach, this book brings socio-psychological, urban studies, social policy and governance perspectives when analyzing the regional development in GBA in China.

Major Arguments of the Book

Policy Background and Research Objectives of the Volume

The present book begins with an introductory chapter (this chapter) providing a brief background of this book project. The introductory chapter highlights the unique features of the book by discussing the major research objectives, key research questions and research design. This chapter also highlights the major features and core arguments of the individual book chapters, thereby serving as a pointer for readers when reviewing and reading the discussions of the different chapters. Chapter 2, which was contributed by Genghua Huang and Ka Wai Tam, highlights the major research foci of the book, and provides the national policy background for GBA development and also the broader political economy context accounting for China's GBA development strategy. This chapter would enable readers to appreciate why and how the Chinese government initiated the GBA development blueprint, and how this regional development strategy is related to the national strategic development through the Belt and Road Initiative introduced a few years ago as globalizing China's initiatives. This chapter draws from the broader political economy perspective, and provides readers with the proper policy contexts for analyzing China's GBA Plan. Given the major research foci and policy background presented in this book, the following discussions are organized into a few sub-themes.

GBA Development: Perceived Challenges and Opportunities

Chapter 3, which was contributed by Alex Yue Feng Zhu, uses empirical studies on GBA as bases in reporting the findings generated from surveys and fieldwork conducted since 2018 to present how Hong Kong residents assess challenges and opportunities when embarking on GBA development plans. Moreover, this chapter utilizes people's perceptions and evaluations as bases in analyzing how people in Hong Kong and other parts of GBA perceive development opportunities and challenges when venturing in regional collaboration and development projects. The major contributions of this chapter are to show the differences between the governments advocating GBA development opportunities and the people's relatively lukewarm responses to GBA opportunities.

Chapter 4 by Alex Yue Feng Zhu draws from the survey examining how Shenzhen and Hong Kong people evaluate their livelihood and competitiveness of their respective cities, and reports and analyses the findings generated from two major surveys related to how Hong Kong people evaluate the emergence of Shenzhen and its impact on the former's regional and global competitiveness. Additionally, this chapter reports how Shenzhen people evaluate the competitiveness of Shenzhen and their willingness to continue to stay in the city for future development. Critical reflections on these surveys evidently show potential conflicts between the two cities, particularly when the central government has planned to offer Shenzhen significantly flexible policy environment to strengthen its leading role in China's national development. This chapter discusses the major challenges for the call for a mega-city development and the rivalry between these cities and the subsequent policy implications.

Cross-Border Mobility: Implications for Social and Public Policy

Responding to the call for more cross-border mobility with more people from Hong Kong and Macau embarking on education, work and residence in GBA, local governments must formulate policy frameworks appropriate for addressing the social welfare and public service needs of new migrants. Chapter 5, which was contributed by Alex Yue Feng Zhu and Ka Ho Mok refers to the youth perspective and attempts to analyze how young people in Hong Kong view migration to GBA as an investment. Time and money are necessary resources to engage in an investment. For young adults, time-related investments can include entrepreneurship activities, studying for higher-education degrees and migration for work and study. This chapter conceptualizes migration to GBA cities in Mainland China as an investment with risks and potential gains. Given a large-scale sample of young adults in Hong Kong, we performed k-mean cluster analysis to identify risk-takers in the migration case who are fully aware of the risks and potential gains and remain willing to migrate to GBA cities to venture for a better life, upward social mobility or other personal objectives. Binary logistic regression was used to assess how biopsychosocial, environmental and participating factors predicted the likelihood of a person becoming a risk-taker and being willing to tolerate the risk associated with migration. The results showed that being female, having experienced visiting a Mainland city and being a full-time employee in the hotel and catering industries are associated with a high likelihood of becoming a risk-taker. Moreover, the findings offered valuable policy implications for promoting GBA plans amongst young adults in Hong Kong.

Chapter 6 moves beyond education and employment and highlights the major policies and reform measures adopted by the central government in promoting social harmony and social cohesion in China. Genghua Huang and Zhaiwen Peng conducted a research, which was set out against the COVID-19 pandemic, examining how citizens based in the nine cities of Guangdong Province respond to the Mainland Chinese government's proposal to provide medical care and support to residents originally from Hong Kong and Macau when migrating to work and live in the GBA area. Huang and Peng's study was conducted in Mainland China, where the COVID-19 pandemic firstly emerged. To flatten the curve of new cases over time, the Chinese government has initiated several decisive actions since the end of January 2020. One of the most effective and dependable actions was the provision of free testing for residents and the removal of excessive out-of-pocket payments for treatment. Given this policy background, residents would be offered 'free treatment' for the disease. Huang and Peng's chapter discusses one of the most controversial topics in Mainland China: whether migrants should be given the same free treatment as residents. Although the number of foreign immigrants in China is relatively low owing to the country's strict immigration control policy, a significant number of Hong Kong residents live in Mainland China. With considerable people mobility from Hong Kong in GBA, local governments in the Bay area should revisit their social policy frameworks to accommodate the 'new migrants' flowing from the different areas of GBA. This chapter critically examines the effectiveness of the social policy and social welfare provisions in meeting the welfare and social policy needs of new migrants for supporting social cohesion and social integration.

Promotion of Quality Living Circle: Social Governance Reform and Policy Learning

Given that amongst the major development goals for GBA is to create a quality living circle for living, working and traveling, this chapter reviews the recent reforms in the government procurement of social services through engaging non-governmental organizations (NGOs) in social service delivery to address citizens' social service needs. Chapter 7 by Chak Kwan Chan and Xue Liu draws from fieldwork and intensive interviews with major stakeholders implementing such a social service management reform in GBA and in Shanghai and Zhejiang Bay Area and Beijing and Bohai Bay Area. Particularly, this chapter offers a regional perspective in understanding the contracting-out social service reforms across different regions in China. Additionally, this chapter analyzes the data generated from the fieldworks, and discusses the experiences of Beijing, Shanghai and Guangzhou when conducting social governance reforms to highlight local variations in contracting out social services. Data of this book were part of a study that examined contracting out social services in China. The contributions of this chapter would enable the wider readership to appreciate the politics of decentralization in social service reforms, as well as welfare regionalism commonly found in the country.

When conceptualizing the state and third sector NGOs through the transfers and transactions of social services, we must be sensitive about the wider political economy context, in which different key players (e.g. the state, market, community and wider civil society) interact to shape the unique state-NGOs relationship. Chapter 8 critically examines how the Chinese government engages NGOs in social service reforms, discussing whether the involvement of NGOs in social governance would facilitate the emergence of the third sector or the civil society at large in China. Specifically, Chak Kwan Chan and Xue Liu, the authors of this chapter, attempt to examine the impact of the policy on the development of NGOs based on the existing literature and a research study conducted by a research team of one of the authors (Mok et al., 2020). Part one of the chapter examines the reasons for the state to commission services to NGOs. Part two and three analyzes the benefits and disadvantages of China's NGOs following their role as welfare contractors. The final part proposes changes to address the existing problems on contracting social services. When reflecting on the contracting social services in Mainland China, Chan and Liu provide new perspectives in analyzing the role of the state in managing complex market transition and state–society relations, particularly when the Chinese state has become an adaptive regulatory state by mobilizing the state sector (at the subnational level) and non-state sectors/actors, as well as markets, to manage increasingly complex social and economic issues.

The analysis offered by Chan and Liu clearly shows the unique approach adopted by the Chinese government in policy learning. Lesson-learning has been conducted by the Chinese government in the last few decades to compensate for late development. However, social engineering in China has clearly revealed the tactical and practical adaptions to the diverse development conditions of the country. The Chinese government has been extremely careful when identifying and adopting any 'best practices' identified elsewhere to preventing the country from disintegration of the state and any violent outcomes from political change resulting from policy learning. Being an adaptive entrepreneurial state, China has been carefully considering its unique social, political and economic contexts when selecting role-models elsewhere. Recently, we have witnessed the creative combination of Confucian values with socialist ideas, searching for a relatively paternalistic way in managing social, economic, political and cultural changes (Fink-Hafner, 2014; Mok, 2017).

Managing Cities in GBA: Regional and Global Governance

The emergence of mega-cities in GBA encounters social integration issues not only from integrating residents coming from the two SARs and nine cities in GBA but also other international students and citizens studying and working in the bay area. In the last few decades, particularly with the strong advocacy for internationalization of higher education, the Chinese government has offered generous scholarships to attract international students to learn in universities across China. Specifically, students from African countries have received various higher-education training in Chinese societies through numerous bilateral and multilateral partnerships in the past two decades. Although the number of students is increasing, there is limited understanding of the political dimensions of their presence and how these students fare in Chinese societies. Chapter 9 contributed by Obert Hodzi and Padmore Adusei Amoah reviews the different types of policies, collaborations and programs in

China and its autonomous regions, which have led to an increase in African students in Chinese societies. This chapter places emphasis on the social conditions of these students in the Guangdong–Hong Kong–Macao GBA, examining how well these international students have been integrated in the local society. The concepts of student mobility, south–south cooperation and people-to-people exchanges are used to explain the novelty and exceptionality of the presence of African students in Chinese societies in GBA. This chapter also reviews the factors that shape the social integration of African students in GBA, and proposes measures to retain potential talents and strengthen Sino-African relations.

Although the unprecedented global health crisis resulting from the COVID-19 pandemic has impacted every country, China has successfully managed to turn the deepening emergency into development opportunities. Chapter 10 by Francis Arthur-Holmes and Ka Ho Mok discusses how the Chinese government proactively reached out to the international community by offering international aid and public health-related support in combating the COVID-19 crisis. Beyond this aspect, we explain how the authoritarian regime commonly conceived by political scientists in the West has enabled China (through the COVID-19 pandemic) to actively promote diplomatic activism through strengthening its 'soft security' and 'soft power'. Using a survey data from GBA in Mainland China, we found that GBA residents support their local governments to be more active and effective in implementing measures to prevent COVID-19 and offering COVID-19 aid in different forms to developing countries. Despite criticisms leveled against the Chinese government for the way the COVID-19 pandemic was handled in the early stages, we argue how China has forged cooperation with different countries whilst acting as a global creditor, thereby asserting its geo-political leadership and enhancing its diplomatic relations with other countries. This chapter presents how the Chinese government has attempted to manage the global health crisis and turned it into opportunity for improving its global governance through reaching out to various countries to offer medical and public health support. Built upon strong support from GBA residents, the Chinese government demonstrates its effort for global engagements by strengthening its 'soft security' and 'soft power' in times of adversity.

Cities, Higher Education and GBA Development from Comparative Perspectives

On the bases of the preceding empirical findings and critical analysis, the concluding chapter (Chapter 11) aims to offer a critical review of how the rapid urbanization in GBA has affected social integration. Accordingly, the following question must be answered: What are the major policy issues and challenges for governance as people's mobility becomes frequent in GBA? This concluding chapter by Ka Ho Mok draws on the experiences of other Bay economies overseas (e.g. New York Bay, Tokyo Bay and Florida Bay), and offers comparative and international perspectives in understanding policy issues and challenges for governance when managing the emergence of cities and the related integration problems. Lastly, this concluding chapter discusses the role of higher education in future GBA development by referring to other successful Bay economies in terms of the contributions of universities to urban development. This concluding chapter also acknowledges the limitations of the present research and indicates a future research agenda.

References

2022 Foundation. (2019). *Creating the Greater Bay Area of the future: Opportunities for Hong Kong*. 2022 Foundation.

Cai, L. J. (2021). Strategic positioning of the Greater Bay Area of Guangdong, Hong Kong and Macao. In S. P. Guo (Ed.), *Guangdong-Hong Kong-Macao Greater Bay Area*. World Scientific.

Cheeseman, N., & Gramont, D. D. (2017). Managing a mega-city: Learning the lessons from Lagos. *Oxford Review of Economics, 33*(3), 457–477.

DBS. (2018). *Asia mega cities in 2030*, DBS Asian Insights. DBS Regional Research Office.

Fink-Hafner, D. (2014). The quest for social harmony: The case of China [Unpublished paper].

Fuchs, R. J., Brennan, E., Lo, F. C., Uitto, J., & Charmie, J. (1994). *Mega-city growth and future*. United Nations University.

GBA Plan. (2019). *Outline development plan for the Guangdong-Hong Kong-Macau Greater Bay Area*. Central Government of China.

Govada, S. S., & Rodgers, T. (2019). Towards smarter regional development of Hong Kong within the Greater Bay Area. In T. M. Vinod Kumar (Ed.), *Smart metropolitan regional development* (pp. 101–171). Springer.

Hu, Z. J. (2019). Research status of Guangdong-Hong Kong-Macao Greater Bay Area. *Open Journal of Social Sciences, 7*(02), 275.

Hui, C. M., Li, X., Chen, T. T., & Lang, W. (2018). Deciphering the spatial structure of China's megacity region: A new bay area—The Guangdong-Hong Kong-Macao Greater Bay Area in the making. *Cities*, *105*, 102168, published online on 24 October 2018.

Jiang, M., Luo, X., & Chen, C. (2018, July). The factors and growth mechanism for smart city: A survey of nine cities of The Guangdong-Hong Kong-Macao Greater Bay Area. In *2018 4th International Conference on Economics, Social Science, Arts, Education and Management Engineering (ESSAEME 2018)*. Atlantis Press.

Li, C. (2021). Economic radiating effect of the Guangdong-Hong Kong-Macao Greater Bay Area in China effects of the Guangdong-Hong Kong-Macao Greater Bay Area. In S. P. Guo (Ed.), *Guangdong-Hong Kong-Macao Greater Bay Area: Planning and global positioning* (pp. 205–259). World Scientific.

Li, C. L., & Kwok, M. T. (2019). Unpacking the plan for the Guangdong-Hong Kong-Macau Greater Bay Area: A mechanism for reform. *China and the World*, *2*(2), 1950010.

Liu, L. H. (2018). *Social governance in China: The role of government and transformation of government functions* (Report No. 85). Institute of Public Administration and Human Resources, Development Research Centre, State Council, People's Republic of China.

Lyu, H. M., Shen, S. L., Zhou, A., & Yang, J. P. (2019). Perspectives for flood risk assessment and management for mega-city metro system. *Tunnelling and Underground Space Technology, 84*, 31–44.

Marshall, J. (2005). Megacity, mega mess. *Nature, 437*(7057), 312–314.

Ministry of Commerce of the People's Republic of China. (2015). *The vision and action in promoting the construction of the Silk Road Economic Belt and the 21st century Maritime Silk Road* [in Chinese]. Ministry of Commerce of the People's Republic of China.

Mok, K. H. (2017). Wither the developmental state? Adaptive state entrepreneurship and social policy expansion in China. In T. Carroll & D. Jarvis (Eds.), *Asia after the developmental state*. Cambridge University Press.

Mok, K. H., Chan, C. K., & Wen, Z. (2020). State-NGOs relationship in the context of China contracting out social services. *Social Policy & Administration, 55*(4), 687–701. https://doi.org/10.1111/spol.12651

State Council of the PRC. (2016). *The 13th five-year plan for national economic and social development of the People's Republic of China*. State Council, the People's Republic of China.

State Council of the PRC. (2019). *Outline development plan for Guangdong-Hong Kong-Macao Greater China Bay Area*. State Council, the People's Republic of China.

Xie, A. L., Postiglione, G. A., & Huang, Q. (2021). The Greater Bay Area (GBA) development strategy and its relevance to higher education. *ECNU Review of Education, 4*(1), 210–221.

Xu, Z. Q., et al. (Eds.). (2019). *Higher education, regional innovation and economic growth: An analysis of the role of University in Bay Area development from comparative perspective*. Guangdong Higher Education Press.

Yeh, A., & Chen, Z. F. (2019). From cities to super mega city regions in China in a new wave of urbanization and economic transition: Issues and challenges. *Urban Studies, 57*(3), 636–654, published online on 9 November 2016.

Yu, Q. W. (2019). Study on the Guangdong-Hong Kong-Macao Greater Bay Area. *Modern Economy, 10*(3), 586–599.

Zhao, G. H. (2021). Economic spatial structure of the Guangdong-Hong Kong-Macao Greater Bay Area. In S. P. Guo (Ed.), *Guangdong-Hong Kong-Macao Greater Bay Area*. World Scientific.

Zhou, X., Lian, H., Ortolano, L., & Ye, Y. (2013). A behavioral model of "muddling through" in the Chinese bureaucracy: The case of environmental protection. *China Journal, 70*, 120–147.

CHAPTER 2

Policy Background for the Greater Bay Area Development in South China

Genghua Huang and Ka Wai Tam

Introduction

The Chinese authority intends to create a world-class city-cluster in Southern China, which includes 11 cities surrounding the Pearl River Delta area and has become known as Guangdong–Hong Kong–Macao Greater Bay Area (GBA). The state's plan for the GBA is to strengthen the cooperation and maximize synergies among the cities based on their common cultural roots, similar customs, and geographical proximity. A more integrated GBA is not only the requirement of industrial upgrading

G. Huang (✉)
Institute of Policy Studies, Lingnan University,
Hong Kong, Hong Kong SAR, China
e-mail: genghuahuang@ln.edu.hk

K. W. Tam
School of Graduate Studies, Lingnan University,
Hong Kong, Hong Kong SAR, China
e-mail: kawaitam@ln.hk

K. H. Mok (ed.), *Cities and Social Governance Reforms*,
Social Policy and Development Studies in East Asia,
https://doi.org/10.1007/978-981-16-9531-5_2

in the region, from "the factory of the world" to international innovation and technology hub, but also a part of the national development strategy to sustain Chinese economic growth and serve as an important connector liaising with the countries along the Maritime Silk Road (Yu, 2019).

The GBA initiative was first introduced in China's 13th Five-Year Plan for the National Economic and Social Development (2016–2020) issued in March 2016, and its whole blueprint was released in the Outline Development Plan for the Guangdong–Hong Kong–Macao Greater Bay Area announced in February 2019, which specified the strategies and key priority areas for the cooperation among the cities in the region. Like many other city-clusters in China such as Yangtze River Delta and Beijing-Tianjin-Hebei Economic Zone (Ye, 2014), the formation of the GBA initiative was led by the central government as well as local states' autonomy. According to the official rhetoric, Xi Jinping, President of China, has "personally planned, personally deployed, personally pushed" this state's grand plan (People's Daily, 2021). Despite top-down regional planning, a "game" relationship exists between the local governments in the process (Fu & Zhang, 2018). The most notable characteristic of the GBA, which distinguishes it from other city-clusters in China and major bay areas in the world, is the existence of three distinct legal and social systems in this region under the "one country, two systems" principle. The GBA will be constrained by the institutional differences among Guangdong, Hong Kong and Macao and face an array of practical hurdles in the way of achieving its ambitious goals of becoming an international first-class bay area and a global economic and business hub.

Drawing from the broader political economy perspective, this chapter aims to provide the readers proper policy contexts for analyzing China's GBA initiative. It proceeds as follows. This chapter will begin by reviewing the evolution process of the GBA. Next, it will describe the profile of the GBA, specifying the socioeconomic conditions of its cities and compared with other major bay areas in the world. Finally, it will present the current cross-border cooperation and governance under the GBA and the challenges for its future development.

The Evolution of the Greater Bay Area

The "bay area" is no longer a purely geographical concept but refers to a special regional economic model. The bay area was first introduced in the studies based on the economic model of San Francisco, exploring the impact of port city-cluster, population, science and technology, and policy coordination on regional development (Schafran, 2013; Volberding, 2011). The GBA comprises the cities surrounding the Pearl River Delta area, including the two Special Administrative Regions of Hong Kong and Macao, and the nine municipalities located in Guangdong Province, namely Guangzhou, Shenzhen, Foshan, Dongguan, Zhuhai, Huizhou, Zhaoqing, Jiangmen, and Zhongshan.

The GBA is not being developed from scratch, but on the basis of robust economic strength and multi-level cooperation among members of the region (Yang, 2006). The cooperation between Guangdong, Hong Kong, and Macao can be traced to the water supply systems to Hong Kong and Macao. After the Second World War, the population of Hong Kong and Macao gradually increased, and the local fresh water supply has been unable to meet the demand. Against this background, Zhuhai began to supply fresh water to Macao in the 1950s, and the Dongshen Water Supply Scheme was also launched in the 1960s to allocate fresh water from Guangdong Province to Hong Kong. China's socioeconomic transformation started in the late 1970s under the policy of reform and opening up. As important measures, Guangdong Province has been entrusted with the task of attracting foreign investment with the auspice of its proximity to wealthy Hong Kong and Macao, and Shenzhen and Zhuhai were designated as special economic zones. Thereafter, many of Hong Kong's enterprises, especially manufacturing enterprises, have moved northward to neighboring cities in the Pearl River Delta, such as Shenzhen and Dongguan, leaving their design, marketing, and other service functions in Hong Kong. It has shaped the "store in the front, factory in the back" cooperation mode under which Guangdong Province has become an important manufacturing base in China, and their products were exported to Europe and America through the transfer station of Hong Kong (Liao & Chan, 2011; Meyer et al., 2012). The combination of the steady capital influx from Hong Kong and the abundant local labor force made the Pearl River Delta in the mainland a "world's factory" at the end of the twentieth century (He & Huang, 2015). On the contrary, Hong Kong's manufacturing industry has been in decline since then, while its tertiary industry was booming, which included finance, insurance, and logistics industries, relying heavily on the export-oriented manufacturing economy of neighboring cities in the Pearl River Delta.

In 1994, Guangdong Province raised the strategy of constructing the Pearl River Delta Economic Zone. In 1998, the Guangdong-Hong Kong

Cooperation Joint Conference was established, aiming to strengthen the coordination of trade, economy, infrastructure development, water and air transport, customs, and passengers between the two places. In 2003, as one of the outcomes of the Joint Conference, the mainland, Hong Kong, and Macao respectively signed the Closer Economic Partnership Arrangement (CEPA), introducing legally binding measures to reduce the market barriers and economic protectionism between the three places (Yang, 2016). The CEPA has been the first formal institutional mechanism for regional economic integration within the GBA. The implementation of CEPA played an important role in helping Hong Kong out of the economic downturn caused by the Asian financial crisis and SARS epidemic, and it also facilitated the access of Guangdong's enterprises to Hong Kong's financial and logistics services and the world market.

Subsequently, a series of new cooperation frameworks have been put forward by local governments, such as Pan-Pearl River Delta Regional Co-operation, Greater Pearl River Delta Townships, Integration of Shenzhen and Hong Kong. However, these cooperation frameworks remained at the conceptual level and lacked substantive and specific measures, which made them difficult to effectively implement. In other words, there was a lack of consensus on a blueprint for the development and integration of the Pearl River Delta (Yang, 2004).

The establishment of the GBA was a milestone in the regional integration in the Pearl River Delta. It is a top-down national strategy, aiming to build the GBA as China's leading economic powerhouse and a quality living circle. This strategy was endorsed by the central government in China's 13th Five-Year Plan (2016–2020) in 2016. It was also written into the work report of the central government in March 2017, and Li Keqiang, China's Premier, proposed to deepen cooperation between the mainland, Hong Kong, and Macao under the GBA initiative at the fifth session of the 12th National People's Congress. However, according to the official rhetoric, the idea of the GBA came from Xi Jinping, China's top leader, who "personally planned, personally deployed, personally pushed" this strategy (People's Daily, 2021). At the 19th National Congress of the Communist Party of China in October 2017, President Xi reaffirmed the national strategy to promote mutually beneficial cooperation between the three places and support the integration of Hong Kong and Macao into the overall development of the country by the construction of the GBA. On February 18, 2019, the Central Committee of the Communist Party of China and the State Council of the People's Republic of China announced the Outline Development Plan for the Guangdong-Hong Kong-Macao Greater Bay Area (referred to as the GBA development outline), which articulated the vision and relevant measures for the GBA initiative and indicated that the construction of the GBA had entered a substantial stage. Different from other previous cooperation frameworks, the GBA initiative is a comprehensive plan, which is not only intended for further eliminating barriers that hinder the free flow of goods and resources in the region, but also emphasizes social cohesion and its active role in China's "Belt and Road Initiative" (Liu, 2019). There are many reasons for Beijing's push for development of the GBA.

Firstly, from the economic perspective, although the Pearl River Delta region made great economic achievements in the late twentieth century, its development has encountered great bottlenecks in recent years. With the rising labor costs in Guangdong Province, many of its manufacturing enterprises began to move to emerging Asian neighbors, such as Malaysia, the Philippines, Vietnam, and so on. The "world's factory" has already ceased to exist except in name. Hong Kong and Macao have been suffering from the singleness of the industry structure. Hong Kong now mainly depends on the financial industry and real estate industry, while Macao relies too much on the gambling industry, which seriously affects the sustainable development of the two places. Against this backdrop, a more integrated GBA was proposed as a solution, and the initiative is expected to create a system in which the mainland cities, Hong Kong, and Macao, are able to complement one another, exerting their competitive advantages and unique strengths so as to enhance the overall competitiveness of the region. At the national level, China's economic development has also slowed down over the past several years. The slowdown, coupled with rising protectionism in the West and the United States, has made the Chinese leadership determined to adjust its export-oriented industrial structure and economy and change extensive growth into high-quality development. The GBA initiative is one of the important measures to promote industrial upgrading and further economic reform in China.

Secondly, from the political perspective, the GBA initiative is partly driven by its attempt to pacify Hong Kong, which has suffered from political instability over recent years, and pursue the rejuvenation of "one country, two systems." Hong Kong was a colony of the United Kingdom, and it was reverted to Chinese sovereignty in the adoption of the one country, two systems arrangement, which is regarded as the cornerstone of Hong Kong's prosperity and stability. However, this constitutional arrangement has faced great challenges since the Occupy Central Movement occurred in the autumn of 2014. Slow economic development, high house prices, and the widening wealth gap are usually regarded as deep-seated problems that caused the political crisis. Thus, accelerating economic development and improving people's livelihood are considered to be key to getting Hong Kong out of trouble (The Government of Hong Kong Special Administrative Region [GovHK], 2019). The GBA initiative is expected to not only align Hong Kong more closely with the mainland socially, but also support Hong Kong's economic development by strengthening its cooperation with mainland cities, thus ensuring the successful implementation of "one country, two systems" (Liu, 2019).

Thirdly, from the perspective of China's international strategy, the GBA could be an important connector in the maritime Silk Road (or twenty-first-century Maritime Silk Road). In concert with the Silk Road Economic Belt, the Maritime Silk Road was proposed by China in 2013, aiming to reconstruct the international order (Berlie, 2020). As one of the starting points of the maritime Silk Road, a more integrated and economically developed GBA could serve as a new driving force for its development (Guo, 2021). Hong Kong is a city with a combination of Chinese and Western cultures, and its economic system and market rules act on international convention, while it has close business relations with Asian and Western countries. As a former Portuguese colony, Macao has a vast business network in Portuguese-speaking countries. Hong Kong and Macao integrated into the GBA could further bridge the countries along the maritime Silk Road and the mainland.

The Profile of the Greater Bay Area

The GBA is one of the most economically developed regions in China. Its GDP accounted for 13% of China's GDP in 2016, while only accounting for less than 1% of the nation's land area (Yu, 2019). Its per capita GDP reached US$19,367 in 2020, which is almost twice the national per capita GDP (Hong Kong Trade Development Council [HKTDC], 2021). According to World Bank statistics, Guangdong has surpassed Australia and South Korea in terms of GDP in 2016, which could justify its description as a "rich country" (Ernst & Young, 2019, p. 7; Yu, 2019).

However, there are great differences among members in the GBA (see Table 2.1). In terms of land area, Zhaoqing is 451 times as large as Macao. In terms of population, Guangzhou is 27 times that of Macao.

Table 2.1 Major Economic Indicators of cities in the Guangdong–Hong Kong–Macau Greater Bay Area (2020)

City	*Land Area (sq. km)*	*Population (mn)*	*GDP[a] (USD bn[b])*	*Per-capita GDP (USD[b])*	*Export (USD bn[b])*	*Utilized FDI (USD bn[b])*
Guangzhou	7434	18.68	362.73	19,422	78.69	7.19
Shenzhen	1997	17.56	401.17	22,846	246.07	8.68
Zhuhai	1736	2.44	50.48	20,693	23.32	2.56
Foshan	3798	9.50	156.82	16,509	59.90	0.67
Huizhou	11,347	6.04	61.21	10,129	24.47	0.81
Dongguan	2460	10.47	139.91	13,367	120.07	1.15
Zhongshan	1784	4.42	45.69	10,342	26.32	0.59
Jiangmen	9507	4.80	46.41	9672	16.32	0.82
Zhaoqing	14,891	4.11	33.51	8147	4.34	0.09
Hong Kong	1110	7.47	346.59	46,325	506.32	74.46[c]
Macao	33	0.68	24.33	35,714	1.35	6.76[c]

Source HKTDC, https://research.hktdc.com/en/article/MzYzMDE5NzQ5
[a]At current market prices
[b]Converted with the yearly average exchange rates
[c]2019 figure

Shenzhen is the largest city in the GBA in terms of economic aggregate, with a GDP of USD 401.17, while Macao, the city with the smallest economic aggregate, has a GDP of only USD 24.33. However, in terms of per capita GDP, an indicator of the sophistication of an economy, Macao ranks second in the GBA after Hong Kong.

The GBA has established a complete modern industrial system. However, its dominant industries are located in different cities, such as high-end equipment manufacturing industry in Guangzhou, information technology industry in Shenzhen, financial services in Hong Kong, gaming tourism in Macao, petroleum and chemical industry in Huizhou and Zhaoqing, and Chinese medicine industry in Zhongshan.

Given that each city in the GBA has its own economic strengths and unique competitiveness, they have been designated different roles in the GBA development outline (see Table 2.2). There are four cities designated as core cities in the GBA development outline: Guangzhou, Shenzhen, Hong Kong, and Macao. Specifically, Guangzhou will be built into a national top-tier gateway city and an international hub for commerce, transportation, culture, and education; Shenzhen is positioned

Table 2.2 Designated role of each city in the GBA

City	*Role in the GBA (according to the GBA development outline)*
Guangzhou	Core city: National top-tier gateway city, international hub for commerce, transportation, culture, and education
Shenzhen	Core city: National economic center, innovation hub with global influence
Zhuhai	Form closer alliance with Macau; advanced equipment manufacturing hub with Foshan; specialist finance in Hengqin
Foshan	Form closer alliance with Guangzhou; advanced equipment manufacturing hub with Zhuhai; manufacturing upgrade and support Hong Kong's "reindustrialization"; high-end service industry
Huizhou	Manufacturing base for green agricultural products
Dongguan	World-class center for electronic equipment and information technology; incubator for new strategic industries
Zhongshan	Innovation center in biomedical technology, especially in the field of Chinese medicine
Jiangmen	Connection point with diasporic Chinese; Yinhu Bay to become an energy conservation and environmental protection industry center and a start-up platform
Zhaoqing	Manufacturing base for green agricultural products
Hong Kong	Core city: International hub for finance, shipping, trading, aviation, offshore RMB, asset management, and risk management
Macao	Core city: International tourism and leisure center, trading hub with Lusophone countries, cultural exchange hub

Source Ernst and Young (2019, p. 3)

as a national economic center and an innovation hub with global influence; Hong Kong will be enhanced in its role as an international hub for finance, shipping, trading, aviation, offshore RMB, asset management, and risk management; and Macao will be developed into a world-class tourism and leisure center and trading hub between China and Lusophone countries. Other cities in the GBA will be developed into satellite cities to support and strengthen the functions of the core cities. For example, Foshan is planned to form a closer alliance with Guangzhou and support Hong Kong's "reindustrialization," and Zhuhai is required to form a closer alliance with Macau and strengthen cooperation with Macao in tourism. In fact, as mentioned above, one of the GBA's initiatives is to exert their competitive advantages and unique strengths so as to maximize synergies between the cities and enhance the overall competitiveness of the region.

The features of the GBA are clearly displayed and compared with other major bay areas in the world in Table 2.3. First, the GBA is the largest one in terms of land area and population. The land area of the GBA is about three times that of the San Francisco Bay Area and the total land area of New York Metropolitan Area and Tokyo Bay Area. The population of Guangzhou is equal to the sum of the other three bay areas.

Table 2.3 Comparison between Guangdong–Hong Kong–Macao Greater Bay Area and other major bay areas in the world (2020)

	Guangdong–Hong Kong–Macao Greater Bay Area	*San Francisco Bay Area*	*New York Metropolitan Area*	*Tokyo Bay Area*
Land area (sq. km)	56,098	17,887	21,479	36,898
Population (mn)	86.17	7.74[c]	19.22[c]	44.34
GDP[a] (US$ bn[b])	1679.3[c]	995.1[c]	1861.2[c]	1991.6[c]
Real GDP growth (%)	4.4[c]	4.0[c]	1.2[c]	1.4[c]
Per-capita GDP (US$)	23,116[c]	128,573[c]	96,853[c]	45,084[c]
Air passenger throughput (mn passenger-times)	101.5	25.8	40.8	40.8
Air cargo and airmail throughput (mn tonnes)	7.66	1.06	1.78	2.72
Port container throughput (mn TEUs)	81.63	2.46	7.59	8.36[c]
GDP share of tertiary industry (%)	66.1	75.0[c,e]	82.4[c,e]	75.9[d]

Source HKTDC, retrieved from https://research.hktdc.com/en/article/MzYzMDE5NzQ5

[a]At current market prices

[b]Converted with the yearly average exchange rates

[c]2019 figure

[d]2018 figure

[e]Estimated figure

Second, the GBA is the most active one in economic development. Its real GDP growth reaches 4.4%, which exceeds that of the San Francisco Bay Area, New York Metropolitan Area, and Tokyo Bay Area. Third, the GBA is a transportation hub. Its air passenger throughput, air cargo and airmail throughput, and port container handling capacity significantly exceed those of other major bay areas in the world.

Cross-Border Cooperation and Governance Under the Greater Bay Area and the Challenges

As mentioned earlier, the cooperation among cities in the Pearl River Delta has a long history. In fact, in the pre-GBA period, cities in the mainland, Hong Kong, and Macao had tried to establish some institutional cooperation mechanisms, but they only focused on economic and trade affairs (Yang, 2006). In contrast, the GBA initiative proposes a comprehensive blueprint that encompasses not only economic and trade cooperation but also infrastructure construction, environmental protection, public service provision, and social development. In other words, the GBA initiative aims to upgrade the inter-city cooperation in Pearl River Delta from "connectivity" to "integration" in governance, economy, society, culture, and so on (Ernst & Young, 2019).

However, there are many difficulties in achieving this goal. One important feature distinguishing the GBA from other bay areas in the world is that there are three distinct legal and social systems in this region. For example, cities in the mainland, Hong Kong, and Macao, are different in governance structure, tax system, and exchange rate system. Against this background, the success of the grand plan is conditional on effective policy coordination and the elimination of various institutional barriers that hinder free mobility of goods and resources (Yu, 2019).

Take the Guangzhou–Shenzhen–Hong Kong Express Rail Link for example. As an important infrastructure facility, the mainland's high-speed railway was extended to Hong Kong in 2018. However, the railway would produce extensive clearance procedures for customs, immigration, and quarantine in Hong Kong and the cities in the mainland as the railway crosses the border between the mainland and Hong Kong. To facilitate the movements of travelers, the governments proposed the "one place and two inspections" (joint checkpoint inspection arrangement) as a solution, which means that travelers could go through the same boundary control procedures at the points of exit and arrival. This is an example of cross-border governance and policy coordination in the GBA, though it has been accompanied by extensive controversy.

In fact, the industrial structures of some cities in the Pearl River Delta overlap to some extent, and the competitions between cities are old and fierce in the region. For instance, both Shenzhen and Hong Kong regard financial industry as their pillar industries, and Hong Kong, Shenzhen, and Guangzhou are facing competition in port cargo, the logistics industry, and the airline industry. In addition, there is only one leading city in each other major bay area in the world, such as San Francisco in the San Francisco Bay Area, New York City in the New York Metropolitan Area, and Tokyo in the Tokyo Bay Area. In the Pearl River Delta, however, there are four "core cities," and in particular, Guangzhou, Shenzhen, and Hong Kong are comparable in terms of economic strength and social maturity. In such a "highly fragmented mega-city region" (Xu & Yeh, 2012), the difficulty of its integration is imaginable. This can partly explain why the previous cooperation mechanism, such as CEPA, has not been effective. Although the central government has been involved in the top-level design of the GBA initiative and the formulation of the GBA development outline, the realization of policy goals depends on the implementation of local governments. This requires that more efforts to be put into cross-city, even cross-border institutional collaboration in economic development as well as social governance.

The vision of the GBA, as stated in the development outline, is to make it not only a global innovation and technology hub but also a high-quality environment for living, working, and traveling. At present, the collaboration within the GBA is still focused on economic and trade affairs, but with the increase of the cross-border mobility of the GBA residents, cross-border governance will be the policy focus in the future. For instance, with convenient transportation, an increasing number of Hong Kong residents and Macao residents are choosing to live in the mainland cities of the GBA. This will generate a large number of issues that need to be responded to by social policies, such as the portability of their welfare benefits in Hong Kong and their eligibility for employment, education, health care, and pensions in the mainland cities.

Concluding Remarks

Geographically, the GBA comprises the eleven cities surrounding the Pearl River Delta area, including the two Special Administrative Regions of Hong Kong and Macao, and the nine municipalities located in Guangdong Province. Despite being the most economically developed region in Southern China, its development has encountered great bottlenecks in recent years. In order to promote the industrial upgrading in the region, from "the factory of the world" to international innovation and technology hub, and create a world-class city-cluster with a high-quality environment for living, working, and traveling, the Chinese authority proposes the GBA initiative and adopts it as a national strategy, while the GBA would also serve as an important connector liaising with the countries along the Maritime Silk Road. One important feature distinguishing the GBA from other bay areas in the world is that there are three distinct legal and social systems in this region. Against this background, the success of the grand plan is conditional on effective policy coordination and the elimination of various institutional barriers that hinder free mobility of goods and resources. At present, the collaboration within the GBA is still focused on economic and trade affairs, but with the increase of the cross-border mobility of the GBA residents, cross-border governance will be the policy focus in the future.

Funding The author(s) disclosed receipt of the following financial support for the research, authorship, and publication of this article: LU Research Committee—Research Seed Fund (Project Number: 102390).

References

Berlie, J. A. (2020). *China's globalization and the belt and road initiative*. Palgrave Macmillan.

Ernst & Young. (2019). *Guangdong–Hong Kong–Macau Greater Bay Area—From connectivity to integration* [Report]. Ernst & Young.

Fu, Y., & Zhang, X. (2018). Two faces of an eco-city? Sustainability transition and territorial rescaling of a new town in Zhuhai. *Land Use Policy, 78*(9), 627–636. https://doi.org/10.1016/j.landusepol.2018.06.007

Guo, S. (2021). *Guangdong–Hong Kong–Macao Greater Bay Area: Planning and global positioning*. World Scientific.

He, A. J., & Huang, G. (2015). Fighting for migrant labor rights in the world's factory: Legitimacy, resource constraints and strategies of grassroots migrant labor NGOs in South China. *Journal of Contemporary China, 24*(93), 471–492. https://doi.org/10.1080/10670564.2014.953851

Hong Kong Trade Development Council (HKTDC). (2021). *Statistics of the Guangdong-Hong Kong-Macao Greater Bay Area*. Retrieved June 14, 2021, from https://research.hktdc.com/en/article/MzYzMDE5NzQ5

Liao, H. F., & Chan, R. C. (2011). Industrial relocation of Hong Kong manufacturing firms: Towards an expanding industrial space beyond the Pearl River Delta. *GeoJournal, 76*(6), 623–639.

Liu, K. (2019). China's Guangdong–Hong Kong–Macao Greater Bay Area: A primer. *The Copenhagen Journal of Asian Studies, 37*(1), 36–56.

Meyer, S., Schiller, D., & Diez, J. R. (2012). The localization of electronics manufacturing in the Greater Pearl River Delta, China: Do global implants put down local roots? *Applied Geography, 32*(1), 119–129.

People's Daily. (2021, May 17). Promote the construction of the Greater Bay Area to make new and greater progress. *People's Daily*. Retrieved June 07, 2021, from http://opinion.people.com.cn/n1/2021/0517/c1003-32104750.html

Schafran, A. (2013). Origins of an urban crisis: The restructuring of the San Francisco Bay Area and the geography of foreclosure. *International Journal of Urban and Regional Research, 37*(2), 663–688. https://doi.org/10.1111/j.1468-2427.2012.01150.x

The Government of Hong Kong Special Administrative Region [GovHK]. (2019). *The chief executive's 2019 policy address* [Government document]. Retrieved April 05, 2021, from https://www.policyaddress.gov.hk/2019/eng/pdf/supplement_full.pdf

Volberding, P. (2011). Engaging Regions in Globalization: The Rise of the Economic Relationship between the San Francisco Bay Area and China. *Berkeley Undergraduate Journal*, *23*(2), 1–32. https://escholarship.org/uc/item/77j9z9wk

Xu, J., & Yeh, A. G. (2012). Re-building regulation and re-inventing governance in the Pearl River Delta China. *Urban Policy and Research, 30*(4), 385–401.

Yang, C. (2004). From market-led to institution-based economic integration: The case of the Pearl River Delta and Hong Kong. *Issues & Studies, 40*(2), 79–118.

Yang, C. (2006). The Pearl River Delta and Hong Kong: An evolving cross-boundary region under "one country, two systems." *Habitat International, 30*(1), 61–86.

Yang, C. (2016). A cross-boundary mega city-region in China under 'two systems': Multi-level governance in the greater Pearl River Delta. In D. Wastl-Walter (Ed.), *The Routledge Research Companion to Border Studies* (pp. 461–478). Routledge.

Ye, L. (2014). State-led metropolitan governance in China: Making integrated city regions. *Cities, 41*, 200–208.

Yu, H. (2019). The Guangdong–Hong Kong–Macau greater bay area in the making: Development plan and challenges. *Cambridge Review of International Affairs*, 1–29. https://doi.org/10.1080/09557571.2019.1679719

CHAPTER 3

Greater Bay Area Cities on Mainland China: Perceptions of Hong Kong Residents

Alex Yue Feng Zhu

Introduction

The governments of Hong Kong and mainland China have been cooperating with the mass media to promote the Greater Bay Area (GBA) plan among the residents of Hong Kong so that they will consider it as a preferable migration choice. Media professionals have devoted themselves to creating a good public image of the GBA by painting pictures of its development through articles, videos, and web pages. They have invited experts to analyze the developmental opportunities and prospects of the GBA and have interviewed people who have been successful as entrepreneurs in mainland GBA cities (Hong Kong Government, 2019). Branding activities driven by government with the objective of advertising the attractiveness of a public object are conceptualized as induced

A. Y. F. Zhu (✉)
Institute of Policy Studies, Lingnan University, Tuen Mun, Hong Kong SAR, China
e-mail: alexzhu@ln.edu.hk

K. H. Mok (ed.), *Cities and Social Governance Reforms*, Social Policy and Development Studies in East Asia,
https://doi.org/10.1007/978-981-16-9531-5_3

communication (Anttiroiko, 2014; Schulz et al., 2019). Induced communication works by screening out the negative and undesirable aspects of the GBA cities on the mainland and by systematically emphasizing the positive features so as to influence the image of the GBA as perceived by the residents of Hong Kong (Pan et al., 2011). This perceived image is intended to shape the perceptions of Hong Kong residents regarding the GBA and motivate them to migrate to mainland GBA cities for work and life (Hawkins et al., 1987; Pan et al., 2011; Xu, 2018). Therefore, the landscape of perceptions of the GBA as held by the residents of Hong Kong is of great significance to the urban planners. The authorities, both in mainland China and in Hong Kong, such as the commerce, immigration and education departments, whose duties are to build a positive image of GBA, are keen to increase their understanding of how the Hong Kong public perceives the mainland GBA cities. This chapter aims to respond to this need and build the required landscape using a strict measurement approach.

In the psychological field, perceived image is a well-grounded construct, which has been studied as public evaluation, opinions, and feelings toward a public object (Arnheim, 1960). Public perception is a mental construct, conceptually overlapping with perceived image. Public perceptions of mainland GBA cities can be interpreted as the impressions that Hong Kong residents have of GBA cities on the mainland, which are reflected through their concerns and motivations when considering a decision to migrate to mainland GBA cities for life and work (Echtner & Ritchie, 1991; Xu, 2018). Public perceptions can be measured empirically by examining a cluster of selected concerns and motivations (Reynolds, 1965). To comprehensively assess public perceptions, it is necessary to consider: (1) institutional concerns and motivations as driven by the specific and differing social, political, and economic systems of Hong Kong and the mainland, and (2) the common and individual concerns that are applicable to any migration activity.

Previous assessments implemented among Hong Kong residents focused only on addressing the landscape of institutional concerns and motivations. Opinions collected among 714 adult Hong Kong residents by the Chinese University of Hong Kong [CUHK] in 2018 revealed that the three most significant institutional concerns were "insufficient freedom of information" (29.3%), "inconvenient transportation" (23.0%), and "issues of food safety" (10.1%). The three most prominent motivations to migrate to mainland GBA cities were "more economic opportunities" (30.9%), "affordable housing prices in Guangdong cities" (16.7%), and "larger living spaces" (12.6%) (CUHK, 2018). Another survey conducted by CUHK one year later (CUHK, 2019) reports the two top institutional concerns as "mainland politics" (20.4%) and "mainland society" (20%), and the two top institutional motivations as "opportunities in the mainland economy" (39.8%) and "cost and quality of life in mainland" (36.8%). Another survey done by the Hong Kong Federation of Youth Groups [HKFYG] (2019) limited participants to young people and found that the top three institutional concerns were "the mainland legal system" (86.0%), "tax issues" (79.9%), and "business institutions" (74.9%), while the top motivation was "rich employment opportunity in mainland" (71.3%).

However, institutional concerns and motivations alone hardly reflect the whole landscape of public perceptions of mainland GBA cities as held by Hong Kong residents. People may hesitate to leave their homeland and migrate to a new place due to a series of common personal concerns, which include abandoning their original employment, social network, lifestyle, and social wellbeing in their home country (Castelli, 2018; Reza et al., 2019). A robust measurement of these individual concerns indirectly reflects the perceptions of mainland GBA cities held by Hong Kong residents. When people have positive perceptions of the GBA, they may systematically report a reduction in their individual concerns. The first objective of this chapter is to address the limitations of previous assessments by adding the measurement and analysis of individual concerns and thereby to present the GBA planners with a fuller landscape of the Hong Kong public's perceptions of mainland GBA cities.

Key to Our Assessment: How Do Young, Well-Educated Professionals in Hong Kong Perceive the Cities of Mainland GBA?

The central government of China followed an innovation-driven developmental mode in building the GBA, which relies heavily on the scientific and technological fields in which young people are concentrated (Liao & Meng, 2020). The strategic goal outlined by the government was that the migration of young citizens from Hong Kong to live, study, work, and perform business activities in mainland GBA cities should be facilitated (Yu, 2019). Against a background where the current economic structures in Hong Kong are unlikely to provide an effective channel by which young people can break a pattern of intergenerational poverty, the Hong

Kong government actively encouraged young people to migrate to mainland GBA cities and to see this as an opportunity to achieve upward social mobility (Census and Statistics Department, 2018; Mok, 2016; Zheng et al., 2019).

To achieve a deep level of cooperation between Hong Kong and the mainland GBA cities, the mainland government prioritized the improvement of soft power, namely human capital, by creating strategies to attract talent, which would improve the existing operations and in particular, the financial, international business, and educational practices in the GBA (Li & Kwok, 2019). As an international financial hub with a good reputation and powerful influence, Hong Kong has a large pool of financial talent with members who could play important roles in integrating the financial services of the GBA with those of Hong Kong. To benefit from the role of Hong Kong in attracting an inflow of international financial capital, mainland GBA cities are eager to have access to the financial professional network of Hong Kong and to motivate financially talent from Hong Kong to serve on the mainland and to contribute to the development of the mainland financial institutions (Yu, 2019). The Belt-and-Road initiative created a platform for Hong Kong and the mainland GBA cities to compete with one another in international business. It became evident that the superior conditions in Hong Kong enable it to attract and retain international business and trade talent. It would therefore appear to be a shortcut for the mainland GBA cities to enlist this talent to improve the competitiveness and performance of their own business operations (Lin et al., 2019). Furthermore, higher educational institutions in Hong Kong are well-known for their institutional autonomy and internationalization, which enable them to cultivate innovative talent in young people with a global vision and competitiveness (Xie et al., 2020). Mainland GBA cities endeavor to facilitate cross-border academic and research collaboration to enable the higher education sector on the mainland to benefit from the premium human capital in the higher education sector in Hong Kong and thereby to improve their own capability in innovation and knowledge production (Xie et al., 2020).

To realize the strategic goal of attracting young, well-educated, talented high-end professionals from Hong Kong to migrate to the mainland GBA cities, the mainland and Hong Kong governments have together implemented a comprehensive set of migration policies. The professional qualifications of Hong Kong residents are now recognized by the mainland GBA cities (GBA Development Plan, 2019). Economic incentives, such as direct financial assistance for start-up business and tax reductions, are provided to young people from Hong Kong who intend to run entrepreneurial businesses in mainland GBA cities (Hong Kong Trade Development Council, 2019; Zhang et al., 2019).

However, the policy context is not the only factor, it is also important for GBA planners to investigate the perceptions of the GBA among the young, well-educated, high-end professionals they hope to attract from Hong Kong. Therefore, the second objective of this chapter is to compare the perceptions of mainland GBA cities (as measured by individual concerns) of both younger and older Hong Kong residents, of those with higher and lower educational achievements, and of professionals and non-professionals. Considering that current policy clearly targets the young, well-educated, professionals, we hypothesize that younger Hong Kong residents will have fewer individual concerns about living in mainland GBA cities compared to older residents (Hypothesis 1). We hypothesize that those with a higher educational level will have fewer individual concerns about living in mainland GBA cities compared to those with lower educational achievements (Hypothesis 2). We also hypothesize that professional workers will have fewer concerns about living in mainland GBA cities compared to non-professional workers (Hypothesis 3).

Method

Procedures and Participants

The target population for the assessment was Hong Kong adult residents aged 18 or older. We adopted a random sampling approach to establish a connection between the sample and the general population of Hong Kong residents. We selected a sample of families by randomly selecting the last two digits of phone numbers of families in Hong Kong. The research team then called the selected families, and if the family was successfully connected, the research team randomly selected one qualified household member and invited him or her to join the assessment. The research team was comprised of staff members with research experience from the School of Graduate Studies at Lingnan University and from the Center for Hong Kong, Macao and Pearl River Delta Studies at the Sun Yat-sen University. This team supervised and participated in the whole data collection process. The field study was performed between 15 and

27 August 2019. Ethical approval was issued by the Research Committee of Lingnan University three months before data collection.

Altogether, 1033 adults completed an interview, giving a response rate of 30.7%. At a 95% confidence level, sample error was controlled at 3%. Gender was well balanced (females 52.7%). The majority of the participants were born in Hong Kong (69.8%), while 25.9% were born in mainland China, and 4.3% were born elsewhere. The younger group (aged 18–34), the middle group (aged 35–59) and the older group (aged 60 or above) accounted for 20, 39.5 and 40.5%, respectively. Of the whole sample, 14.8% of participants had received elementary education or less, those whose highest educational level was middle school, high school, diploma and associate degree together made up 55.3%, while those who had graduated with a bachelor's degree or above accounted for 29.9% of the group. A total of 42.4% of all respondents had a full-time job. In terms of occupational classes, those employed in a higher occupational class (i.e. senior management, professional, and associated professional) together accounted for 22.0%.

Measures

To assess institutional concerns, we created a full list of concerns reflecting various institutional arrangements between Hong Kong and the mainland. The list was produced by combining the concerns listed in three previous assessments, and it included concerns about the legal system, air quality, freedom of information, citizenship, healthcare services, taxation, social wellbeing, market freedom, government efficiency, transportation, public security, and food security (CUHK, 2018, 2019; HKFYG, 2019). Following previous designs, we invited the respondents to choose the three concerns that they perceived to be the most significant in inhibiting their decision to migrate to mainland GBA cities. Similarly, to assess institutional motivations, we created a full list of the advantageous aspects of the mainland GBA cities and asked the respondents to select the three that they perceived as the most important in motivating them to migrate to mainland GBA cities. The list contained all the positive aspects of the GBA as mentioned in previous assessments, and included driving the development of the Hong Kong economy, low living costs, transportation, technological innovation, economic prospects, advanced studies, psychological well-being, cultural capital, employment opportunities, housing conditions, and entertainment (CUHK, 2018, 2019; HKFYG, 2019).

We also used a four-item measurement where the answers were calibrated into a 11-point scale from 0 (not worried at all) to 10 (very worried about it) to assess individual concerns. The four items were "finding a job in mainland GBA cities," "losing my social network in Hong Kong," "getting used to lifestyle on the mainland," and "losing the social welfare of Hong Kong" (Zhu et al., 2021). The Cronbach Alpha across the four items was 0.80.

Data Analysis Plan

Following the analysis plan used in the previous surveys, we created two figures to report the frequency of each institutional concern and motivation. The three most important institutional concerns and motivations emerged from simple comparisons. Group comparisons for individual concerns were conducted by using a strict approach where latent means were compared after removing the measurement errors and establishing measurement invariance (Kim et al., 2017; Steinmetz et al., 2009). We used 35 as the cut-off age to differentiate between younger and older participants (Zhu et al., 2021). The group with higher educational achievements consisted of those with a bachelor's degree or above, while the rest were put into the group with lower educational achievements. Participants employed as a senior executive officer, a professional, or an associate professional were identified as professionals, while the others were identified as non-professional labor.

A comparison of latent group means for individual concerns (i.e. an indirect reflection of perceptions of mainland GBA cities) was considered meaningful when the members of two groups interpreted four individual concerns indifferently. We estimated the mean of the latent individual concerns in the multi-group measurement model. The mean of the latent construct of one group was set to 0. We constrained both measurement weights and measurement intercepts to be equal, and tested if the model fit had changed significantly. The insignificant change was a signal of measurement invariance, which indicated that members of both groups interpreted four individual concerns indifferently and we could proceed by testing the difference of two latent means. On the basis of constraining both measurement weights and intercepts of all observed items, we checked if the model fit changed significantly after constraining the two latent means as equal. If two latent means were found to be significantly different under measurement invariance, we could proceed with comparing the means between the two groups. Since the mean of one group was set at 0, we just needed to check if the estimated mean of another group was positive or negative.

If the measurement invariance could not be established, we re-estimated the model by freeing the intercepts, setting the variance of the latent individual concerns as 1, and constraining each pair of measurement weights in sequence for the purpose of assessing how latent individual concerns were differently associated with each specific concern.

Results

Frequencies reported in Figs. 3.1 and 3.2 reveal that the top three concerns were "food security," "public security," and "transportation," while the top three motivations were "entertainment," "housing conditions," and "employment opportunities."

For latent individual concerns, measurement invariance of equal measurement weights and equal intercepts was established between the younger group and the older group (CMIN = 14.76, $p = 0.14$). The results of the measurement model with measurement invariance are reported in Fig. 3.3. Under the measurement invariance, the latent means across the two groups were found to be significantly different (CMIN = 16.99, $p < 0.001$). Since the latent mean of the younger group was set as 0, the negative latent mean of the older group ($M = -0.79$, $p < 0.001$), indicated that the younger group was more concerned about migrating to mainland GBA cities than the older group.

The data also supported the establishment of equal measurements between the groups with higher and lower educational achievements (CMIN = 16.38, $p = 0.09$). The results of the measurement model with equal measurement weights and intercepts are reported in Fig. 3.4. Under the measurement invariance, the difference of latent means across the two groups was found to be insignificant (CMIN = 1.23, $p = 0.27$). Thus, the conclusion can be drawn that the individual concerns of participants with higher and lower educational levels were the same.

Intergroup analysis between professional and non-professional participants did not support the measurement invariance (CMIN = 26.66, $p < 0.01$). The results of the measurement model with equal measurement weights and intercepts are reported in Fig. 3.5. The unconstrained model results with freed measurement weights and intercepts are reported in Fig. 3.6. Checking the difference of each pair of measurement weights

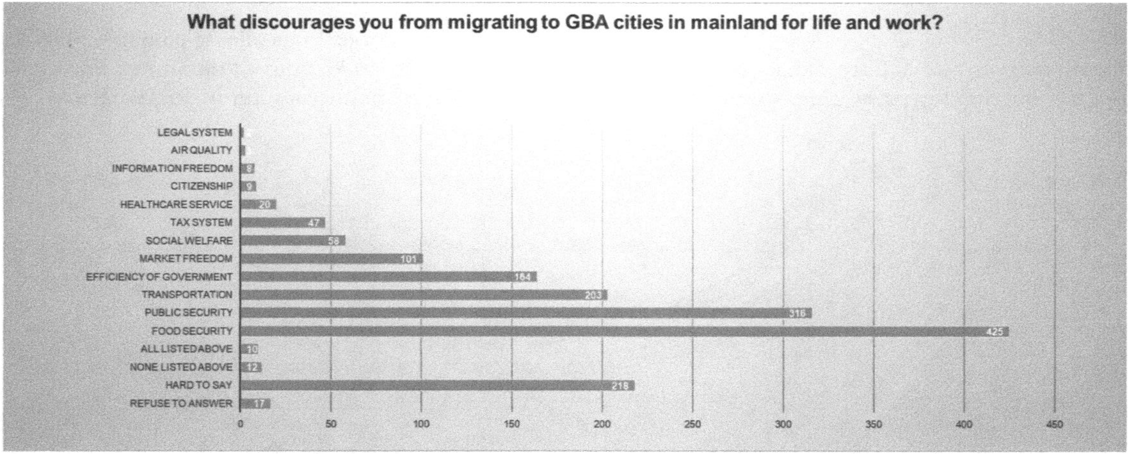

Fig. 3.1 Frequency of institutional concerns about mainland GBA cities (*Note* As respondents can choose up to three options, the total frequency exceeds the sample size [$N = 1033$]. All frequencies reported were weighted by age and gender)

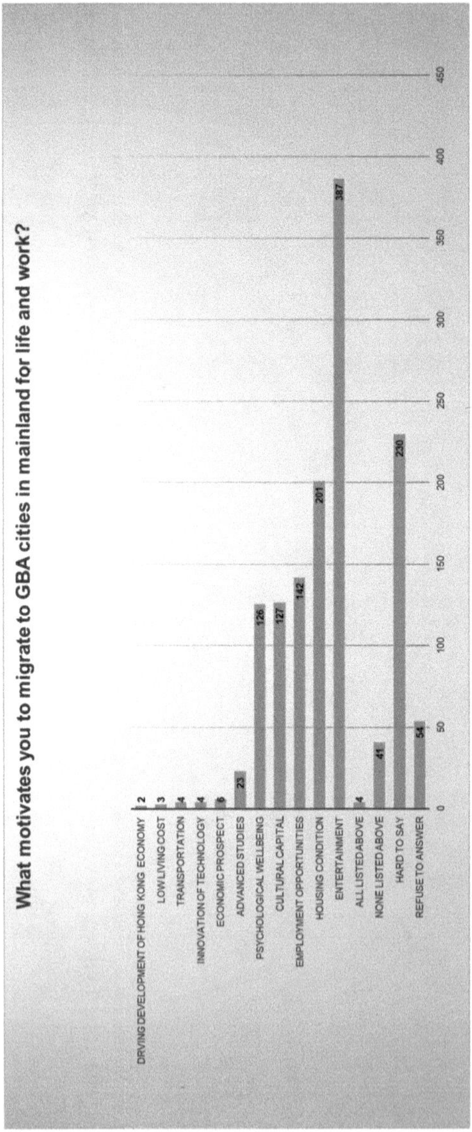

Fig. 3.2 Frequency of institutional motivations to migrate to mainland GBA cities listed by respondents (*Note* As respondents can choose up to three options, the total frequency exceeds the sample size [$N = 1033$]. All frequencies reported were weighted by age and gender)

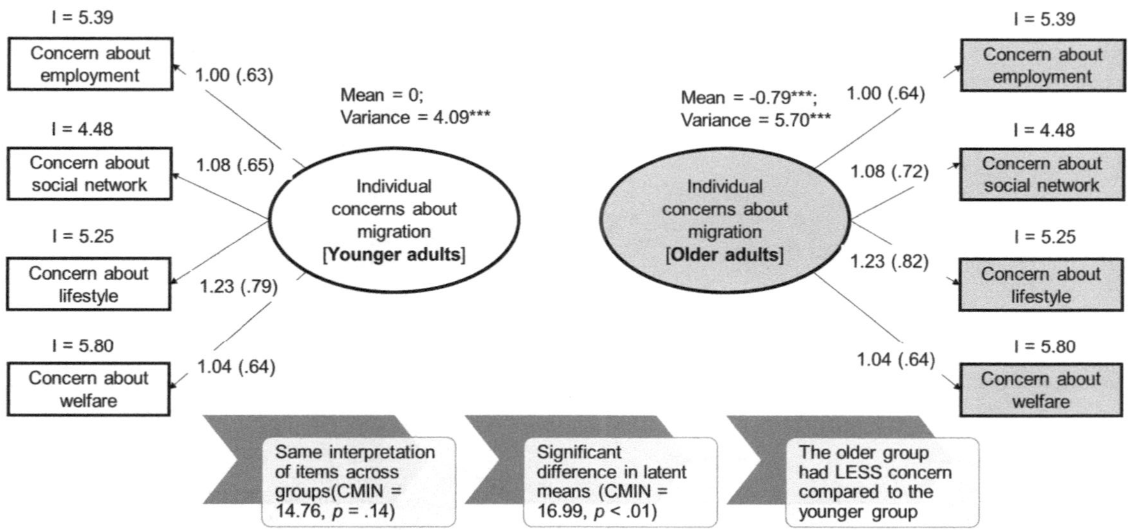

Fig. 3.3 Comparing the latent means of individual concerns about mainland GBA cities of younger and older Hong Kong residents (*Note* N [younger group] = 208; N [older group] = 825. I = intercept of the item. Results are produced after constraining weights and intercepts. For all unstandardized, standardized weights [in parenthesis], and intercepts, $p < 0.001$, *** $p < 0.001$)

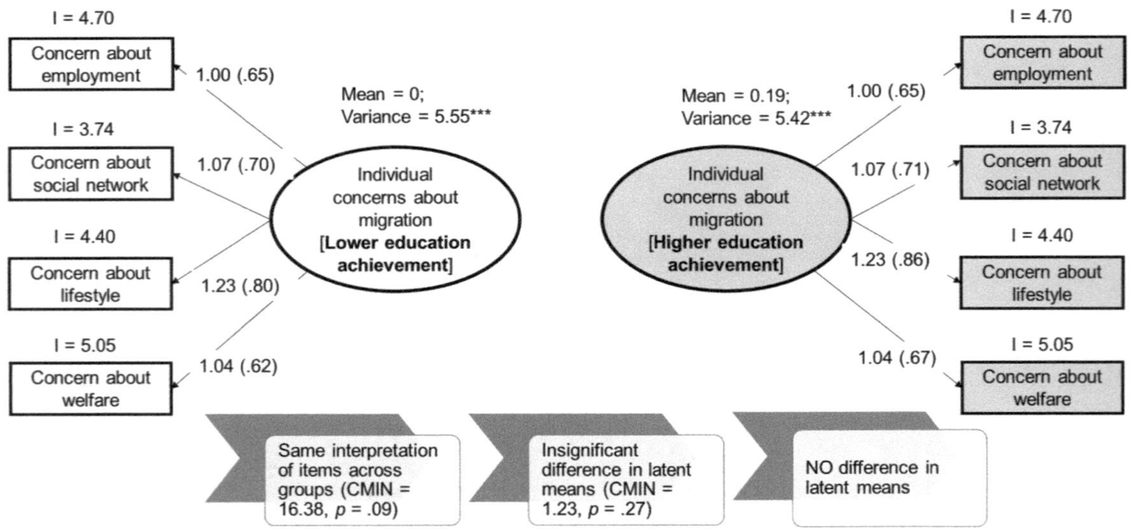

Fig. 3.4 Comparing latent means of individual concerns about mainland GBA cities of Hong Kong residents with lower and higher educational achievements (*Note* N [lower educational achievement] = 626; N [higher educational achievement] = 386. I = intercept of the item. Results are produced after constraining weights and intercepts. For all unstandardized, standardized weights [in parenthesis], and intercepts, $p < 0.001$, *** $p < 0.001$)

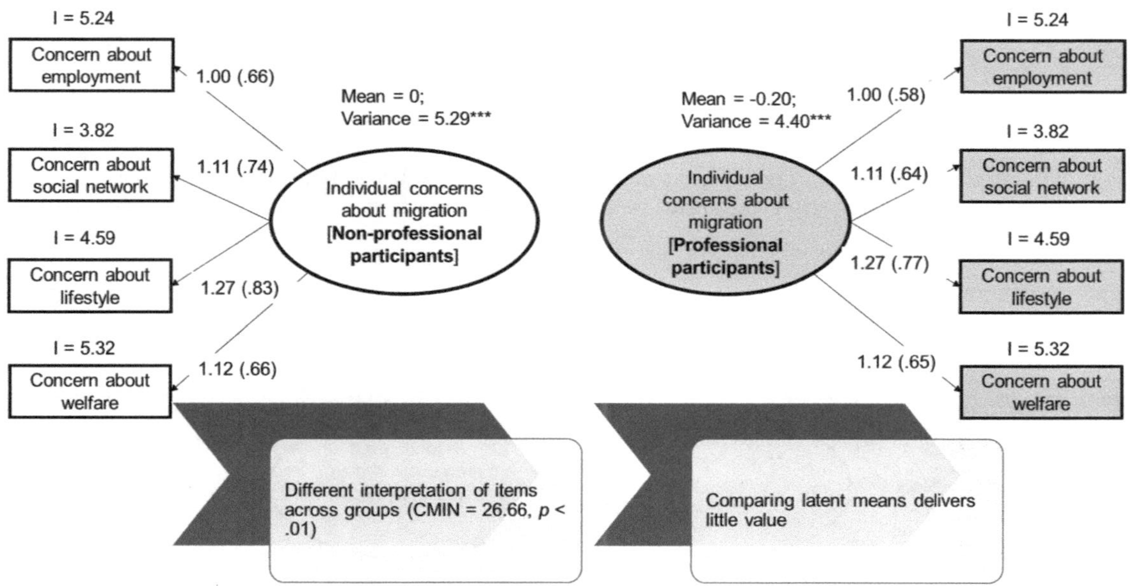

Fig. 3.5 Comparing latent means of individual concerns about mainland GBA cities of professionals and non-professionals (*Note* N [professionals] = 286; N [non-professionals] = 215. I = intercept of the item. Results are produced after constraining weights and intercepts. For all unstandardized, standardized weights [in parenthesis], and intercepts, $p < 0.001$, *** $p < 0.001$)

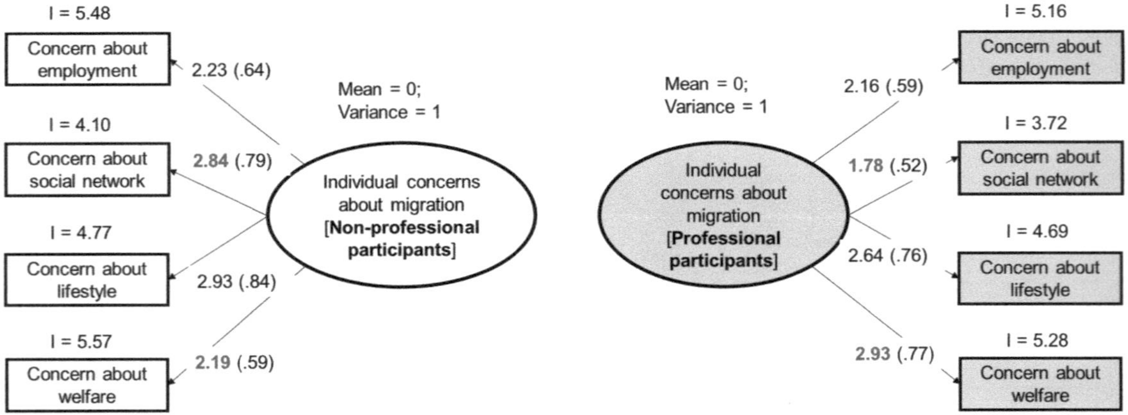

Fig. 3.6 Different interpretations of individual concerns about mainland GBA cities by professional and non-professional workers (*Note* N [professionals] = 286; N [non-professionals] = 215. I = intercept of the item. Results of unconstrained model are reported)

in sequence, we found that the association between latent individual concerns and concern about losing the social network of Hong Kong, and the association between latent individual concerns and concern about losing social welfare of Hong Kong were significantly different between the two groups (CMIN = 10.23, $p < 0.01$; CMIN = 4.02, $p < 0.05$). Among the professionals, latent individual concerns were more strongly associated with concern about losing the social welfare of Hong Kong ($B = 2.93$ vs. $B = 2.19$, $p < 0.001$) and less strongly associated with concern about losing the social network of Hong Kong ($B = 1.78$ vs. $B = 2.84$, $p < 0.001$) as compared with the concerns of the non-professional participants.

Discussion

Against the background of the three previous assessments (CUHK, 2018, 2019; HKFYG, 2019), this chapter reports on the full range of the Hong Kong public's perceptions of mainland GBA cities by assessing the institutional concerns and motivations that are related to the differences in institutional arrangements between the mainland and Hong Kong. It also considers the individual concerns that are common in all migratory activities. To enable our assessment to deliver more value to GBA planners who are interested in encouraging well-educated, professional, and talented young people in Hong Kong to move to the mainland for life and work, we assessed the difference in individual concerns between different age groups, different educational groups, and between professionals and the non-professional labor force.

Since we adopted more complete and comprehensive lists for exploring institutional concerns and motivations, it is not surprising to note that our findings were not fully consistent with those reported by CUHK (2018). Among the top three institutional concerns emerging from our data, two are consistent with those reported by CUHK (2018), namely "food security" and "transportation." Since our assessment was conducted one year later, it should be noted that the induced communication activities undertaken in the interim to promote the GBA cities had not been successful in eliminating the concerns of Hong Kong residents about food security issues and the lack of convenient transportation. When grouping all the institutional concerns into the four categories of life, economy, culture, and politics, we note that both food security and transportation issues belong in the life category. Policy makers may interpret this finding in two ways: Compared to economic, cultural, and political issues, Hong Kong residents are more concerned about issues relating to quality of life and whether the mainland government is capable of addressing these issues. Another explanation is that the Hong Kong residents are fully aware that the mainland is unlikely to make any substantial change in its economic, political, or cultural operations in the short run, so they are just hoping to see improvements in public administration and public service, which are also listed as important development goals for mainland cities in the GBA Development Plan (2019). CUHK (2018) reported "information freedom," as another institutional concern, while our figures indicate that "public security" is an important concern. As information freedom sounds more like a political issue, and public security is closely related to quality of life, we may infer that there has been a shift in institutional concerns from the political domain to the life domain between 2018 and 2019. The three top motivations emerging in our study are consistent with those identified by CUHK (2018), namely employment opportunities, housing conditions, and commodity prices (low costs in various consumption fields, including entertainment). GBA planners may consider that their induced communication in these three economic fields has been very successful in shaping the perceptions of the public in Hong Kong.

Regarding individual concerns, it is alarming to see that the younger participants reported more individual concerns than the older respondents. The central government of China is particularly wanting younger people to migrate to the GBA and to integrate into mainland society, and the development of key technological industries in the GBA requires young manpower (Liao & Meng, 2020; Yu, 2019). Negative perceptions of the GBA among young people send a signal to the GBA planners that the policy currently supported might be failing to address the critical needs of younger people. The standardized coefficient comparison reveals that individual concerns are most strongly associated with concerns about lifestyle, relative to other concerns. The current GBA plan might fail to be attractive to Hong Kong's young people if it fails to address the lifestyle differences between Hong Kong and the mainland cities (Du, 2019; Shan, 2018).

We did not find a significant reduction in individual concerns among well-educated participants relative to their less-educated counterparts. Since the GBA plan was designed to attract better-educated people to move to the mainland (Li & Kwok, 2019; Lin et al., 2019; Xie et al., 2020), policy makers have to acknowledge that the support given by current policy may be too general and fail to address the unique needs of well-educated Hong Kong residents. The current policy focuses on creating economic incentives, but it is increasingly evident that for Hong Kong residents, who achieved their higher educational qualifications with the purpose of obtaining social and cultural capital, migration to the mainland would mean abandoning the very social and cultural assets they have accumulated in Hong Kong (Armstrong & Hamilton, 2013; Borgen, 2015). Existing social and cultural connections within the Hong Kong community might be meeting the unique needs of the well-educated people. Promoting cooperation and establishing business links between Hong Kong residents on the mainland and those in Hong Kong may be a potential solution.

We found that professional and non-professional people interpreted individual concerns differently, causing a direct comparison to deliver little value. The unstandardized coefficient comparison revealed that losing social welfare in Hong Kong was a more serious concern and losing a social network in Hong Kong was a less serious concern among professional people relative to their non-professional counterparts. As improving the welfare scheme on the mainland is a huge and costly project that cannot be completed in the short term, GBA planners on the mainland might consider using induced communication to send a signal to the public in Hong Kong to indicate that they have a strategic plan for transforming the welfare scheme in the mainland GBA cities, and thereby give the public, and particularly professional people, greater confidence and motivation toward migration.

Limitations

Two limitations have to be reported that have influenced the scientific properties of this work. First, when performing a comparison of measurement models between two age groups, the group sizes were not balanced. The same concern emerged when we compared two groups with different educational achievements. Future studies should reconsider the items observed to ensure that the measurement invariance is successfully established between professionals and non-professionals so as to enable a more effective comparison of individual concerns between the two groups, which is a matter of great interest to the GBA planners.

References

Anttiroiko, A. V. (2014). *The political economy of city branding*. Routledge.

Armstrong, E., & Hamilton, L. (2013). *Paying for the party: How college maintains inequality*. Harvard University Press.

Arnheim, R. (1960). *Art and visual perception: A psychology of the creative eye*. University of California Press.

Borgen, N. T. (2015). College quality and the positive selection hypothesis: The 'second filter' on family background in high-paid jobs. *Research in Social Stratification and Mobility, 39*, 32–47.

Castelli, F. (2018). Drivers of migration: Why do people move? *Journal of Travel Medicine*. https://doi.org/10.1093/jtm/tay040

Census and Statistics Department. (2018). *General household survey*. Census and Statistics Department.

Chinese University of Hong Kong. (2018). *Hong Kong people's evaluation of development opportunity and challenge in the Greater Bay Area*. Chinese University of Hong Kong.

Chinese University of Hong Kong. (2019). *Survey findings on public opinion on the outline Development Plan for the Guangdong-Hong Kong-Macao Greater Bay Area*. Chinese University of Hong Kong.

Du, Y. (2019, October). A discussion on furniture rental service for urban migrants in China—from the gain of a lifestyle design research in Hong Kong & Beijing. In *IOP Conference Series: Materials Science and Engineering* (Vol. 616, No. 1, p. 012034). IOP Publishing.

Echtner, C. M., & Ritchie, J. R. B. (1991). The meaning and measurement of destination image. *Journal of Tourism Studies, 2*(2), 2–12.

GBA Development Plan. (2019). *Outline of development plan for the Guangdong-Hong Kong-Macau Greater Bay Area*. Central Government of China.

Hawkins, R. P., Pingree, S., & Adler, I. (1987). Searching for cognitive processes in the cultivation effect adult and adolescent samples in the United States and Australia. *Human Communication Research, 13*(4), 553–557.

Hong Kong Federation of Youth Groups. (2019). *Removal barriers for enabling Hong Kong young people to work in the Greater Bay Area*. Hong Kong Federation of Youth Groups.

Hong Kong Government. (2019). *The speech of Chief Executive at the opening ceremony of the first Guangdong-Hong Kong-Macao Greater Bay Area Media Summit in Guangzhou*. Hong Kong Government Press.

Hong Kong Trade Development Council. (2019). *Guangdong looks to boost prospects of young GBA entrepreneurs*. Retrieved December 1, 2021 from https://hkmb.hktdc.com/en/1X0AHJUL/hktdc-research/Guangdong-Looks-to-Boost-Prospects-of-Young-GBA-Entrepreneurs

Kim, E. S., Cao, C., Wang, Y., & Nguyen, D. T. (2017). Measurement invariance testing with many groups: A comparison of five approaches. *Structural Equation Modeling: A Multidisciplinary Journal, 24*(4), 524–544.

Li, L. C., & Kwok, M. T. (2019). Unpacking the plan for the Guangdong-Hong Kong–Macao greater bay area: A mechanism for reform. *China and the World, 2*(2), 1–20.

Liao, Y., & Meng, L. (2020). Research on social psychology and young people's action in the construction of Guangdong-Hong Kong-Macao Greater Bay Area. *Journal of Social and Political Sciences, 3*(1), 152–175.

Lin, X., Chen, D., Han, J., Chen, T., & Li, C. (2019). A study on the role of Guangdong-Hong Kong-Macao Greater Bay Area based on the Belt and Road Initiative. *Journal of Economics and Business*. https://ssrn.com/abstract=3434491

Mok, K. H. (2016). Massification of higher education, graduate employment and social mobility in the Greater China region. *British Journal of Sociology of Education, 37*(1), 51–71.

Pan, S., Tsai, H., & Lee, J. (2011). Framing New Zealand: Understanding tourism TV commercials. *Tourism Management, 32*(3), 596–603.

Reynolds, W. H. (1965). The role of the consumer in image building. *California Management Review, 7*(3), 69–76.

Reza, M. M., Subramaniam, T., & Islam, M. R. (2019). Economic and social well-being of Asian labour migrants: A literature review. *Social Indicators Research, 141*(3), 1245–1264.

Schulz, P., Shehu, E., & Clement, M. (2019). When consumers can return digital products: Influence of firm-and consumer-induced communication on the returns and profitability of news articles. *International Journal of Research in Marketing, 36*(3), 454–470.

Shan, W. (2018). Post-materialism: What divides youth in Hong Kong, Taiwan and mainland China. *East Asian Policy, 10*(03), 87–98.

Steinmetz, H., Schmidt, P., Tina-Booh, A., Wieczorek, S., & Schwartz, S. H. (2009). Testing measurement invariance using multigroup CFA: Differences between educational groups in human values measurement. *Quality & Quantity, 43*(4), 599–616.

Xie, A., Postiglione, G. A., & Huang, Q. (2020). The Greater Bay Area (GBA) development strategy and its relevance to higher education. *ECNU Review of Education, 4*(1), 210–221. https://doi.org/10.1177/2096531120964466

Xu, D. (2018). *How can city image be cultivated: Understanding the influence of media communication on people's perceptions of city image and evaluations of and behavioral intentions toward a city*. Doctoral Dissertation.

Yu, H. (2019). The Guangdong-Hong Kong-Macau greater bay area in the making: Development plan and challenges. *Cambridge Review of International Affairs*, 1–29. https://doi.org/10.1080/09557571.2019.1679719

Zhang, C., Huang, X., Qu, X., Zhong, Y., & Niu, B. (2019, July). The influence of entrepreneurial environment and entrepreneurial cognitive capital on youth entrepreneurial motivation: Take Shenzhen as an example. In *Proceedings of 2019 16th International Conference on Service Systems and Service Management* (ICSSSM) (pp. 1–6). Institute of Electrical and Electronics Engineers.

Zheng, V., Hsiao, H. H. M., Wan, P. S., & Wong, K. (2019). Young people's sense of fairness and social action: A survey analysis of Taiwan, Hong Kong, and Macao. *Asian Journal of Comparative Politics, 5*(3), 270–287. https://doi.org/10.1177/2057891119844602

Zhu, A. Y. F., Mok, K. H., & Huang, G. H. (2021). Migrating to GBA cities in mainland China: Assessing a model of psychological distance among Hong Kong working adults. *Analyses of Social Issues and Public Policy*. https://doi.org/10.1111/asap.12235

CHAPTER 4

Competition for Premium Human Resources: Cooperation and Rivalry Between Hong Kong and Shenzhen

Alex Yue Feng Zhu

Introduction

Since the late 1970s, Hong Kong and Shenzhen have been cooperating through industrial complementation. Benefiting from its own low-cost human resources and from the inflow of technology and international capital from Hong Kong, Shenzhen has grown into a regional and international manufacturing hub that has consistently supplied commodities to Hong Kong and has helped sustain the development of Hong Kong as a center of service, business, and trade in the Asian Pacific Region (Li & Kwok, 2019). This effective level of cooperation has enabled the gross domestic product (GDP) of Shenzhen to increase rapidly, with

A. Y. F. Zhu (✉)
Institute of Policy Studies, Lingnan University, Tuen Mun, Hong Kong SAR, China
e-mail: alexzhu@ln.edu.hk

K. H. Mok (ed.), *Cities and Social Governance Reforms*, Social Policy and Development Studies in East Asia, https://doi.org/10.1007/978-981-16-9531-5_4

an annual growth rate of around 35% before 1995 and around 14% between 1995 and 2014 (National Bureau of Statistics of China, 2015). In the early phase of this cooperation, a substantial proportion of GDP in Shenzhen was produced by labor-intensive assembly industries (Chen & Ogan, 2017). Having established a basic accumulation of capital, Shenzhen started to outsource its low-tech and high-pollution productions and invested in scientific and technological innovations to facilitate its industrial transformation. This was accompanied, supported, and fostered by human capital, identified as *premium human resources* (Chen & Ogan, 2017).

Similar to Shenzhen, scientific and technological innovation was not a focus of the development in Hong Kong during the early phase of its cooperation with Shenzhen. Under its more laissez-faire policies, business and entrepreneurs in Hong Kong exploited the new technologies available in the international market, and this strengthened the role of Hong Kong as an international trade hub specializing in providing intermediary services (Carney & Davies, 1999; Howard, 1999). With the exception of its financial service industries, which are able to offer innovative services equal to the level offered by European countries, the other three pillar industries in Hong Kong (tourism, trading and logistics, and professional and producer services) have not been able to offer innovative products directly to their mainland customers (Sharif & Baark, 2008). Although its traditional service mode sustained the economic growth of Hong Kong when the mainland adopted an open-door policy, its period of strong growth ended with the global financial crisis in 2008, which forced Hong Kong to transform into a knowledge-intensive and innovation-based service economy (World Bank, 2019). As with Shenzhen, the transformation called for the involvement of *premium human resources* to be engaged in business, service, and management innovations.

Looking Forward: Cooperation and Rivalry Between Hong Kong and Shenzhen for Premium Human Resources

Both Hong Kong and Shenzhen desire premium human resources to support effective innovation systems that will facilitate their own industrial transformation. The construction of a cross-border innovation ecosystem for the sharing of human capital can benefit both Hong Kong and Shenzhen, and is therefore of great interest to both governments. In the ideal scenario, the joint ecosystem would be composed of a mutually complementary and reinforcing innovation network with a regional knowledge cluster supported by professionals from both sides (Carayannis et al., 2018). A free and flexible cross-border personnel flow would be a critical prerequisite for this scenario. Undeniably, the free mobility of talented people would further activate rivalry between Hong Kong and Shenzhen in attracting and retaining premium human resources.

The Quadruple Helix Model proposes that an innovative system grows within the dynamics of government, universities, industries, and society (Stoltenberg, 1984). The competitiveness of the innovative governance, higher education, pillar industries, and social development in Shenzhen and Hong Kong are already complementary (Kang & Jiang, 2020). The Shenzhen government closely manages and dominates the direction of its industrial innovation, and it adopts policy tools that prompt social capital to be invested in research and development (R&D) activities. In comparison, the role of the Hong Kong government is more like a promoter or facilitator, as it is committed to following its laissez-faire ideology. Therefore, the scale of private and public investment in industrial innovation in Hong Kong is far smaller than that in Shenzhen (Kang & Jiang, 2020). However, R&D activities in Hong Kong universities have achieved global excellence, while in Shenzhen the development of higher education has fallen behind other major cities in mainland China, such as Beijing and Shanghai (QS World University Rankings, 2021). Since 2017, the complementary advantages of the two cities have facilitated a series of joint projects with the aim of building a cross-border innovation ecosystem (e.g. the Hong Kong–Shenzhen Innovation and Technology Park in Lok Ma Chou Loop), within which talented people are encouraged to move cross-border frequently to engage in cooperative innovative activities.

The Guangdong-Hong Kong-Macao Greater Bay Area (or Greater Bay Area, GBA hereafter) Plan was introduced in February 2019 to further expand cooperation between Hong Kong and Shenzhen, and it facilitated the development of a joint innovation ecosystem (GBA Development Plan, 2019). Under the GBA Plan, educational achievements and professional qualifications are recognized in the city cluster, friendly migration policies are implemented, and migration procedures are simplified (GBA Development Plan, 2019). Strong policy support facilitated the mobility of premium human resources in the GBA, but inevitably it also activated competition for human capital. This chapter is not concerned with a comparison of the migration policies of Hong Kong and Shenzhen but is devoted to a comparison that considers which city has the more competitive social and economic environment for the retention of premium human resources. In addition to thinking about how to attract an inflow of talented people, city planners need to carefully assess whether their city environment favors premium human resources and whether it is sufficiently competitive to prohibit an outflow of human capital.

Relative Deprivation: An Indicator of City Competitiveness in the Retention of Premium Human Resources

The concept "relative deprivation" is frequently cited in the migration literature as a motivation for emigrating from a home country (Flippen, 2013; Jin, 2016; Quinn, 2006; Stark & Taylor, 1991; Stark & Yitzhaki, 1988). People normally select a reference group in their home country and assess their own relative economic and social status as compared to that of the reference group; an unsatisfied assessment outcome increases their willingness to leave their home country (Stark & Taylor, 1991). Relative deprivation can be measured either objectively or subjectively. Objective relative deprivation reflects actual differences in household income, family income, health status, tax level, and monetary social welfare between a particular population group and the reference group (Boyle et al., 2004; Flippen, 2013; Liu et al., 2019). Subjective relative deprivation is understood as a feeling that the city environment does not favor a particular group in comparison to the reference group, or the development direction of a city does not benefit a particular group as compared to the reference group (Akay et al., 2017; Jin, 2016). In this study, the target population is the premium human resources group who are younger, better-educated, or have a higher income. Thus, we aimed to compare their sense of relative deprivation compared with counterparts who are older, less educated, or who have lower incomes. To integrate both the objective and subjective measures, we utilized a two-step approach to assess perceived relative deprivation by premium human resources. First, we asked residents to report their subjective assessment of *selected variables* reflecting various aspects of well-being. Then, we calculated the objective differences for these variables between our target population group (the younger, better-educated, or higher-income respondents) and their counterparts. Any negative objective difference could be interpreted as relative deprivation. Inversely, a positive and large difference identified in one city as compared to the other city, revealed that the policies of that city were more favorable to human capital. We may reasonably infer that premium human resources will therefore be less likely to emigrate, and that this city will be more competitive in the knowledge and innovation economy.

Variables for Comparison

Against a background where both Hong Kong and Shenzhen are focusing on developing innovative clusters and high-technology industries in executing the GBA plan, the creative class thesis is an appropriate theoretical framework by which to identify ***variables*** for comparison (Florida, 2002, 2003, 2005; Florida et al., 2008). The traditional human capital model and the social capital model posit career opportunities and social networks as two critical factors in the retention of human capital, where human capital is measured as educational achievement and working experience (Maning & Darnton, 2006). The creative class theory is not entirely new, but was developed on the basis of the human capital model and the social capital model. Creative class theory focuses on just one type of human capital, namely creative capital, and proposes two basic notions (Florida, 2002): First, knowledge, talent, and creative capital play a decisive role in the development of innovation clusters and therefore determine the development of a knowledge-driven economy (Darchen & Tremblay, 2010; Florida, 2003). Second, other than career opportunities and social networks, the openness of a city to creativity and the perceived creativity of a city's industries are also of great interest to talented people: they are more willing to live in a city where they believe creativity and knowledge can flourish, whether now or in the future (Darchen & Tremblay, 2010; Florida, 2003).

The creative class thesis also posits that talented people need a stable and comfortable environment to unleash their potential for creativity, which upholds the importance of quality of life in a place of residence (Clifton, 2008). Pilati and Tremblay (2007) proposed a series of quality of life factors that have been shown to influence the effectiveness of creative work and the vitality of a city. These include level of tolerance, lifestyle, housing costs, population density, density of green places, convenience of transportation, and public services. Since previous research has been unable to reach a consensus as to whether the human capital model (e.g. career opportunities), the social capital model (e.g. business cooperation), or creative class thesis (e.g. creativity of industries, all quality of life indicators) was more important in explaining the decisions of talented people to live in a particular city (Donegan et al., 2008; Hoyman & Faricy, 2009; Westlund & Calidoni, 2010), we have included all these variables for comparison in this research. For convenience in creating our research hypotheses, we reorganized the variables into two categories, namely, perceived economic environment variables and perceived quality-of-life variables. The former consists of economic development, city development, career opportunities, business opportunities, business cooperation, and creativity of industries. The latter consists of education, healthcare, social well-being, housing, environmental protection, well-being of the next generation, and general quality of life.

The latest global city ranking of sustainable economic competitiveness reveals that both Hong Kong and Shenzhen performed far better than other Chinese cities, with Hong Kong (ranked 7th globally and 1st in China) being more competitive in sustaining economic growth compared to Shenzhen (ranked 19th globally and 2nd in China) (United Nations & Chinese Academy of Economic Strategy, 2020). Thus, we hypothesize that Hong Kong is more competitive than Shenzhen in retaining premium human resources (Hypothesis 1). The research report by Mercer (2019) reveals that neither Hong Kong nor Shenzhen performed well in the quality of life they offer to residents, while the performance of Shenzhen (ranked 132nd globally) was considerably worse than that of Hong Kong (ranked 71st globally). Therefore, we hypothesize that the quality of life in both Hong Kong and Shenzhen is not competitive in retaining premium human resources, but that the situation in Shenzhen is worse than that in Hong Kong (Hypothesis 2).

Method

Sampling and Samples

We identified two projects that had been managed by our team and extracted their datasets to achieve a comparison between Hong Kong and Shenzhen. The Joint Research Center for the Greater Bay Area-Social Policy and Governance of Lingnan University (LU) was entrusted by the Public Opinion Program of LU to implement a large-scale survey among Hong Kong residents in September 2019 to assess the competitiveness of Hong Kong relative to the mainland GBA cities. The survey covered the subjective assessment of two variables involving the economic environment and five variables about quality of life. The target population was Hong Kong adults aged 18 or over, and the participants were identified by randomly selecting residential telephone numbers based on the last two digits of the Hong Kong residential directory. Data were successfully collected from 1216 Hong Kong adults (53.7% female), with a response rate of 31.3%. As we were defining "premium human resources" as people who were younger, well-educated, or had a higher income, we were particularly interested in the proportions of these three sociodemographic attributes in the sample. Descriptive statistics revealed that younger people, aged between 18 and 29, made up 15.3% of the sample. Well-educated people with their highest educational achievement being an associated degree or above made up 35.9%. Higher-income participants were those with a monthly income of HKD 30,000 or above, and they made up 41.5% of the sample.

We commissioned a mainland survey company to survey Shenzhen residents about their consumption habits in 2018. The survey assessed five variables relating to the economic environment and three variables about quality of life, which were similar to those in the Hong Kong survey. The target population for the Shenzhen survey was adults aged 18 to 75, which was almost the same as that in Hong Kong. Using a stratified random sampling strategy, the final sample consisted of 1007 participants (50.3% male) and was evenly distributed between four residential districts in Shenzhen. To achieve an effective comparison between Hong Kong and Shenzhen, the same criteria were used to define younger, well-educated, and higher-income participants. Those aged 18 to 29 were defined as the younger group, which comprised 33.5% of the whole sample. Well-educated participants were those with at least an associate degree, and made up 64.3% of the sample. As a cost of living comparison revealed that Shenzhen residents are able to maintain the same standard of living (including rental costs) as they could in Hong Kong with a monthly income of just 50% compared to that in Hong Kong (Numbeo, 2021), the cut-off value differentiating higher and lower incomes in the Shenzhen sample was set as RMB 12,500 (1RMB = 1.25 HKD). Those with a higher income made up 25.4% of the sample.

Measures

In the survey implemented in Hong Kong, participants were invited to rate their satisfaction on two economic environment variables (economic development and career opportunities), and five quality of life variables (education, healthcare, social well-being, housing, and environmental protection), on a scale from 1 (very unsatisfied) to 10 (very satisfied). In the survey implemented in Shenzhen, participants were invited to indicate their agreement to eight statements that described economic environment and quality of life in Shenzhen. All answers were calibrated on a five-point scale from 1 (totally disagree) to 5 (fully agree). The five items assessing perceived economic environment were "Shenzhen is a city of economic prosperity," "Shenzhen is a place filled with business opportunities," "Shenzhen is a place to meet new people for business cooperation," "Shenzhen is a place for personal career development," and "Industries in Shenzhen are creative." The three items assessing perceived quality of life were "Shenzhen is a good place for the development of the next generation," "Shenzhen has a beautiful natural environment," and "The life quality of residents in Shenzhen is very high." (Table 4.1).

Data Analysis Plan

First, we needed to calculate the difference between the variables for the economic environment and the quality of life domains between two contrasting groups (e.g. between the younger and the older participants, between the well-educated and the less-educated people, and between those with higher and lower incomes) in both the Hong Kong and Shenzhen samples. Second, we needed to calculate the effect sizes of all differences obtained in the first step and then compare the effect sizes between the two samples. As the variables measured in the two surveys were not exactly the same, we paired variables that were similar. A total of ten pairs were created for comparison, which are identified in Tables 4.2, 4.3 and 4.4 by the same color. For example, in Table 4.2, career opportunities in the Hong Kong sample are paired with business opportunities, business cooperation, and career opportunities in the Shenzhen sample for the comparison. Statistical mean difference was calculated, and an independent sample t test was implemented to check the significance of the difference. Before calculating the effect size, an F test was performed to test the equal variance assumption for each

Table 4.1 Decision rules for comparison

	Mean difference of a variable between contrasting groups in Hong Kong	*Mean difference of a variable between contrasting groups in Shenzhen*	*Effect size of the difference in Hong Kong*	*Effect size of the difference in Shenzhen*	*Conclusion*
Scenario 1	Positive and significant	Negative and significant	–	–	Hong Kong is competitive; Shenzhen is not competitive
Scenario 2	Positive and significant	Insignificant	–	–	Hong Kong is competitive; Shenzhen is not competitive
Scenario 3	Positive and significant	Positive and significant	Larger	Smaller	Both are competitive; Hong Kong is more competitive than Shenzhen
Scenario 4	Positive and significant	Positive and significant	Smaller	Larger	Both are competitive; Shenzhen is more competitive than Hong Kong
Scenario 5	Negative and significant	Positive and significant	–	–	Shenzhen is competitive; Hong Kong is not competitive
Scenario 6	Insignificant	Positive and significant	–	–	Shenzhen is competitive; Hong Kong is not competitive
Scenario 7	Negative and significant	Negative and significant	Larger	Smaller	Neither are competitive; Hong Kong is worse

(continued)

Table 4.1 (continued)

	Mean difference of a variable between contrasting groups in Hong Kong	*Mean difference of a variable between contrasting groups in Shenzhen*	*Effect size of the difference in Hong Kong*	*Effect size of the difference in Shenzhen*	*Conclusion*
Scenario 8	Negative and significant	Negative and significant	Smaller	Larger	Neither are competitive; Shenzhen is worse
Scenario 9	Negative and significant	Insignificant	–	–	Neither are competitive; Hong Kong is worse
Scenario 10	Insignificant	Negative and significant	–	–	Neither are competitive; Shenzhen is worse
Scenario 11	Insignificant	Insignificant	–	–	Neither are competitive; unable to compare

variable between two contrasting groups. Glass's delta was reported as the effect size when the equal variance assumption was violated (e.g. the *F* value calculated was significant). When equal variance between contrasting groups was confirmed, Hedges' *g* was reported as the effect size when two contrasting groups were of very different sample size; Cohen's *d* was reported as the effect size if two contrasting groups were of similar sample size.

When all effect sizes were prepared, we followed a prior fixed decision rule for conducting the comparisons. This decision rule is presented in Table 4.1. Due to the limited space, we have not displayed all possible scenarios, but show only the 11 scenarios most likely to occur. The table can be improved further if the results of statistics used in this study, or in future studies, are generated for scenes that are not included in this table.

Table 4.2 Comparing differences in subjective assessment on the city of residence between younger and older people in Hong Kong and Shenzhen

Hong Kong							Shenzhen						
Indicator	Mean difference	Equal variance	t	Cohen's d	Glass's delta	Hedges' g	Indicator	Mean difference	Equal variance	t	Cohen's d	Glass's delta	Hedges' g
Economic environment							**Economic environment**						
Economic development	0.619	$F = 5.26^{*}$	$t(460) = 4.18^{**}$	.28	**.31**	.27	City development	-0.12	$F = 1.64$	$t(999) = -2.32^{*}$	.15	.15	**.15**
Career opportunities	-0.024	$F = 6.78^{**}$	$t(463) = -0.164$	-	-	-	Business opportunities	-0.01	$F = 1.05$	$t(1001) = -0.11$	-	-	-
Quality of life							Business cooperation	0.01	$F = 0.01$	$t(1001) = 0.29$	-	-	-
Education	0.01	$F = 2.93$	$t(1181) = 0.08$	-	-	-	Career opportunities	-0.07	$F = 1.07$	$t(1002) = -1.37$	-	-	-
Healthcare	-0.60	$F = 5.17^{*}$	$t(457) = -3.98^{***}$	.27	**.29**	.26	Creativity of industries	-0.06	$F = 2.34$	$t(1003) = -1.21$	-	-	-
Social well-being	-0.86	$F = 5.55^{*}$	$t(464) = -5.71^{***}$	.39	**.42**	.37	**Quality of life**						
Housing	-0.77	$F = 6.05^{*}$	$t(452) = -5.24^{***}$	.36	**.38**	.35	Well-being of next generation	-0.12	$F = 3.21$	$t(989) = -1.79$	-	-	-
Environmental protection	-0.29	$F = 5.57^{*}$	$t(473) = -2.05^{***}$	.14	**.15**	.13	Environmental protection	-0.05	$F = 0.20$	$t(1005) = -0.95$	-	-	-
							General quality of life	- 0.10	$F = 0.01$	$t(1005) = -1.97^{*}$	.13	.13	**.14**

Note Mean difference = Mean (younger group) – Mean (older group). Glass's delta was reported as the effect size when the equal variance assumption was violated. Hedges' g was reported as the effect size when the equal variance assumption was not violated, but the two groups were of very different sample size. Cohen's d was reported as the effect size if two groups had similar standard deviations and were of similar sample size. Variables with the same color could be compared. Effect size reported in the grey blank was used for comparison. * $p < 0.05$, ** $p < 0.01$, *** $p < 0.001$

Table 4.3 Comparing the difference of subjective assessment on the city of residence between well-educated and less well-educated people in Hong Kong and Shenzhen

Hong Kong							Shenzhen						
Indicator	Mean difference	Equal variance	t	Cohen's d	Glass's delta	Hedges' g	Indicator	Mean difference	Equal variance	t	Cohen's d	Glass's delta	Hedges' g
Economic environment							**Economic environment**						
Economic development	0.56	F = 19.91***	t (1005) = 4.21***	.25	**.28**	.25	City development	0.06	F = 0.92	t (999) = 1.24	-	-	-
Career opportunities	0.28	F = 12.85***	t (966) = 2.12*	.13	**.14**	.13	Business opportunities	0.00	F = 0.49	t (1001) = 0.06	-	-	-
Quality of life							Business cooperation	0.01	F = 0.01	t (1001) = 0.90	-	-	-
Education	-0.03	F = 8.32**	t (962) = -0.22	-	-	-	Career opportunities	0.05	F = 0.33	t (1002) = -1.07	-	-	-
Healthcare	-0.23	F = 3.77	t (1155) = -1.60	-	-	-	Creativity of industries	0.11	F = 0.02	t (1003) = 2.55*	.16	.17	**.16**
Social well-being	-0.32	F = 7.28**	t (975) = - 2.35*	.14	**.16**	.14	**Quality of life**						
Housing	-0.08	F = 4.41*	t (941) = -0.63	-	-	-	Development of next generation	-0.09	F = 7.53**	t (989) = -1.46	-	-	-
Environmental protection	0.02	F = 3.61	t (1135) = 0.11	-	-	-	Environmental protection	0.03	F = 0.66	t (1005) = -0.66	-	-	-
							General quality of life	-0.03	F = 0.00	t (1005) = -0.58	-	-	-

Note Mean difference = Mean (well-educated group) – Mean (less well-educated group). Glass's delta was reported as the effect size when the equal variance assumption was violated. Hedges' g was reported as the effect size when the equal variance assumption was not violated, but the two groups were of very different sample size. Cohen's d was reported as the effect size if two groups had similar standard deviations and were of similar sample size. Variables with the same color could be compared. Effect size reported in the grey blank was used for comparison. * $p < 0.05$, ** $p < 0.01$, *** $p < 0.001$

Table 4.4 Comparing differences in subjective assessment of the city of residence between higher-income and lower-income people in Hong Kong and in Shenzhen

Hong Kong							Shenzhen						
Indicator	Mean difference	Equal variance	t	Cohen's d	Glass's delta	Hedges' g	Indicator	Mean difference	Equal variance	t	Cohen's d	Glass's delta	Hedges' g
Economic environment							**Economic environment**						
Economic development	0.32	$F = 0.81$	$t\,(471) = 1.65$	-	-	-	City development	-0.02	$F = 1.02$	$t\,(978) = -0.41$	-	-	-
Career opportunities	0.66	$F = 1.88$	$t\,(467) = 3.32$**	.31	.32	**.31**	Business opportunities	-0.07	$F = 0.00$	$t\,(980) = -1.16$	-	-	-
Quality of life							Business cooperation	0.06	$F = 0.60$	$t\,(980) = 1.13$	-	-	-
Education	0.17	$F = 0.05$	$t\,(470) = 0.79$	-	-	-	Career opportunities	0.05	$F = 0.09$	$t\,(981) = 0.97$	-	-	-
Healthcare	0.10	$F = 0.00$	$t\,(475) = 0.50$	-	-	-	Creativity of industries	-0.01	$F = 13.35$**	$t\,(501) = -0.19$	-	-	-
Social well-being	0.39	$F = 0.07$	$t\,(468) = -1.89$	-	-	-	**Quality of life**						
Housing	0.33	$F = 0.88$	$t\,(472) = -1.65$	-	-	-	Well-being of next generation	0.10	$F = 1.83$	$t\,(968) = 1.48$	-	-	-
Environmental protection	0.25	$F = 0.95$	$t\,(475) = 1.26$	-	-	-	Environmental protection	0.09	$F = 1.50$	$t\,(984) = 1.62$	-	-	-
							General quality of life	0.04	$F = 2.32$	$t\,(984) = 0.71$	-	-	-

Note Mean difference = Mean (higher-income group) − Mean (lower-income group). Glass's delta was reported as the effect size when the equal variance assumption was violated. Hedges' ***g*** was reported as the effect size when the equal variance assumption was not violated, but the two groups were of very different sample size. Cohen's ***d*** was reported as the effect size if two groups had similar standard deviations and were of similar sample size. Variables with the same color could be compared. Effect size reported in the grey blank was used for comparison. ** $p < 0.01$

Results

Table 4.2 reports the differences in the subjective assessment of the city of residence between younger and older people in Hong Kong and Shenzhen, respectively. Regarding the economic environment, the statistical results led us to analyze the two pairs of variables highlighted in blue (economic development vs. city development, and economic development vs. creativity of industries). In Hong Kong, the younger respondents were more satisfied with the economic development than their older counterparts (t [460] = 4.18, $p < 0.01$, Glass's delta = 0.31), while the younger respondents in Shenzhen were less satisfied with the city development compared to their older counterparts (t [999] = –2.32, $p < 0.05$, Hedges' $g = 0.15$). These results fit scenario 1 in the decision rule. We found significant and positive differences in perceived economic development between the two age groups in Hong Kong, but insignificant differences in the perceived creativity of industries between the age groups in Shenzhen. This situation fits scenario 2. Both scenarios 1 and 2 indicate that the economic environment in Hong Kong is more competitive than that in Shenzhen.

Regarding quality of life, the statistical results led us to analyze the three pairs of variables highlighted in purple (e.g. healthcare vs. general quality of life) and one pair of variables highlighted in yellow (i.e. environmental protection vs. environmental protection). In Hong Kong, younger people were less satisfied with the healthcare services (t [457] = -3.98, $p < 0.001$, Glass's delta = 0.29) compared to their older counterparts; whereas in Shenzhen, the younger participants rated quality of life lower compared to their older counterparts, but with a smaller effect size (t [1005] = –1.97, $p < 0.05$; Hedges' $g = 0.14$). The situation fits scenario 7 in the decision rules. Analysis of the results for the pairs "social well-being vs. general quality of life" and "housing vs. general quality of life" also fit scenario 7. In Hong Kong, the younger adults were less satisfied with the environmental protection (t [473] = –2.05, $p < 0.001$, Glass's delta = 0.15); whereas in Shenzhen, there was no significant difference in perceived environmental protection between the two age groups (t [1005] = –0.95; $p > 0.05$). This situation fits scenario 9. Both scenarios 7 and 9 indicate that the quality of life in both Hong Kong and Shenzhen are not competitive, with the situation in Hong Kong being worse than that in Shenzhen.

Table 4.3 reports the differences in the subjective assessments of the city of residence between well-educated and less well-educated people in both Hong Kong and Shenzhen. Regarding the economic environment, the statistical results motivated us to analyze all five pairs highlighted in blue and green. In Hong Kong, the average rating for economic development among well-educated individuals was higher than that among the less well-educated (t [1005] = 4.21, $p < 0.001$, Glass's delta = 0.28). In Shenzhen, the average rating for creativity of industries was higher among well-educated individuals than among their counterparts, but the effect size of the difference was smaller (t [1003] = 2.55, $p < 0.05$, Hedges'g = 0.16). The situation fits scenario 3. In Hong Kong, satisfaction about career opportunities was higher among well-educated participants compared to the less well-educated ones (t [966] = 2.12, $p < 0.05$, Glass's delta = 0.14); in Shenzhen, average ratings for career opportunities did not differ significantly between the two education groups (t [1002] = –1.07; $p > 0.05$). This situation fits scenario 2. Analysis results of the other three pairs (i.e. economic development vs. city development, career opportunities vs. business opportunities, and career opportunities vs. business cooperation) also fit scenario 2. Both scenarios 2 and 3 support the notion that the economic environment of Hong Kong is more competitive than that in Shenzhen.

Regarding quality of life, the statistical results allowed us to analyze just one pair of variables, which are highlighted in purple in Table 4.3 (i.e. social well-being vs. general quality of life). Well-educated participants in Hong Kong were less satisfied with social well-being compared to their less-educated counterparts (t [975] = –2.35, $p < 0.05$, Glass's delta = 0.16), while in Shenzhen the difference in the subjective assessment of general quality of life was not significant between the two education groups (t [1005] = –0.58; $p > 0.05$). The situation fits scenario 9 in that neither Hong Kong nor Shenzhen was seen as competitive in offering a high quality of life to their well-educated residents, while the situation in Hong Kong was worse.

Table 4.4 reports difference in the subjective assessment of their city of residence between higher-income and lower-income people in both Hong Kong and Shenzhen. The statistical results supported the analysis of three pairs of variables in the economic environment, which are highlighted in green (e.g. career opportunities vs. career opportunities). In Hong Kong, the average rating of career opportunities among higher-income respondents was higher than that among lower-income respondents (t [467] = 3.32, $p < 0.01$, Hedges' $g = 0.31$); the Shenzhen sample shows that there was no statistical difference in the subjective assessment of career opportunities (t [981] = 0.97; $p > 0.05$) between the two income groups. This situation fits scenario 2. Analysis of the results of the other two pairs also fits scenario 2. In scenario 2, the economic environment of Hong Kong is seen as more competitive than that in Shenzhen.

The findings in Tables 4.2, 4.3 and 4.4 *consistently* show that: (1) the economic environment of Hong Kong is more competitive than that of Shenzhen in retaining premium human resources; (2) the quality of life in neither Hong Kong nor Shenzhen is competitive in retaining premium human resources, with the situation in Hong Kong being worse. Hypothesis 1 is thus well supported, and Hypothesis 2 is partially supported.

Discussion

The GBA Plan removed barriers to enable Hong Kong and Shenzhen to implement cooperation in innovation, but the resulting free mobility of talented people has activated rivalry for premium human resources. There is a need for policy makers in both Hong Kong and Shenzhen to assess the competitiveness of their economic and social systems in attracting and retaining knowledgeable, creative, and young talented people. As an addition to the comparison of performance via the traditional macro-level economic and social indicators (Mercer, 2019; United Nations & Chinese Academy of Economic Strategy, 2020), this chapter offers a new entry point for such a comparison. We quantified the sense of relative deprivation among the premium human resources in both cities and adopted it as an indirect indicator to predict the future competitiveness of the two cities. As our indicator is human capital oriented, it is particularly powerful in assessing the sustainability of the economic growth of a city in the innovation-and knowledge-driven economy.

In the domain of the economic environment, the results of our comparison echo the latest global city rankings for sustainable economic competitiveness, which show that the performance and sustainability of the Hong Kong economy is far better than that of Shenzhen (United Nations & Chinese Academy of Economic Strategy, 2020). The convergence of the results from the two comparisons reveals that the human capital in Hong Kong could be better utilized and integrated into its industries to push its economic growth, relative to Shenzhen. A perceived relative deprivation in economic opportunities among young, well-educated, or higher-income people was not found in Hong Kong but was found in Shenzhen. Compared to Shenzhen, the premium human resources in Hong Kong looked more positively at the economic prosperity of their city and believed more strongly that the economic environment of their city was friendly to them. Although the Shenzhen government has been creating and implementing policies to attract creative talent, its current economic environment seems to fail to meet the needs of premium human resources. Policy makers in Shenzhen might need to conduct a systematic reflection and take action to avoid the risk of losing human capital through the joint innovation ecosystem.

Regarding quality of life, our findings partially echo the report by Mercer (2019). Consistent with that report, the quality of life in both Hong Kong and Shenzhen seem to be uncompetitive in terms of retaining premium human resources. However, the competitiveness of Hong Kong was found to be even lower, which is the opposite of the rankings in the Mercer report (Mercer, 2019). We can identify several possible reasons why the sense of relative deprivation in quality of life was stronger among younger, well-educated, or higher-income people in Hong Kong compared to those in Shenzhen. Hong Kong's population is rapidly aging, and the latest government report reveals that the proportion of residents aged 65 or above had reached 17.9% in 2018 (Office of the Government Economist, 2019). In an aging society, a significant proportion of public resources has to be allocated to meet the basic needs of the elderly, among which are public healthcare resources (Lam, 2017; Wu et al., 2019). Recent research shows that rising housing costs in Hong Kong have almost broken the connection between house ownership and income (as well as educational level), making house ownership increasingly linked to wealth level; even young, well-educated, and high-income Hong Kong residents find it a struggle to afford ownership of a private house (Forrest & Xian, 2018; Lee, 2019). All of these factors may activate a sense of relative deprivation among Hong Kong's premium human resources. Our inferences should be formally assessed by future research projects. In comparison, Shenzhen is a city of immigrants where the median age of all residents is only 33 years (Commerce Bureau of Shenzhen Municipality, 2021). As temporary immigrants, most young, well-educated, and high-income residents are more likely to care about business opportunities and career development, while house ownership, health, and quality of life might not be priority concerns before they become permanent residents of Shenzhen (Liu et al., 2018). This might explain why the sense of relative deprivation in quality of life among premium resource individuals in Shenzhen was not as serious as that in Hong Kong.

Limitations

Although we have presented evidence to address a critical policy issue, two limitations should be highlighted that might erode the scientific value of this chapter. First, although the time interval between the fieldwork in Hong Kong and that in Shenzhen was not long, the Hong Kong survey was conducted several months later than that in Shenzhen. Second, there was a difference in survey instruments between the two surveys. Among all the pairs of variables available for comparison, only three pairs were exactly the same, while the others were only similar. However, neither of these limitations can outweigh the important contribution made by this study: a new indicator (e.g. relative deprivation of premium human resource individuals) was proposed to understand the competitiveness of Hong Kong and Shenzhen. The new indicator needs to be evaluated, as it could affect the completion of the core mission of the GBA plan, namely optimizing the use of human capital in the city cluster to achieve industrial transformation.

References

Akay, A., Bargain, O., & Zimmermann, K. F. (2017). Home sweet home? Macroeconomic conditions in home countries and the well-being of migrants. *Journal of Human Resources, 52*(2), 351–373.

Boyle, P., Norman, P., & Rees, P. (2004). Changing places. Do changes in the relative deprivation of areas influence limiting long-term illness and mortality among non-migrant people living in non-deprived households? *Social Science & Medicine, 58*(12), 2459–2471.

Carney, M., & Davies, H. (1999). From entrepot to entrepot via merchant manufacturing: Adaptive mechanisms, organizational capabilities and the structure of the Hong Kong economy. *Asia Pacific Business Review, 6*(1), 13–32.

Carayannis, E. G., Grigoroudis, E., Campbell, D. F., Meissner, D., & Stamati, D. (2018). The ecosystem as helix: An exploratory theory building study of regional co-opetitive entrepreneurial ecosystems as Quadruple/Quintuple Helix innovation models. *R&D Management, 48*(1), 148–162.

Chen, X., & Ogan, T. L. (2017). China's emerging Silicon Valley: How and why has Shenzhen become a global innovation centre. *European Financial Review, 2017*(1), 55–62.

Clifton, N. (2008). The "creative class" in the UK: An initial analysis. *Geografiska Annaler: Series B, Human Geography, 90*(1), 63–82.

Commerce Bureau of Shenzhen Municipality. (2021). *Business environment of Shenzhen*. Retrieved from http://www.sz.gov.cn/en_szgov/business/environment/content/post_1343686.html.

Darchen, S., & Tremblay, D. G. (2010). What attracts and retains knowledge workers/students: The quality of place or career opportunities? The cases of Montreal and Ottawa. *Cities, 27*(4), 225–233.

Donegan, M., Drucker, J., Goldstein, H., Lowe, N., & Malizia, E. (2008). Which indicators explain metropolitan economic performance best? Traditional or creative class. *Journal of the American Planning Association, 74*(2), 180–195.

Flippen, C. (2013). Relative deprivation and internal migration in the United States: A comparison of black and white men. *American Journal of Sociology, 118*(5), 1161–1198.

Florida, R. (2002). The economic geography of talent. *Annals of the Associations of American Geographers, 92*(4), 743–755.

Florida, R. (2003). Cities and the creative class. *City & Community, 2*(1), 3–19.

Florida, R. (2005). *Cities and the creative class*. Routledge.

Florida, R., Mellander, C., & Stolarick, K. (2008). Inside the black box of regional development—Human capital, the creative class and tolerance. *Journal of Economic Geography, 8*(5), 615–649.

Forrest, R., & Xian, S. (2018). Accommodating discontent: Youth, conflict and the housing question in Hong Kong. *Housing Studies, 33*(1), 1–17.

GBA Development Plan. (2019). *Outline development plan for the Guangdong-Hong Kong-Macau Greater Bay Area*. Beijing: Central Government of China.

Howard, D. (1999). The future shape of Hong Kong's economy: Why high-technology manufacturing will prove to be a myth. In A. W. Chan, W. S. Chow, P. Fosh, E. Snape, & R. Westwood (Eds.), *Hong Kong management and labour: Continuity and change* (pp. 43–58). Routledge.

Hoyman, M., & Faricy, C. (2009). It takes a village: A test of the creative class, social capital, and human capital theories. *Urban Affairs Review, 44*(3), 311–333.

Jin, L. (2016). Migration, relative deprivation, and psychological well-being in China. *American Behavioral Scientist, 60*(5–6), 750–770.

Kang, Y., & Jiang, J. (2020). Revisiting the innovation systems of cross-border cities: The role of higher education institution and cross-boundary cooperation in Hong Kong and Shenzhen. *Journal of Higher Education Policy and Management, 42*(2), 213–229.

Lam, A. H. Y. (2017). Strategies of Hong Kong's healthcare system in ageing population. In official conference proceedings of the *Asian Conference on Ageing & Gerontology*. The University of Hong Kong.

Lee, J. (2019). *Housing, home ownership and social change in Hong Kong*. Routledge.

Li, L. C., & Kwok, M. T. (2019). Unpacking the plan for the Guangdong-Hong Kong–Macao greater bay area: A mechanism for reform. *China and the World, 2*(2), 1950010.

Liu, T., Feng, H., & Brandon, E. (2018). Would you like to leave Beijing, Shanghai, or Shenzhen? An empirical analysis of migration effect in China. *Plos One, 13*(8), e0202030.

Liu, Y., Zhang, F., Liu, Y., Li, Z., & Wu, F. (2019). Economic disadvantages and migrants' subjective well-being in China: The mediating effects of relative deprivation and neighbourhood deprivation. *Population, Space and Place, 25*(2), e2173.

Maning, T. J., & Darnton, J. (2006). Social diversity and economic development in the metropolis. *Journal of Planning Literature, 21*(2), 153–168.

Mercer. (2019). *Vienna tops Mercer's 21st quality of living ranking*. Retrieved from https://www.mercer.com/newsroom/2019-quality-of-living-survey.html (Accessed on 1 December 2021).

National Bureau of Statistics of China. (2015). *Chinese statistics digest*. National Bureau of Statistics of China.

Numbeo. (2021). *Cost of living comparison between Shenzhen and Hong Kong* [Data file]. Retrieved from https://www.numbeo.com/cost-of-living/compare_cities.jsp?country1=China&city1=Shenzhen&country2=Hong+Kong&city2=Hong+Kong (Accessed on 1 December 2021).

Office of the Government Economist. (2019). *Population ageing trend of Hong Kong*. Retrieved from https://www.hkeconomy.gov.hk/en/pdf/el/el-2019-02.pdf (Accessed on 1 December 2021).

Pilati, T., & Tremblay, D. G. (2007). Le développement socio-économique de Montréal: La cité créative et la carrière artistique comme facteurs d'attraction? *Canadian Journal of Regional Science, 30*(3), 475–495.

QS World University Rankings. (2021). *Ranking Table Block*. Retrieved from https://www.topuniversities.com/university-rankings/world-university-rankings/2021 (Accessed on 1 December 2021).

Quinn, M. A. (2006). Relative deprivation, wage differentials and Mexican migration. *Review of Development Economics, 10*(1), 135–153.

Sharif, N., & Baark, E. (2008). From trade hub to innovation hub: Hong Kong. In C. Edquist & L. Hommen (Eds.), *Small country innovation systems: Globalization, change and policy in Asia and Europe* (pp. 194–234). Edward Elgar Cheltenham.

Stark, O., & Taylor, J. E. (1991). Migration incentives, migration types: The role of relative deprivation. *The Economic Journal, 101*(408), 1163–1178.

Stark, O., & Yitzhaki, S. (1988). Labour migration as a response to relative deprivation. *Journal of Population Economics, 1*(1), 57–70.

Stoltenberg, C. D. (1984). China's special economic zones: Their development and prospects. *Asian Survey, 24*(6), 637–654.

United Nations & Chinese Academy of Economic Strategy. (2020). *Global urban competitiveness report*. UN Habitat.

Westlund, H., & Calidoni, F. (2010, July). The creative class, social capital and regional development in Japan. In *Review of Urban & Regional Development Studies: Journal of the Applied Regional Science Conference* (pp. 89–108). Blackwell Publishing Asia.

World Bank. (2019). *GDP growth (annual %) – Hong Kong SAR, China* [Data file]. Retrieved from https://data.worldbank.org/indicator/NY.GDP.MKTP.KD.ZG?locations=HK (Accessed on 1 December 2021).

Wu, X., Law, C. K., & Yip, P. S. F. (2019). A projection of future hospitalisation needs in a rapidly ageing society: A Hong Kong experience. *International Journal of Environmental Research and Public Health, 16*(3), 473–484.

CHAPTER 5

Understanding Migration into Greater Bay Area Cities in Mainland China as an Investment for Hong Kong Young Adults

Alex Yue Feng Zhu and Ka Ho Mok

Introduction

Investment activities are encouraged by policy makers, educators, financial experts, and social workers, as they build an effective avenue to maintain the value of the risk-taker's monetary resources and appreciate his

A. Y. F. Zhu (✉)
Institute of Policy Studies, Lingnan University, Tuen Mun, Hong Kong SAR, China
e-mail: alexzhu@ln.edu.hk

K. H. Mok
Institute of Policy Studies, Lingnan University, Hong Kong, China
e-mail: kahomok@ln.edu.hk

K. H. Mok (ed.), *Cities and Social Governance Reforms*, Social Policy and Development Studies in East Asia,
https://doi.org/10.1007/978-981-16-9531-5_5

or her financial assets. For economically disadvantaged individuals, shouldering the risk and engaging in investment activities creates a chance to achieve upward social mobility (Almenberg & Dreber, 2015; Barberis et al., 2006; Georgarakos & Pasini, 2011; Grinblatt et al., 2011; Guiso & Jappelli, 2005; Hong et al., 2004; Mishra, 2018; Sivaramakrishnan et al., 2017; Van Rooij et al., 2011). However, literature does not put adequate emphasis on a special type of resource, time, which is particularly important among young adults who have not accumulated enough monetary resources to engage in financial investment activities. Young adults may choose to take the risk of uncertainties and invest valuable time into university studies, entrepreneurship activities, or migration to another economy for a better life, or they may refuse to invest in the future and live on a stable income generated from their current employment (Geldhof et al., 2014; Heckman & Montalto, 2018).

Investment for the future has become a critical issue among Hong Kong young adults. A number of research studies have indicated that upward social mobility has gradually ceased in the community (Census and Statistics Department, 2018; Mok, 2016; Zheng et al., 2019). A comparative study conducted in the Greater China region among 1000 young adults aged between 18 and 35 revealed that the percentage of young people who perceived that they had insufficient opportunities to move upward was the highest in Hong Kong, comprising 61.9% of the respondents; whereas in Taiwan, it was 55.1%, and in Macau, it was 38.4%. Mok (2016) surveyed 500 students at a Hong Kong public university and found that 77.9% thought that opportunities for upward social mobility were diminishing. The Census and Statistics Department (2018) found that within the last five years, the number of young people, aged 25 to 29, who were promoted as managers, administrators, and professionals has ceased its stable growth of the previous ten years, with a decrease from 13.6% in 2015 to 10.1% in 2017.

In February 2019, the Chinese government announced its development plan for the Guangdong Mainland China-Hong Kong-Macau Greater Bay Area (GBA Plan, hereafter). Making reference to other world-leading Bay areas with successful bay economies, the GBA Plan not only calls for megacity cluster development (Hui et al., 2018), but also dramatically changes capital and manpower requirements for the GBA and creates a heavy demand for talent in finance, law, business innovation, and business English, all of which are favorable to Hong Kong college graduates (Bai & Li, 2020). Migrating to GBA cities in Mainland China for life and work is an investment with both substantial risk and the potential outcome of betterment of life. Policy makers packaged and promoted migration to GBA cities in Mainland China as "a valuable personal investment" and conducted a series of surveys to explore how the current generation of young adults in Hong Kong perceived migration to GBA cities in Mainland (Chinese University of Hong Kong, 2018; Hong Kong Federation of Youth Groups, 2019; Mok, 2019). The surveys asked young adults to determine their level of confidence in the prospects for GBA development, concern with institutional differences and other migration-related concerns between Hong Kong and Mainland China, and interest in migrating to Mainland China for life and work in the future.

However, when conceptualizing migration to GBA cities in Mainland China as an investment, we do not care about confidence, concern, or migration intention alone but are interested in identifying people who are fully aware of potential gain and risk and are willing to take the risk. In other words, current literature calls for more assessment to identify the real risk-takers who are fully aware of both the development prospects of GBA cities in Mainland China and the risk of migration and are still willing to consider migrating to Mainland China in the future. This study adopted a refined survey instrument to collect perceptions on GBA cities in Mainland China among a large-scale sample of Hong Kong young adults. We aim to address two objectives: first, to identify risk-takers who are willing to invest time to venture into GBA cities in Mainland China by clustering potential benefit, risk, and behavioral intention; second, to adopt the framework of risk tolerance to assess how predisposing and participating factors affect the likelihood of becoming a risk-taker in the migration case.

Becoming a Risk-Taker: Predisposing and Participating Factors

When the Expected Utility Theory (EUT) and Modern Portfolio Theory (MPT) were cited to explain risk tolerance in the field of financial investment, risk tolerance was deemed as constant and unable to be altered (Markowitz, 1952; Von Neumann & Morgenstern, 1947). The EUT emphasizing the reduced marginal utility of additional wealth determines that people will not be willing to take additional risk to get additional return once their utility has almost been maximized. The MPT posits that people will only be willing to take risks when the potential return is high; risk tolerance depends on the attribute of an investment product but not on the biopsychosocial variables of a person or the external environment he or she faces. As an essential development, the Prospect Theory (PT) emerged and was validated after a series of clinical experiments. The PT posits that risk tolerance is related to biopsychosocial and environmental factors and can be altered by exposure to different participating scenarios (Kahneman & Tversky, 1979). The PT opened a gate for the research of risk tolerance and facilitated the development of a framework of predisposing and participating factors affecting the development of risk tolerance (Grable, 2016).

Predisposing Predictors: Biopsychosocial Factors

Predisposing factors are comprised of biopsychosocial and environmental factors, which can hardly be controlled and manipulated by policy makers (Irwin, 1993). Typical biopsychosocial factors affecting risk tolerance are gender, self-esteem, and personal and family social-economic status, while environmental factors focus on social network and social interaction (Grable, 2016). Ho et al. (1994) posited that females show more interest in taking risks to venture for the betterment of their futures compared to males, as females' life expectancy is longer. However, when measuring risk tolerance in an objective manner by assessing risk-taking investment behaviors, researchers consistently documented that males, rather than females, are more likely to take risks, as reflected by trading more frequently and holding riskier investment portfolios (Cupples et al., 2013; Fisher & Yao, 2017; Grable et al., 2009; Neelakantan, 2010). Compared to financial investment products in the previous studies, migration to the GBA for life and work, as an investment of time and energy, is a long-term investment that people cannot quit in the short run; young adults have to shoulder a huge loss if the investment outcome is not favorable. Thus, we tend to cite the notion of Ho et al. (1994) and posit that females are more likely to take the risk and migrate to GBA cities in Mainland, for their innate future perspective.

Positive self-esteem was documented as a critical psychological attribute that is associated with a higher likelihood of taking risks (Baumeister et al., 2003). It can be understood as the confidence in personal skills, capabilities, and competence (Williams & Galliher, 2006).

The uncertain outcomes of investment activities inevitably erode confidence, causing stress and tension, all of which may reduce positive self-esteem; those with high positive self-esteem are more likely to manage the loss of confidence in the investment well and are more likely to have courage to partake in investment activities (Gondaliya & Dhinaiya, 2016). Most people with positive self-esteems become high achievers in different professional fields after risky investments (Bragues, 2005). Adopting the theory in the case of migration, we tend to believe that those who have established positive self-esteem about personal skills and competence are more likely to invest time to venture for betterment of life in GBA cities in Mainland China.

Regarding the association between economic status and risk tolerance, research documents both positive and negative relationships. A rational pathway indicates that people with stable employment, higher incomes, higher levels of accumulated wealth, and better family economic backgrounds should be more willing to take risk and engage in investments, as they have stronger capabilities to shoulder the loss if the outcomes are not favorable (Hallahan et al., 2004; Watson & McNaughton, 2007). Meanwhile, individuals with low economic statuses can also be strongly motivated to join investment activities with risk to alter their disadvantaged economic statuses (Anbar & Eker, 2010; Faff et al., 2008). We tend to posit that the behaviors of the latter cannot be used to define risk tolerance, as people tend to ignore the risk of an investment product and just focus on the potential benefit when there is a strong need to improve economic status by investment; risk tolerance cannot be defined when investors are not fully aware of the risk and the potential harm. We strictly define ***risk-takers*** in the migration case as those who are fully aware of the risk and the potential gain and still consider migration. We believe economic status will promote the likelihood of becoming a risk-taker in the migration context. In comparison, the effect of educational achievements on risk tolerance is less controversial, as individuals with higher educational levels can better understand the importance of investment in lifelong financial planning and the critical role of taking risk in facilitating upward social mobility (Anbar & Eker, 2010). Thus, Hong Kong residents with higher-education degrees are more likely to deem migration to GBA cities in Mainland China as a valuable investment opportunity and take it to venture for the future.

Predisposing Predictors: Environmental Factors

Aside from biopsychosocial factors, environmental influence may also subconsciously shape attitudes toward risk-taking and the decision to engage in investment activities. *Investment* can be interpreted as a social activity; people may find an investment activity more attractive when they notice their friends engaging in it (Hong et al., 2004). Demonstrating the same level of risk tolerance as their friends conveys willingness to integrate into the social network (Brown et al., 2008). Alternatively, information and knowledge offered by successful investors in the social network can motivate others to model their risk-taking behaviors, which explains the relationship between environmental influence and risk tolerance as a process of social learning (Bursztyn et al., 2014; Ostrovsky-Berman & Litwin, 2019). Research conceptualizes the environmental influence in the process of investment decision-making as interactive activities with parents, children, colleagues, and peers; findings reveal a consistent attitudinal and behavioral pattern between an individual and others with social ties (Black et al., 2017; Duflo & Saez, 2003; Li, 2014). For young adults born and based in Hong Kong, the GBA Plan is a new opportunity, and it might still take time for migration to GBA cities in Mainland China to grow into a social phenomenon in Hong Kong. However, if a person has a relative in Mainland China, they are likely to hear the stories of venturing for a better life in GBA cities and develop interest in taking the risk and considering migration.

Participating Factors

Compared to biopsychosocial and environmental factors, which can hardly be affected by policy intervention, participating factors (i.e. knowledge and cognition about the investment product) are more easily altered by marketing tools and promotion programs. When an individual looks positively at the prospect of an investment product and is fully aware of its risk, he or she has to overcome the last challenge before becoming a risk-taker and formally making an investment: accumulating adequate knowledge regarding the product. Knowledgeable people may feel that it is effortless to complete all procedures in the investment process (Grable, 2016; Wang, 2009). Knowledge about the product also creates a cognitive system that is totally independent from personal attributes to receive and digest all new information about the product, facilitating positive interactions between individuals and product providers (Wang, 2006, 2009). Knowledgeable individuals tend to categorize all information about the product and reach an investment decision in a more efficient manner; in comparison, those with less knowledge have to process fragmented information, which postpones the decision-making (Awais et al., 2016; Bayar et al., 2020).

In the migration case, knowledge about GBA cities in Mainland China is built either on the basis of top-down information (i.e. information from both Hong Kong and Mainland governments to Hong Kong residents) or down-down information (i.e. information generated from direct interaction with Mainland residents and institutions). Both governments systematically promoted the GBA Plan in the traditional and new media, highlighting the provision of direct financial assistance and tax reductions for Hong Kong professionals (Yu, 2019; Zhang et al., 2019). The GBA Plan clearly indicates that young entrepreneurs from Hong Kong and Mainland residents can benefit equally from the employment and entrepreneurship support policies (Hong Kong Trade Development Council [HKTDC], 2019). By visiting Mainland China for study and business purposes, people may accumulate rich experience and skills of interacting with the Mainland people, social system, and economic institutions. Realizing both risk and development prospects, these top-down and down-down information channels can facilitate the migration decision-making. International studies clearly suggest the influence of tourism (previous visit and emotional attachment) and occupation on migration intention behavior. Nonetheless, we must realize that the information that helps to determine migration varies depending on socio-demographics. Males and females may have different concerns when choosing to migrating from native metropolitan to non-metropolitan areas (Taima & Asami, 2020). Thus, we believe that people who learn more about policies in support of the GBA Plan and those who have visited Mainland China before with site visit experiences and emotional attachment (environmental change as Adams, 2012 argued) are more likely to become risk-takers and consider migrating to GBA cities for development.

Research Hypotheses

Supported by the literature, we hypothesize that Hong Kong young adults who are female, report higher perceived competence and skills in the labor market, are economically advantaged, have higher educational qualification, have relative(s) in Mainland China, have learned about equal rights in GBA cities in Mainland China, and have visited GBA cities before tend to be risk-takers, while those born in Hong Kong and with negative self-esteem are unlikely to become risk-takers and invest time to venture for a better life in GBA cities in Mainland China.

Method

Sampling and Sample

We commissioned an international data service provider to survey a representative sample of the Hong Kong population. The interviewers completed the fieldwork between 25 March 2019 and 1 April 2019. As the United Nations (2019) indicates that adults younger than 35 have a higher tendency to migrate, the survey targets of this study are limited to young adults aged between 18 and 35 in Hong Kong. We successfully invited 1214 young adults to join the assessment. The ratio of the number of participants in three territories (i.e. Hong Kong Island, Kowloon, and the New Territories) was around 2:3:5, close to the real ratio in the Hong Kong population (Census and Statistics Department, 2019). Half of the participants were male, and the other half were female. Among all respondents, 14.3% were born in Hong Kong, while the rest were born either in GBA cities or other cities in Mainland China. As for economic status, 79.9% of participants were employed full-time, and 11.7% were full-time students. In terms of educational achievement, most individuals in the sample had an undergraduate degree or above (61.3%), followed by those with a high-school diploma only (16.1%), a postsecondary diploma (10.8%), and an associate's degree (8.9%). Sample attributes are detailed in Table 5.1.

Table 5.1 Descriptive statistics ($N = 1214$)

	Frequency (proportion)
Demographic variable	
Male	607 (50.0%)
Economic status	
Full-time employed	970 (79.9%)
Student	142 (11.7%)
Part-time employed	57 (4.7%)
Unemployed	24 (2.0%)
Housewife	20 (1.6%)
Not specified	1 (0.1%)
Educational achievement	
No formal schooling	2 (0.2%)
Primary school	4 (0.3%)
Junior middle school	23 (1.9%)
High school	196 (16.1%)
Secondary diploma	131 (10.8%)
Associate's degree	108 (8.9%)
Undergraduate degree or above	744 (61.3%)
Not specified	6 (0.5%)
Industry	
Financial service	133 (11.0%)
Trade and retailing	179 (14.7%)
Education	127 (10.5%)
Public service	125 (10.3%)
Health and social work	113 (9.3%)
Business logistics	74 (6.1%)
Hotel and catering	54 (4.4%)
Housing	46 (3.8%)
Agricultural and architecture	64 (5.3%)
Others	113 (9.3%)
Occupational class	
Senior executive	147 (12.1%)
Professional	246 (20.3%)
Associate professional	164 (13.5%)
Clerical support workers	294 (24.2%)
Service and sales workers	76 (6.3%)
Craft and related workers	15 (1.2%)
Plant and machine operators and assemblers	12 (1.0%)
Elementary occupations	23 (1.9%)
Others	51 (4.2%)

(continued)

Table 5.1 (continued)

	Frequency (proportion)
Not specified	186(15.3%)
Occupational class of father	
Senior executive	116 (9.6%)
Professional	157 (12.9%)
Associate professional	61 (5.0%)
Clerical support workers	99 (8.2%)
Service and sales workers	69 (5.7%)
Craft and related workers	73 (6.0%)
Plant and machine operators and assemblers	79 (6.5%)
Elementary occupations	192 (15.8%)
Others	368 (30.3%)
Income class	
HKD 10,000 or below	39 (3.2%)
HKD 10,000–HKD 1,4999	143 (11.8%)
HKD 15,000–HKD 19,999	249 (20.5%)
HKD 20,000–HKD 24,999	200 (16.5%)
HKD 25,000–HKD 29,999	118 (9.7%)
HKD 30,000–HKD 34,999	110 (9.1%)
HKD 35,000–HKD 39,999	67 (5.5%)
HKD 40,000 or above	102 (8.4%)
Not specified	186 (15.3%)

Measurement

Biopsychosocial Factors

To measure negative self-esteem, we asked the respondents to indicate the perceived difficulty of finding a job in Hong Kong, and the answers were calibrated in a five-point scale from 1 (very easy) to 5 (very difficult). Participants with full-time jobs were coded as 1, while others were coded as 0. Educational achievements were coded from 1 (no formal schooling) to 7 (undergraduate or above). Personal occupational classes and occupational classes of father were coded from 1 (elementary occupations) to 8 (senior executive). Monthly incomes were coded as eight classes from 1 (HKD 10,000 or below) to 4 (HKD 40,000 or above).

Environmental Factors
Participants born in Hong Kong were coded as 1, while those not born in Hong Kong were coded as 0. Participants who had relative(s) in Mainland China were coded as 1, while others were coded as 0.

Participating Factors
We asked participants if they had learned about equal rights of Hong Kong residents and Mainland residents in the GBA cities and if they had visited a Mainland city in the past 12 months. The answer "yes" was coded as 1, while the answer "no" was coded as 0.

Variables Used for Cluster Analysis
Based on the items validated in the previous surveys, the research team developed a seven-item scale that captured situational concerns about economic institutions and social governance in GBA cities in Mainland China. Seven items captured the risks of economic status, social and life status, cultural integration, free information access, and educational issues of the next generation. Participants were invited to indicate their agreement on a five-point scale from 1 (not worried about it at all) to 5 (very worried about it). Cronbach's alpha across the seven items was 0.82. Situational concerns were calculated by totaling the scores. We assessed the potential gain of migration by asking young people to indicate their agreement to two items on a five-point scale from 1 (strongly disagree) to 5 (strongly agree). These items were "The GBA will be prosperous in the future" and "The GBA will bring development opportunities to Hong Kong's young people." Participants were also invited to report their intentions to migrate to the GBA, to both live and work, by answering one question on a five-point scale from 1 (absolutely will not consider) to 5 (absolutely will consider).

Data Analysis

K-mean cluster analysis was run to categorize all participants into four groups based on four standardized indicators: situational concerns, confidence about the GBA's future, confidence about development opportunities in the GBA, and migration intention. By analyzing the mean of each indicator in each group, we identified the group "risk-taker." All members in this group were well aware of the risks and potential benefits of migration and were still willing to consider migration as a personal investment opportunity. At the next stage, we adopted binary logistic regression to regress on the likelihood of becoming a risk-taker on biopsychosocial variables, environmental variables, and participating variables to assess their unique contributions to the group membership. Considering that industrial backgrounds may equip participants with unique perceptions about the GBA Plan, and affect social-economic statuses and risk tolerance, nine industrial variables were created and added to the model as controls.

Results

K-mean cluster analysis categorized all participants in four groups, as displayed in Table 5.2. The first group could be labeled as "optimist," as this group had the highest confidence in the GBA (M = 0.83; SD = 0.52), the highest confidence in the GBA development opportunity (M = 0.81; SD = 0.50), the lowest situational concerns (M = −1.18; SD = 0.68), and the highest migration intention (M = 0.98; SD = 0.56). Members in this group were aware of the potential gain of migrating to GBA cities in Mainland China but seemed unaware of the risk associated with the migration. We labeled the second group as "pessimist," as its members went to the opposite extreme: they had the lowest confidence in the GBA (M = −1.43; SD = 0.60), the lowest confidence in

Table 5.2 Mean and standard deviations of the four clusters on the four key variables regarding the GBA

	Optimist (N = 307)		*Pessimist (N = 210)*		*Risk-Taker (N = 378)*		*Indifferent (N = 319)*		*F*	*p*
	Mean	*SD*	*Mean*	*SD*	*Mean*	*SD*	*Mean*	*SD*		
Situational concerns	−1.18	0.68	1.03	0.58	0.34	0.57	−0.02	0.76	541.24	0.00
Intention to migrate	0.98	0.56	−1.21	0.44	0.23	0.82	−0.37	0.68	499.55	0.00
Confidence in the GBA prospect	0.83	0.52	−1.43	0.60	0.52	0.51	−0.42	0.65	845.73	0.00
Confidence in GBA job opportunities	0.81	0.50	−1.41	0.52	0.67	0.38	−0.60	0.55	1317.57	0.00

Note The *K*-mean cluster analysis was performed
GBA, Greater Bay Area; SD, Standard deviation

the GBA development opportunity (M = –1.41; SD = 0.52), the highest situational concerns (M = 1.03; SD = 0.58), and the lowest migration intention (M = –1.21; SD = 0.44). Members of the "pessimist" group only paid attention to the risk of migration but were not aware of the potential gain. The third group reported higher confidence in the GBA (M = 0.52; SD = 0.51), higher confidence in the GBA development opportunity (M = 0.67; SD = 0.38), higher situational concerns (M = 0.34; SD = 0.57), and higher migration intention (M = 0.23; SD = 0.82). The psychological status of this group well matched the definition of risk-takers: being fully aware of risk and potential gain and still willing to consider migration as an investment. Thus, this group was labeled as "risk-taker." The four indicators in the fourth group were all lower: lower confidence in the GBA (M = –0.42; SD = 0.65), lower confidence in the GBA development opportunity (M = –0.60; SD = 0.55), lower situational concerns (M = –0.02; SD = 0.76), and lower migration intention (M = –0.37; SD = 0.68). Members in this group seemed to be indifferent to the GBA Plan, so we labeled them as "indifferent." As reported in Fig. 5.1, the proportion of risk-takers was highest in the sample (31.1%), followed by indifferent (26.3%) and optimist (25.3%), and the percentage of pessimist (17.3%) was the lowest.

As shown in Table 5.3, binary logistic regression found that other than gender, all other biopsychosocial and environmental factors could not affect the likelihood of becoming a risk-taker in the migration case. Males were less likely to become risk-takers (OR = 0.63; $p < 0.01$). As for participating factors, results supported that having experience visiting a Mainland city increased the likelihood of being a risk-taker (OR = 2.01; $p < 0.001$). Full-time employees in the hotel and catering industries, compared to those in other industries, were less likely to become risk-takers (OR = 0.40; $p < 0.05$).

Our models generated a series of other findings. Being male (OR = 1.43; $p < 0.05$), having a relative in GBA cities in Mainland China (OR = 1.49; $p < 0.01$), learning about equal rights (OR = 1.65; $p < 0.01$), and Mainland-visit experience (OR = 2.18; $p < 0.001$) increased the likelihood of being an optimist, while negative self-esteem (OR = 0.74; $p < 0.001$) and being born in Hong Kong (OR = 0.45; $p < 0.001$) reduced the likelihood. Those who had negative self-esteem (OR = 1.36; $p < 0.001$), had a full-time job (OR = 1.94; $p < 0.05$), and were born in Hong Kong (OR = 3.90; $p < 0.01$) were more likely to become pessimists, while those with Mainland-visit experience were less likely (OR

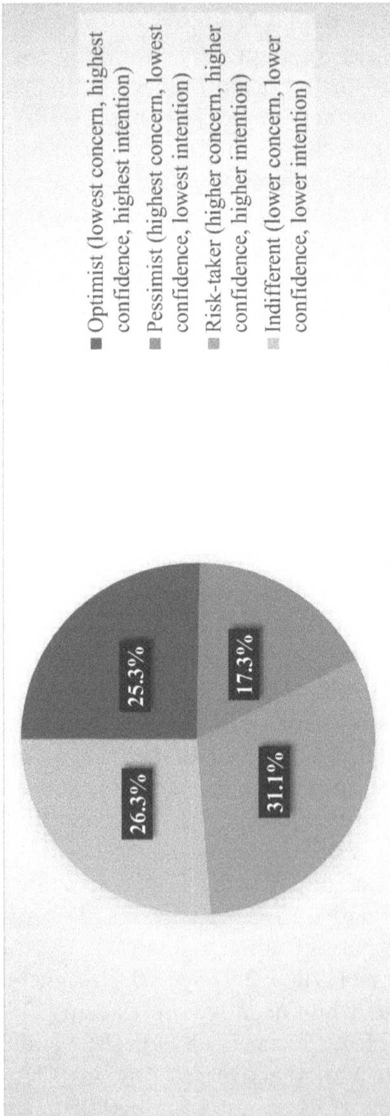

Fig. 5.1 The distribution of respondents among the four clusters ($N = 1214$) (*Note* The K-mean cluster analysis was performed)

Table 5.3 Results of binary logistic regressions ($N = 1214$)

	Optimist		*Pessimist*		*Risk-Taker*		*Indifferent*	
	OR	*p*	*OR*	*p*	*OR*	*p*	*OR*	*p*
Biopsychosocial factors								
Being male	**1.43**	**0.017**	1.18	0.336	**0.63**	**0.001**	1.04	0.799
Negative self-esteem	**0.74**	**0.000**	**1.36**	**0.000**	0.89	0.071	**1.26**	**0.001**
Having a full-time job	1.06	0.798	**1.94**	**0.018**	0.97	0.869	**0.60**	**0.017**
Educational achievement	0.84	0.003	1.11	0.159	0.98	0.702	**1.14**	**0.026**
Occupational class	1.03	0.682	1.12	0.127	1.03	0.592	**0.87**	**0.018**
Occupational class of father	1.02	0.635	0.93	0.075	1.03	0.429	1.01	0.821
Monthly income	1.02	0.638	1.01	0.922	1.02	0.592	0.95	0.268
Environmental factors								
Born in Hong Kong	**0.45**	**0.000**	**3.90**	**0.001**	1.20	0.328	1.18	0.434
Having a relative living in GBA cities in Mainland China	**1.49**	**0.007**	0.72	0.060	1.13	0.368	**0.71**	**0.019**
Participating factors								
Having learned about equal rights in GBA cities in Mainland China	**1.65**	**0.001**	1.30	0.134	0.88	0.327	**0.62**	**0.001**
Having visited Mainland China in the past 12 months	**2.18**	**0.000**	**0.27**	**0.000**	**2.01**	**0.000**	0.83	0.229
Control variables								
Industry: Financial service	0.85	0.601	0.70	0.276	0.77	0.314	2.05	0.009
Industry: Trade and retailing	1.63	0.070	0.52	0.044	0.71	0.163	1.43	0.168
Industry: Education	0.83	0.542	0.72	0.320	0.97	0.890	1.59	0.085
Industry: Public service	1.46	0.202	0.90	0.746	0.94	0.819	0.76	0.382
Industry: Health and social work	1.03	0.924	0.81	0.533	1.06	0.841	1.19	0.562
Industry: Business logistics	1.08	0.824	0.63	0.263	1.30	0.393	0.86	0.668
Industry: Hotel and catering	1.73	0.156	0.52	0.156	**0.40**	**0.032**	**2.02**	**0.042**
Industry: Housing	0.62	0.305	0.68	0.424	1.35	0.396	1.52	0.290
Industry: Agricultural and architecture	1.14	0.728	0.70	0.389	0.93	0.830	1.47	0.269
Constant	0.85	0.755	0.01	0.000	0.36	0.042	0.34	0.043
Nagelkerke R^2	0.178		0.186		0.064		0.100	

OR, Odds Ratio; GBA, Greater Bay Area

= 0.27; $p < 0.001$). Negative self-esteem (OR = 1.26; $p < 0.01$) and higher educational achievement (OR = 1.14; $p < 0.05$) increased the likelihood of being indifferent to the GBA Plan, while having a full-time job (OR = 0.60; $p < 0.05$), being in a higher occupational class (OR = 0.87; $p < 0.05$), having a relative in GBA cities in Mainland China (OR = 0.71; $p < 0.05$), and being aware of equal rights (OR = 0.62; $p < 0.01$) reduced the likelihood.

Discussion

This research interpreted the migration to GBA cities in Mainland China as an investment; identified young adults in Hong Kong who were willing to take risks and consider migrating to GBA cities in Mainland China; and adopted a three-level framework to assess the factors promoting the likelihood of becoming a risk-taker in the migration case. Compared to previous measurements of risk tolerance, our approach is more creative and closer to the conceptual definition of risk tolerance. Our cluster analysis differentiated risk-takers (i.e. knowing both risk and benefit and being willing to take the risk) from those who only pay attention to risk (i.e. pessimist) or benefit (i.e. optimist) and those who do not care about this investment product at all (i.e. indifferent). We found from our sample that the proportion of risk-takers exceeded that of the three other groups. The results are favorable to the Hong Kong government, which promotes migration to the GBA in Mainland China as a strategy to achieve upward social mobility; results are also favorable to the Mainland government, which promotes the GBA Plan as a strategy to achieve regional integration. As Laurila (2011) argued, government's centralized policy intervention would contribute to the efficient allocation of people. Hence, providing policy as incentives to encourage people's mobility from native metropolitan to non-metropolitan areas for work and residence plays an important role to inter-region mobility as clearly revealed by the experiences in other East Asian countries (Kincannon et al., 2005; Kwon, 2003). Although both governments actively introduced the GBA plan to young adults in Hong Kong and have aimed to increase the number of participants, they may prefer to see more-responsible participants who have carefully assessed the risk and potential benefit and thus determined to join (i.e. risk-takers) rather than fanatic participants who ignore the risk and deem the GBA Plan as a perfect gift instead of an investment product (i.e. optimist).

Just as expected, females compared to males were more likely to take the risk and migrate, which is consistent with the biological attribute of females that they are more forward-looking and favor investing in products that last for a long period (Ho et al., 1994). We did not find other predisposing factors that could drive people to become risk-takers, but this actually should not disappoint policy makers. Predisposing factors are normally used to identify primary targets of policy intervention. Since most predisposing factors were found to be insignificant in this study, the roles of participating factors were highlighted in promoting risk tolerance (Wang, 2006, 2009). Interestingly, we detected only the positive effect of having an experience of visiting a Mainland city (first-hand knowledge about the GBA) but did not find the impact of learning about equal rights (a type of top-down socialization). This means that to encourage more young adults to take the risk and consider migrating to GBA cities in Mainland China for life and work, funding a visit to Mainland China seems more effective than specific policy support. Similar findings are also reported by Taima and Asami (2020) when young people in Japan make their decisions to move from metropolitan to non-metropolitan areas. In addition, whether people when planning for migrating to work would also consider whether the future places that they plan to go are inclusive enough. Being treated equally and feeling being socially included is also important, as it would affect peoples' migration intention, such observations are particularly common for Chinese citizens making plans for inter-city migration in China (Hu & Wang, 2019). However, we need to acknowledge that our findings indicate equal rights had no effect on generating risk-takers; the consolation is that it could reduce the likelihood of becoming indifferent to the GBA Plan. Besides, we need to highlight the negative side effect of both Mainland visits and learning about equal rights: both of them may create more optimists, who can be seen as irresponsible investors who ignore the investment risk.

Different from previous studies assessing the perceptions of the GBA among Hong Kong young adults, this study did not directly comment on the migration attitude and decision but focused on evaluating the combination of attitude and behavior by introducing the framework of developing risk tolerance. Like promoting responsible investment decision-making, we recommend a systematic thinking pattern of assessing risk and benefit, tolerating risk, and making decisions in the migration case. Our findings offered entry points for policy makers to train young adults to become risk-takers. Future studies may follow our design by considering the time of young people as a valuable financial resource and adopting the models in the field of investment decision-making and financial risk tolerance to assess activities among young people related to time investment, like entrepreneurship and studying abroad.

References

Adams, H. (2012). *Migration decision-making under environmental change.* Doctoral dissertation, University of East Anglia.

Almenberg, J., & Dreber, A. (2015). Gender, stock market participation and financial literacy. *Economics Letters, 137*, 140–142.

Anbar, A., & Eker, M. (2010). An empirical investigation for determining of the relation between personal financial risk tolerance and demographic characteristic. *Ege Academic Review, 10*(2), 503–523.

Awais, M., Laber, M. F., Rasheed, N., & Khursheed, A. (2016). Impact of financial literacy and investment experience on risk tolerance and investment decisions: Empirical evidence from Pakistan. *International Journal of Economics and Financial Issues, 6*(1), 73–79.

Bai, J., & Li, H. (2020, January). Review of researches on talent cultivation models and approaches under the background of Guangdong-Hong Kong-Macao Greater Bay Area. In *2019 International Conference on Management Science and Industrial Economy* (MSIE 2019). Paris, France: Atlantis Press.

Bayar, Y., Sezgin, H. F., Öztürk, Ö. F., & Şaşmaz, M. Ü. (2020). Financial literacy and financial risk tolerance of individual investors: Multinomial Logistic Regression Approach. *SAGE Open, 10*(3), 2158244020945717.

Barberis, N., Huang, M., & Thaler, R. H. (2006). Individual preferences, monetary gambles, and stock market participation: A case for narrow framing. *American Economic Review, 96*(4), 1069–1090.

Baumeister, R. F., Campbell, J. D., Krueger, J. I., & Vohs, K. D. (2003). Does high self-esteem cause better performance, interpersonal success, happiness, or healthier lifestyles? *Psychological Science in the Public Interest, 4*(1), 1–44.

Black, S., Devereux, P., Lundborg, P., & Majlesi, K. (2017). On the origins of risk-taking in financial markets. *The Journal of Finance, 72*(5), 2229–2278.

Bragues, G. (2005). Business is one thing, ethics is another: Revisiting Bernard Mandeville's 'the fable of the bees.' *Business Ethics Quarterly, 15*(2), 179–203.

Brown, J., Ivkovic, Z., Smith, P., & Weisbenner, S. (2008). Neighbors matter: Causal community effects and stock market participation. *The Journal of Finance, 63*(3), 1509–1531.

Bursztyn, L., Ederer, F., Ferman, B., & Yuchtman, N. (2014). Understanding mechanisms underlying peer effects: Evidence from a field experiment on financial decisions. *Econometrica, 82*(4), 1273–1301.

Census and Statistics Department. (2018). *General household survey*. Census and Statistics Department.

Census and Statistics Department. (2019). *Hong Kong annual digest of statistics*. Census and Statistics Department.

Chinese University of Hong Kong. (2018). *Hong Kong people's evaluation of development opportunity and challenge in the Greater Bay Area*. Chinese University of Hong Kong.

Cupples, S., Rasure, E., & Grable, J. E. (2013). Educational achievement as a mediator between gender and financial risk tolerance: An exploratory study. *Ewha Journal of Social Sciences, 6*, 151–180.

Duflo, E., & Saez, E. (2003). The role of information and social interactions in retirement plan decisions: Evidence from a randomized experiment. *The Quarterly Journal of Economics, 118*(3), 815–842.

Faff, R., Mulino, D., & Chai, D. (2008). On the linkage between financial risk tolerance and risk aversion. *Journal of Financial Research, 31*(1), 1–23.

Fisher, P. J., & Yao, R. (2017). Gender differences in financial risk tolerance. *Journal of Economic Psychology, 61*, 191–202.

GBA Plan. (2019). *Outline development plan for the Guangdong-Hong Kong-Macau Greater Bay Area*. Central Government of China.

Georgarakos, D., & Pasini, G. (2011). Trust, sociability, and stock market participation. *Review of Finance, 15*(4), 693–725.

Geldhof, G. J., Porter, T., Weiner, M. B., Malin, H., Bronk, K. C., Agans, J. P., ... Lerner, R. M. (2014). Fostering youth entrepreneurship: Preliminary findings from the young entrepreneurs study. *Journal of Research on Adolescence, 24*(3), 431–446.

Gondaliya, V., & Dhinaiya, G. (2016). Assessing financial risk tolerance: Do demographic, socioeconomic and attitudinal factors work? *International Journal of Marketing & Financial Management, 4*(5), 32–38.

Grable, J. E. (2016). Financial risk tolerance. In J. J. Xiao (Ed.), *Handbook of consumer finance research* (pp. 19–31). Springer.

Grable, J. E., McGill, S., & Britt, S. (2009). Risk tolerance estimation bias: The age effect. *Journal of Business and Economics Research, 7*(7), 1–12.

Grinblatt, M., Keloharju, M., & Linnainmaa, J. (2011). IQ and stock market participation. *The Journal of Finance, 66*(6), 2121–2164.

Guiso, L., & Jappelli, T. (2005). Awareness and stock market participation. *Review of Finance, 9*(4), 537–567.

Hallahan, T. A., Faff, R. W., & McKenzie, M. D. (2004). An empirical investigation of personal financial risk tolerance. *Financial Services Review, 13*(1), 57–78.

Heckman, S. J., & Montalto, C. P. (2018). Consumer risk preferences and higher education enrollment decisions. *Journal of Consumer Affairs, 52*(1), 166–196.

Ho, K., Milevsky, M. A., & Robinson, C. (1994). Asset allocation, life expectancy, and shortfall. *Financial Services Review, 3*, 109–126.
Hong, H., Kubik, J. D., & Stein, J. C. (2004). Social interaction and stock-market participation. *The Journal of Finance, 59*(1), 137–163.
Hong Kong Federation of Youth Groups. (2019). *Removal barriers for enabling Hong Kong young people to work in the Greater Bay Area*. Hong Kong Federation of Youth Groups.
Hong Kong Trade Development Council [HKTDC]. (2019). *Guangdong looks to boost prospects of young GBA entrepreneurs*. Retrieved from https://hkmb.hktdc.com/en/1X0AHJUL/hktdc-research/Guangdong-Looks-to-Boost-Prospects-of-Young-GBA-Entrepreneurs (Accessed on 1 December 2021).
Hu, W. Y., & Wang, R. (2019). Which Chinese cities are more inclusive and why? *Cities, 86*, 51–61.
Hui, C. M., Li, X., Chen, T. T., & Lang, W. (2018). Deciphering the spatial structure of China's megacity region: A new bay area – The Guangdong-Hong Kong-Macau Greater Bay Area in the making. *Cities, 105,* 102168.
Irwin, C. E. (1993). Adolescence and risk taking: How are they related? In N. J. Bell & R. W. Bell (Eds.), *Adolescent risk taking*. Sage.
Kahneman, D., & Tversky, A. (1979). Prospect theory: An analysis of decision under risk. *Econometrica, 47*(2), 263–291.
Kincannon, C. L., He, W., & West, L. A. (2005). Demography of ageing in China and the United States and economic well-being of their older populations. *Journal of Cross-Cultural Gerontology, 20*(3), 243–255.
Kwon, T. H. (2003). The transformation of Korean life: Demographic trends and social implications. *Social Indicators Research, 62*, 19–38.
Laurila, H. (2011). Optimisation of city size. *Urban Studies, 48*(4), 737–747.
Li, G. (2014). Information sharing and stock market participation: Evidence from extended families. *The Review of Economics and Statistics, 96*(1), 151–160.
Markowitz, H. (1952). Portfolio selection. *Journal of Finance, 7*(1), 77–91.
Mishra, R. (2018). Financial literacy, risk tolerance and stock market participation. *Asian Economic and Financial Review, 8*(12), 1457–1471.
Mok, K. H. (2016). Massification of higher education, graduate employment and social mobility in the Greater China region. *British Journal of Sociology of Education, 37*(1), 51–71.
Mok, K. H. (2019). Calling for regional development and collaboration: Young people's perceptions and evaluations of the development opportunity in the Greater Bay Area in South China. *Paper presented at 2019 International Symposium on Regionalization and Development of the Greater Bay Area*, National Chengchi University.
Neelakantan, U. (2010). Estimation and impact of gender differences in risk tolerance. *Economic Inquiry, 48*, 228–233.

Ostrovsky-Berman, E., & Litwin, H. (2019). Social network and financial risk tolerance among investors nearing and during retirement. *Journal of Family and Economic Issues, 40*(2), 237–249.

Sivaramakrishnan, S., Srivastava, M., & Rastogi, A. (2017). Attitudinal factors, financial literacy, and stock market participation. *International Journal of Bank Marketing, 35*(5), 818–841.

Taima, M., & Asami, Y. (2020). Determinants and policies of native metropolitan young workers' migration toward non-metropolitan areas in Japan. *Cities, 102*, 1–10.

United Nations. (2019). *International migration report*. The United Nations.

Van Rooij, M., Lusardi, A., & Alessie, R. (2011). Financial literacy and stock market participation. *Journal of Financial Economics, 101*(2), 449–472.

Von Neumann, J., & Morgenstern, O. (1947). *Theory of games and economic behavior*. Princeton University Press.

Wang, A. (2006). The effects of audience knowledge on message processing of editorial content. *Journal of Marketing Communications, 12*(4), 281–296.

Wang, A. (2009). Interplay of investors' financial knowledge and risk taking. *The Journal of Behavioral Finance, 10*(4), 204–213.

Watson, J., & McNaughton, M. (2007). Gender differences in risk aversion and expected retirement benefits. *Financial Analysts Journal, 63*(4), 52–62.

Williams, K. L., & Galliher, R. V. (2006). Predicting depression and self-esteem from social connectedness, support, and competence. *Journal of Social and Clinical Psychology, 25*(8), 855–874.

Yu, H. (2019). The Guangdong-Hong Kong-Macau Greater Bay Area in the making: Development plan and challenges. *Cambridge Review of International Affairs*, 1–29. https://doi.org/10.1080/09557571.2019.1679719

Zhang, C., Huang, X., Qu, X., Zhong, Y., & Niu, B. (2019, July). The influence of entrepreneurial environment and entrepreneurial cognitive capital on youth entrepreneurial motivation: Take Shenzhen as an example. In *Proceedings of 16th International Conference on Service Systems and Service Management* (pp. 1–6). Institute of Electrical and Electronics Engineers.

Zheng, V., Hsiao, H. H. M., Wan, P. S., & Wong, K. (2019). Young people's sense of fairness and social action: A survey analysis of Taiwan, Hong Kong, and Macao. *Asian Journal of Comparative Politics, 5*(3), 270–287.

CHAPTER 6

Combating the COVID-19 Pandemic and Enhancing Social Integration: Health Coverage Support for Hong Kong Residents in the GBA

Genghua Huang and Zhaiwen Peng

Background

International population mobility is a significant challenge for the management of the coronavirus (COVID-19) pandemic, an ongoing public health crisis spreading around the world. The suspension of flights

G. Huang (✉)
Institute of Policy Studies, Lingnan University,
Hong Kong, Hong Kong SAR, China
e-mail: genghuahuang@ln.edu.hk

Z. Peng
Research Center for Social Security, Sun Yat-Sen
University, Guangzhou, China
e-mail: pengzhaiwen@163.com

K. H. Mok (ed.), *Cities and Social Governance Reforms*,
Social Policy and Development Studies in East Asia,
https://doi.org/10.1007/978-981-16-9531-5_6

and other traffic has been adopted as an important measure to avoid more cases of imported infection by many countries during the pandemic, but these measures mean that most migrant populations, including migrates, migrant and seasonal workers, international students, and others, have to stay in their host nations. Therefore, equitable access to health and social services in their migrant-receiving areas is crucial, and the World Health Organization (WHO) specifically issued guidance to Member States and partners calling for the inclusion of migrants and the removal of any excessive out-of-pocket payments for COVID-19-related health services (WHO, 2020). However, host nations may encounter a dilemma when considering their policy responses. On the one hand, these changes would allow migrant populations to benefit from limited and valuable medical resources, even free medical services, designed for local residents. On the other hand, the exclusion of migrant populations from the welfare system and public health services, such as free testing, diagnostics, care, and treatment, would increase the risk of outbreaks in these populations (WHO, 2020) and present an additional threat to local public health due to the externalities of the pandemic (Dimick et al., 2017, 2018). In this context, it is vital to understand public attitudes toward migrant populations' access to public health services and welfare benefits, as these attitudes explain policy responses (Harold, 1975; Michael, 1988; Richard & Guy, 1978; Ronald, 1990). The current study was conducted in China, where the COVID-19 pandemic first emerged. To flatten the curve of new cases over time, the Chinese government has taken several decisive actions since the end of January 2020. One of the most effective and dependable actions was the provision of free testing for local residents and the removal of excessive out-of-pocket payments for treatment. Treatment for COVID-19 costs an average of RMB 17,000 (USD 2400) per patient, and 65% of the cost is covered by basic medical insurance (Global Times, 2020). In addition, in early February, China announced that the other 35% of COVID-19 patients' medical costs would be subsidized by local governments. In other words, local residents would be offered "free treatment" for the disease.

One of the most controversial topics in China is whether migrates should be given the same free treatment as local residents. The number of foreign immigrants in China is relatively small due to the country's strict immigration control policy (Miao & Wang, 2017). Yet, there is a significant number of Hong Kong residents living in Mainland China. According to Hong Kong government statistics, there were about 41,000

Hong Kong residents—aged 18 and over—who had taken up residence in the mainland in 2001, accounting for about 0.8% of Hong Kong's population aged 18 and over; while these figures rose to 155,000 and 2.8%, respectively, in 2007–2008 (Census and Statistics Department [C&SD], 2009; see Fig. 6.1). In addition to sharing a similar culture and living habits, the key reasons why these residents decide to live in the mainland include lower cost of living (43.1%), better living environment (24.2%), retirement (25.8%), and convenience for work in the mainland (13.4%) (C&SD, 2009). The accommodations of the majority of Hong Kong residents who have moved to the mainland are located in Guangdong—a mainland province bordering Hong Kong. In 2007–2008, the statistics show that 83.0% of those who had taken up residence in the mainland resided in Guangdong province (C&SD, 2009; see Fig. 6.2).

Based on the special institutional arrangement of "one country, two systems," Hong Kong's financial system and social security system are independent of those in Mainland China. Therefore, Hong Kong residents are usually considered migrant populations when they move to Mainland China. Recently, with the national strategy of the construction of the Guangdong-Hong Kong-Macao Greater Bay Area and a series of favorable policies for cross-border living and working, more and more Hong Kong residents have chosen to reside in Guangdong, especially in the GBA cities in Guangdong. Figures from the Hong Kong government

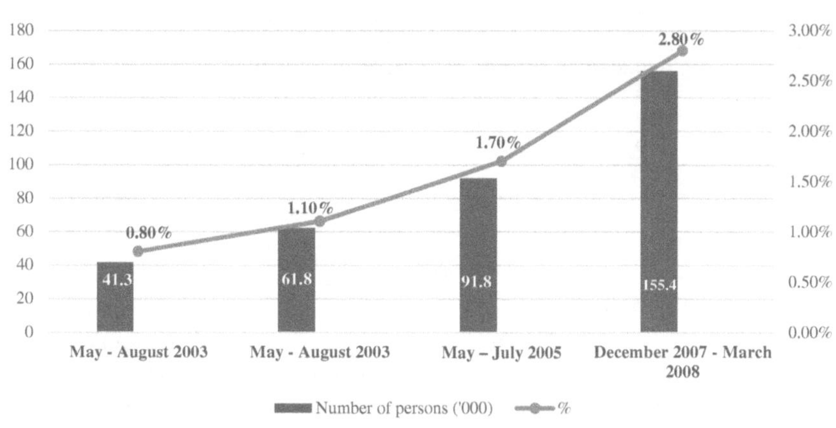

Fig. 6.1 Number of Hong Kong residents (aged 18 and over) living in mainland China (*Source* C&SD [2009])

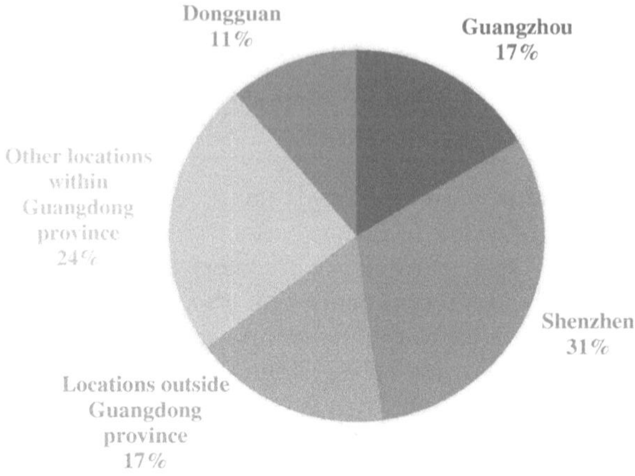

Fig. 6.2 Distribution of Hong Kong residents (aged 18 and over) living in the mainland (December 20) (*Source* C&SD [2009])

Table 6.1 Hong Kong residents in the Guangdong Province (2013–2019)

Reference time point	*Age group*					*Total*
	0–14	*15–24*	*25–44*	*45–64*	*≥ 65*	
Mid-2013	220,100	19,600	71,900	137,400	67,600	516,700
Mid-2014	218,800	21,000	70,400	135,700	70,900	516,600
Mid-2015	218,700	22,000	68,300	134,000	73,100	516,000
Mid-2016	220,500	23,000	68,400	134,000	75,200	521,000
Mid-2017	223,800	24,500	70,100	135,200	77,400	531,000
Mid-2018	220,700	26,400	72,600	137,100	81,000	537,700
Mid-2019	199,000	28,700	76,400	147,600	90,200	541,900

Source C&SD (2020)

show that there were about 542,000 Hong Kong residents in Guangdong in mid-2019, and most of them were older adults and children (see Table 6.1) (C&SD, 2020). During the current outbreak of COVID-19, some Hong Kong residents were also infected with the virus, and the debate about whether they should get the free treatment has aroused widespread public attention. Given this context, this study will investigate Guangdong residents' attitudes toward Hong Kong people's access to local public health services and welfare benefits.

Given this context, this study will investigate Guangdong residents' attitudes toward Hong Kong people's access to local public health services and welfare benefits. This study proposes two key research hypotheses based on a literature review.

Research Hypotheses

COVID-19 Infection Externalities, Health Security Risk, and Attitudes Toward Migrates' Health Coverage

Self-interest hypothesis is one of the mainstreaming theories that explain an individual's social policy preference (Linos & West, 2003; Reeskens & Van Oorschot, 2015; Svallfors, 2004). According to self-interest hypothesis, local residents who are healthy or at a relatively low risk of communicable disease exposure will be more likely to support health coverage for infectious diseases for migrates, since they will have less need for health care than those who are in poorer health or at a high risk of infectious disease exposure. In addition, the exclusion of migrant populations from public health services, such as free testing, diagnostics, care, and treatment, would increase the risk of outbreaks in these populations (WHO, 2020) and present an additional threat to local public health due to the externalities of the pandemic. The negative externalities of infectious diseases may further prompt healthy local residents to support health coverage for infectious diseases for migrates.

After considering the externalities of COVID-19, we derived the following hypothesis:

Hypothesis I Individuals with higher health security ratings, a lower demand for health services, and greater concern about the risk of infectious diseases are more supportive of extending coverage for COVID-19 testing and treatment to migrates.

Impressions of Migrates' Home Country or Place and Attitudes Toward Extending Health Services to Migrates

The politics of social policy on immigration are also influenced by the reciprocal relationship between home country and host country (Hainmueller & Hopkins, 2015). The friendliness/inclusiveness of public policy in migrates' home country or place exerts a feedback effect on the policy preferences of the host country regarding the welfare eligibility of migrates (Eugster, 2018; Jordan, 2013). Thus, the impressions of migrates' home country or place may influence local residents' attitudes toward extending health services to migrates.

From this line of reasoning, this study formulated the second hypothesis:

Hypothesis II Individuals who rate migrates' home country or place as more inclusive and friendly are more supportive of extending health coverage of COVID-19 testing and treatment to migrates.

Materials and Methods

Data Collection

The data used in this study came from an online survey conducted in March 2020. The survey targeted adults aged 18 and older who were local residents of nine cities in Guangdong province. These cities included Guangzhou, Shenzhen, Zhuhai, Dongguan, Foshan, Huizhou, Zhongshan, Jiangmen, and Zhaoqing, all of which are part of the Guangdong-Hong Kong-Macao Greater Bay Area. To ensure that the survey sample was a representative sample of the nine cities, we included respondents from all regions and of different demographic characteristics. We also employed weighting to match the characteristics of the survey sample with the characteristics of the general population. Weighting was calculated using data from the Guangdong Statistical Yearbook. The survey was approved by the Sub-Committee on Research Ethics and Safety of the Research Committee of author's affiliation. The sample size was 1040, and STATA 15.0 was used in the statistical analysis.

Dependent Variable

The survey included a question on public support for migrant healthcare coverage, which was the dependent variable in this study. The survey asked, "If a resident from Hong Kong is infected with COVID-19 in your city, do you support offering them the same free treatment that locals enjoy?" The options offered were "Yes," "No," and "Don't know." Responses were collected using a two-point scale where "Yes = 1" and "No or Don't know = 0," since this study used logistic regression analysis to test the research hypotheses.

Explanatory Variables

To test the first research hypothesis, respondents' subjective health statuses were collected using a five-point Likert-type scale ranging from "1 = very bad" to "5 = very good." The second explanatory variable was related to respondents' perceptions of the risk of the local pandemic. The question read, "How do you evaluate the trend of the COVID-19 pandemic in your city?" Responses were collected using an 11-point scale ranging from "0 = very pessimistic" to "10 = very optimistic."

To test the second research hypothesis, this survey asked respondents to evaluate the performance of the Hong Kong government. The question read, "How do you evaluate the Hong Kong governments' performance in epidemic prevention and control?" The responses were measured using an 11-point scale ranging from "0 = very bad" to "10 = very good."

Another explanatory variable was related to participants' overall impressions of Hong Kong. The survey invited respondents to indicate to what extent they agreed with the following statements: "Hong Kong is an inclusive city," "Hong Kong is an open city," and "Hong Kong is a friendly city." Responses were collected using a five-point Likert-type scale ranging from "1 = strongly disagree" to "5 = strongly agree."

Control Variable

The survey also collected respondents' individual-level characteristics as control variables in the logistic regression analysis. The characteristics were as follows: age group (18–29 = 1; 30–39 = 2; 40–49 = 3; 50–59 = 4; 60+ = 5), gender (male = 1; female = 0), occupation (farmer;

individual business; employees of enterprises and government-sponsored institutions; private entrepreneurs; national civil servants; students; other), and educational attainment (middle school or below = 1; high school = 2; college (diploma) = 3; bachelor = 4; master or above = 5).

Results

Descriptive Statistics

The results demonstrated that 63.48% of respondents supported the provision of free treatment to Hong Kong people infected with COVID-19. Approximately half of the respondents thought their health statuses were "very good" (10.38%) or "good" (44.13%). The survey revealed that most respondents were optimistic about the trend of the local pandemic, creating a curve that was skewed right of the distribution of their responses (mean = 9.508, SD = 1.428). As mentioned above, this survey also asked participants to evaluate their overall impressions of Hong Kong. Only 16.16, 29.81, and 30.96% of the participants agreed (or strongly agreed) that "Hong Kong is an inclusive city," "Hong Kong is an open city," and "Hong Kong is a friendly city," respectively.

The descriptive statistics for the key variables used in this study are outlined in Table 6.2.

Table 6.2 Descriptive statistics for the variables used in this study

Variable	*Mean (SD)*
Dependent variables	
Support for migrant health coverage	0.635 (0.482)
Health security risk variables	
Subjective health status	3.505 (0.879)
Perceptions of the risk of the local pandemic	9.508 (1.428)
Impressions of immigrants' home countries	
Evaluation of the Hong Kong government's performance	7.386 (2.105)
Inclusive	2.898 (1.048)
Open	3.767 (0.93)
Friendly	3.011 (1.01)
Demographic variables	
Age (five groups: 1–5)	2.414 (0.641)
Gender	0.507 (0.5)
Educational attainment (five groups: 1–5)	3.599 (0.757)

Multiple and Logistic Regression Analyses

To test hypothesis I, the set of health security risk variables was added to Model 1, controlling for age, gender, educational attainment, and occupation. The dependent variable specified in the third section was regressed, and the results of this logistic regression analysis are presented in Table 6.3. The findings demonstrated that subjective health status was positively associated with support for migrant health coverage. Specifically, individuals who perceived themselves to be in good health tended to support the provision of free COVID-19 treatment to Hong Kong people, while those who perceived themselves to be in bad health tended to oppose it. In addition, Model 1 also revealed that the degree of optimism about the local pandemic was positively associated with support for migrant healthcare coverage. It implies that individuals who were optimistic about the local pandemic tended to support sharing medical resources with migrants. Therefore, Model 1 supports hypothesis I.

To test research hypothesis II, the set variables about impressions of migrates' home country were added to Model 2. Similarly, Model 2 controlled for age, gender, educational attainment, and occupation. As seen in Table 6.3, respondents' evaluations of the Hong Kong government's performance were positively associated with support for the provision of free COVID-19 treatment to Hong Kong people. Individuals' overall impressions of Hong Kong also influenced their attitudes toward this issue. Individuals who considered Hong Kong to be an inclusive or friendly city tended to support the sharing of medical resources with Hong Kong people in their cities. Thus, Model 2 supports hypothesis II.

The dependent variable was regressed on two sets of explanatory variables together in Model 3 (see Table 6.3). It turned out to be interesting: On the one hand, the effect of health security risk variables on the support for extending health services to Hong Kong people is no longer significant, under control over individual impressions of Hong Kong; On the other hand, however, the positive correlation between the support for health coverage for Hong Kong people and individual impressions of Hong Kong is still significant, when controlling for health security risk variables. Research hypothesis II received stronger empirical confirmation in this study, with better impressions of a place leading to more supportive of extending health coverage for the migrant populations from that place.

Table 6.3 Multiple and logistic models explaining the support for migrant healthcare coverage

	(1)	*(2)*	*(3)*
Health security risk variables			
Subjective health status	0.126* (1.72)		0.0743 (0.93)
Perceptions of the risk of the local pandemic	0.0812* (1.78)		0.0155 (0.32)
Impressions of immigrants' home countries			
Evaluation of the Hong Kong government's performance		0.0860** (2.35)	0.0812** (2.12)
Inclusive		0.266*** (2.97)	0.266*** (2.97)
Open		0.121 (1.37)	0.119 (1.35)
Friendly		0.381*** (4.42)	0.379*** (4.39)
Control variables			
Age	– 0.197* (–1.83)	– 0.245** (–2.03)	– 0.243** (–2.02)
Male, gender	0.479*** (3.65)	0.404*** (2.91)	0.400*** (2.88)
Individual business, occupation	– 0.878 (–1.09)	– 0.965 (–1.09)	– 0.965 (–1.09)
Employees of enterprises and government-sponsored institutions, occupation	– 1.171 (–1.54)	– 1.196 (–1.41)	– 1.210 (–1.43)
Private entrepreneurs, occupation	– 1.073 (–1.30)	– 1.013 (–1.11)	– 1.038 (–1.14)
National civil servants, occupation	– 1.066 (–1.20)	– 0.872 (–0.87)	– 0.878 (–0.88)
Students, occupation	– 1.015 (–1.32)	– 1.144 (–1.34)	– 1.155 (–1.35)
Other, occupation	– 1.131 (–1.36)	– 1.274 (–1.38)	– 1.270 (–1.38)
Educational attainment	0.00446 (0.05)	0.0812 (0.82)	0.0767 (0.77)
_cons	0.673 (0.69)	– 1.144 (–1.17)	– 1.476 (–1.36)
N	1040	1040	1040
chi2	27.21	111.9	112.3

Note *** $p < 0.01$; ** $p < 0.05$; * $p < 0.10$

Discussion and Conclusion

The study is one of the first attempts to quantify the drivers of public support for health coverage for migrates in less developed countries during the COVID-19 pandemic. To address the challenge of the pandemic, many countries provide free diagnostic and treatment services to their citizens. However, migrant populations, including migrates, migrant and seasonal workers, international students, and others, are usually excluded from this policy arrangement due to lack of citizenship or coverage by social health insurance in the host nations. If migrant populations are not adequately protected against the financial consequences of COVID-19-related health expenses, the risk of outbreaks in immigrant populations can increase and present an additional threat to local public health. Given these considerations, the world health organization called on Member States and partners to integrate migrant populations into their health structures and avoid excessive out-of-pocket payments for COVID-19-related health services (WHO, 2020).

The self-interest hypothesis argues that local residents would consider their needs prior to the wellbeing of migrant populations; therefore, the public may not support the extension of welfare services to migrate at a time of crisis when public service and welfare resources are scarce (Van Oorschot & Uunk, 2007). In fact, a large number of existing literature material have shown that, the public health crisis and the resulting economic crisis would generally undermine public support for international assistance (Bodenstein & Faust, 2017; Heinrich et al., 2016; Henson & Lindstrom, 2013). However, the attitudes of local residents may be affected by the externalities of the pandemic, which complicates local residents' attitudes toward migrant populations' access to free health service under the public health crisis. Our empirical study finds that due to the negative externalities of infectious diseases, individuals with higher health security ratings, lower demand for health services, and greater concern about the risk of infectious diseases are more supportive of extending health services to migrant populations. In addition, impressions of migrates' home country or place may also alter this prediction created by the self-interest hypothesis. This study finds that the impressions of migrates' home country or place will exert a feedback effect on the welfare attitudes of citizens in the host country. Individuals who rate migrates' home country or place as inclusive and friendly are more supportive of extending health services to migrates.

According to Johns Hopkins Coronavirus Resource Center, the COVID-19 pandemic has spread to 188 countries or regions around the world, while the overall number of infections has surpassed 64 million by 3 Dec 2020 (Johns Hopkins Coronavirus Resource Center, 2020). According to the COVID-19 pandemic prediction model created by the Center for Infectious Disease Research and Policy at the University of Minnesota, the epidemic is likely to last until 2022 if there is no cure for the COVID-19 and the vaccine (Kissler et al., 2020).

Public support for health coverage for migrates in the COVID-19 Pandemic is influenced by infection externalities and impressions of migrates' home country or place. This study provides preliminary findings about the characteristics and causes of public support for health coverage for migrants during the pandemic. It also outlines a series of crucial implications for social cohesion and social integration in the GBA. The establishment of the GBA was a milestone in the regional integration in the Pearl River Delta. As a top-down national strategy, one of its aims is to build the GBA as a quality living circle. In fact, in the pre-GBA period, the cooperation between cities in the mainland, Hong Kong, and Macao mostly focused on economic and trade affairs. In contrast, the GBA initiative proposes a comprehensive blueprint that encompasses not only economic and trade cooperation but also public service provision and social integration. Since the release of the GBA development outline in February 2019, the Chinese authority has introduced a series of policy measures to facilitate Hong Kong people to work and live in the mainland cities of the GBA (Constitutional and Mainland Affairs, 2020). These measures give Hong Kong people access to some public services in the mainland, such as education, employment, and social security. Indeed, these measures may encourage more Hong Kong people to move to the mainland, aligning Hong Kong more closely with the mainland socially. However, these public services need additional public finance, so local public attitudes should not be ignored. In addition, a series of social incidents broke out in Hong Kong in the second half of 2019, which would change the impression of some mainland residents on Hong Kong and their support for social integration. In brief, COVID-19, public attitudes, and public services and welfare benefits have an important impact on the social cohesion in the GBA, and there is a need for more research to be done to understand the relationship among them.

Funding The author(s) disclosed receipt of the following financial support for the research, authorship, and publication of this article: LU Research Committee—Research Seed Fund (Project Number: 102390).

References

Bodenstein, T., & Faust, J. (2017). Who cares? European public opinion on foreign aid and political conditionality. *Journal of Common Market Studies, 55*(5), 955–973.

Census and Statistics Department (C&SD). (2009). *Thematic household survey report—Characteristics of Hong Kong residents having resided/having stayed substantially in the mainland of China*. Census and Statistics Department.

Census and Statistics Department (C&SD). (2020). *Statistics on Hong Kong residents usually staying in Guangdong*. Census and Statistics Department. Retrieved September 10, 2020, from https://www.censtatd.gov.hk/hkstat/sub/sp150.jsp?productCode=D5320188

Constitutional and Mainland Affairs. (2020, September 29). Facilitation Measures for Hong Kong People. Retrieved April 05, 2021, from https://www.cmab.gov.hk/en/issues/facilitation_measures.htm

Dimick, M., Rueda, D., & Stegmueller, D. (2017). The altruistic rich? Inequality and other-regarding preferences for redistribution. *Quarterly Journal of Political Science, 11*(4), 385–439.

Dimick, M., Rueda, D., & Stegmueller, D. (2018). Models of other-regarding preferences, inequality, and redistribution. *Annual Review of Political Science, 21*(1), 441–460.

Eugster, B. (2018). Immigrants and poverty, and conditionality of immigrants' social rights. *Journal of European Social Policy, 28*(5), 452–470.

Global Times. (2020, March 29). China spends $2,395 on average for each COVID-19 patient. *Global Times*. Retrieved April 05, 2021, from https://www.globaltimes.cn/content/1184060.shtml

Hainmueller, J., & Hopkins, D. J. (2015). The hidden American immigration consensus: A conjoint analysis of attitudes toward immigrants. *American Journal of Political Science, 59*(3), 529–548.

Harold, L. W. (1975). *The Welfare State and Equality: Structural and ideological roots of public expenditure*. University of California Press.

Henson, S., & Lindstrom, J. (2013). "A mile wide and an inch deep"? Understanding public support for aid: The case of the United Kingdom. *World Development, 42*, 67–75.

Heinrich, T., Kobayashi, Y., & Bryant, K. A. (2016). Public opinion and foreign aid cuts in economic crises. *World Development, 77*, 66–79.

Johns Hopkins Coronavirus Resource Center. (2020). *COVID-19 Map*. Retrieved March 29, 2020, from https://coronavirus.jhu.edu/map.html

Jordan, J. (2013). Policy feedback and support for the welfare state. *Journal of European Social Policy, 23*(2), 134–148.

Kissler, S. M., Tedijanto, C., Goldstein, E., Grad, Y. H., & Lipsitch, M. (2020). Projecting the transmission dynamics of SARS-CoV-2 through the postpandemic period. *Science, 368*(6493), 860–868.

Linos, K., & West, M. (2003). Self-interest, social beliefs, and attitudes to redistribution: Re-addressing the issue of cross-national variation. *European Sociological Review, 19*(4), 393–409.

Miao, L., & Wang, H. Y. (2017). *International Migration of China: Status, policy and social responses to the globalization of migration*. Springer.

Michael, H. (1988). *Principles of Group Solidarity*. University of California Press.

Page, K. R., Venkataramani, M., Beyrer, C., & Polk, S. (2020). Undocumented U.S. immigrants and Covid-19. *New England Journal of Medicine*, *382*(21), e62.

Reeskens, T., & Van Oorschot, W. (2015). Immigrants' attitudes towards welfare redistribution: An exploration of role of government preferences among immigrants and natives across 18 European welfare states. *European Sociological Review, 31*(4), 433–445.

Richard, R., & Guy, P. (1978). *Can government go bankrupt?* Basic Books.

Ronald, I. (1990). *Culture shift in advanced society*. Princeton University Press.

Svallfors, S. (2004). Class, attitudes and the welfare state: Sweden in comparative perspective. *Social Policy and Administration, 38*(2), 119–138.

Van Oorschot, W., & Uunk, W. (2007). Welfare spending and the public's concern for immigrants: Multilevel evidence for eighteen European countries. *Comparative Politics, 40*(1), 63–82.

World Health Organization [WHO]. (2020). *Preparedness, prevention and control of coronavirus disease (COVID-19) for refugees and migrants in non-camp settings: Interim guidance*. Retrieved April 08, 2021, from https://apps.who.int/iris/bitstream/handle/10665/331777/WHO-2019-nCoV-Refugees_Migrants-2020.1-eng.pdf

CHAPTER 7

Variations on Contracting Out Social Services in China's Cities: The Case of Beijing, Shanghai and Guangzhou

Chak Kwan Chan and Xue Liu

Introduction

Nationwide policy variations are a common phenomenon in China. Local governments have been widely reported to constantly reinterpret and modify central government's policy according to local circumstances. This scenario has led to 'systematic deviation from the original intention of the policies' (Zhou, 2010). Variations are also an outcome of the central government's policy implementation because central officials only define a national policy framework, and local government officials are given some space to work out the details according to available resources and needs

C. K. Chan (✉) · X. Liu
Asia-Pacific Institute of Ageing Studies, Lingnan University, Hong Kong, China
e-mail: chakkwanchan@ln.edu.hk

K. H. Mok (ed.), *Cities and Social Governance Reforms*, Social Policy and Development Studies in East Asia, https://doi.org/10.1007/978-981-16-9531-5_7

(Duckett & Carrillo, 2011). Thus, China's governance is named 'fragmented authoritarianism' because government bureaucrats launch policies 'under diverse local conditions while following the directives of the central government' (Huang & Kim, 2020, p. 344).

Contracting out social services has become China's main welfare strategy. This chapter will illustrate regional differences on the bases of a qualitative study conducted in Beijing, Shanghai and Guangzhou. The chapter is composed of three sections. Section one introduces the recent literature on local policy variations and research background and methodology of the study. Section two reports the key findings, whilst the final section discusses policy implications.

Local Policy Variations and Research Methodology

As illustrated in other chapters of this volume, the Chinese government is using contracting out social services to shift its role from a direct welfare provider to a services monitor. This move is an obvious departure from its former practices and is even described as China's welfare revolution (Chan, 2018). Considering that it is a new national policy, China's central government published some guidelines, and its actual implementation will be decided by local officials.

In China, policy variations at the local level are the consequence of the central government's decentralization approach that aims to ensure the implementation of key national policies. According to Mok and Wu (2013), policy variations come in two forms, including systematic (vertically) and local variations (horizontally). For systematic variation, China's central government encourages local governments to adopt innovative policy methods on the bases of local conditions. In this way, local governments can achieve some national policy objectives. This policy implementation is called 'top-level design and bottom-level innovation'. Local government officials have to manage pressures from the top and from the bottom simultaneously in the process of launching new policies (Huang & Kim, 2020; Zhou, 2010). As for horizontal variation, local governments do not fully follow central government policies but only selectively implement some areas according to their social and financial conditions. This form of variation may exist as a result of local resistance, collusion and local officials' bargains with central authorities (Zhu & Zhao, 2018).

Both the systematic (vertically) and local variations (horizontally) can partly achieve national policy goals, which are also a reflection of financial difficulties of local governments. This contradiction is due to the fact that most policies are actually proposed by China's central government but are financed by local resources. Therefore, local governments make local adjustments according to their financial circumstances (Zhu & Zhao, 2018). Notably, local policy variations provide valuable information for central government's decision-makers to evaluate the impact and effectiveness of a policy and then make the necessary changes (Zhu & Zhao, 2018).

This chapter aims to use the experiences of Beijing, Shanghai and Guangzhou to examine local variations on contracting out social services. The data of this paper were part of a study that examined contracting out social services in China. The study adopted a qualitative approach to gather the concrete experiences of key stakeholders in implementing the new policy. The respondents of this study were from three developed cities of China, including Beijing, Shanghai and Guangzhou. In this article, respondents from Beijing will be referred to code B, from Shanghai S and Guangzhou G. A total of 12 respondents were interviewed in the three economically developed cities, including 3 from Beijing, 4 from Shanghai and 5 from Guangzhou. Concerning the positions of the respondents, 6 were head or associate head of social service agencies, 2 were frontline social workers and 4 were academics involved in running non-governmental organizations (NGOs) or acted as experts for assessing contract bids or contract completion performances. Thematic analysis was adopted to examine the variations in the practices of contracting out social services in the three cities, and the key findings are presented in the following sections.

Key Findings

Who Are Welfare Purchasers?

The political structure of China has led to the creation of multiple welfare purchasers in a city. At the city level, the Civil Affairs Bureau and Social Work Committee are two major departments for purchasing public services in Beijing and Shanghai. Some traditional mass organizations such as the Women Alliance, Disability Alliance and Communist Youth Group have their own resources to buy services for their service groups.

However, these groups are not under the control of the city governments and can freely purchase services for achieving their own objectives. Moreover, lower-level governments can purchase welfare services for their districts, streets and towns. Multiple buyers at the city level and in different levels of governments can be found across the three cities. Under the existing arrangements, coordination scarcely happens on the purchasing services among different government agencies and different levels of governments.

The political power of a government department in a city directly affects its resources for purchasing services. In Beijing and Shanghai, the Social Work Committee and the Civil Affairs Bureau are the main departments for commissioning social services. Their finances come from the city government, thereby affording them other resources to commission large-scale projects than the regional branches of the mass organizations and district governments. More importantly, the administrative structure of a local government affects the purchasing power of a department. For example, the chairman of the Social Work Committee is also a member of the standing committee of the Beijing Municipal Party Committee, which is responsible for building and developing the city. Therefore, the Social Work Committee is more powerful and resourceful in Beijing than its counterpart in Shanghai (B2, p2).

In China, the mass organizations, including the Women Alliance, Disability Alliance and Communist Youth Group, are nationwide organizations and financed by the central government. These organizations are very powerful in a region and are free to use their resources to set up welfare organizations or commission NGOs to provide services for their user groups (B1 and B2). According to a respondent in Beijing, NGOs now receive money from a wide range of funding sources and obtain service contracts from various types of government agencies (B1, p1). In addition, lower-level governments and semi-official bodies such as the Street Offices and Resident Associations commissioned NGOs to do projects (B2).

The scale of contracted projects will likely be affected by local leaders' attitudes on social welfare. For example, senior officials of Guangzhou City consider purchasing services as an effective strategy to shift the provision of public services to the third sector. Therefore, the Civil Affair Bureau and lower-level governments introduce large-scale purchasing services. The contract period of the projects will even be increased from the current three years to five years instead of one year in Beijing and

Shanghai. In this way, welfare workers of NGOs will be more stable in launching services to consolidate their work (G4).

A few of the major barriers to welfare contracting in China are insufficient NGOs and limited contacts between government agencies and NGOs. Government officials tend to offer contracts to organizations that they are familiar with or have a good reputation as the auditing department of a city will strictly scrutinize the use of public money. Therefore, bureaucrats tend to avoid taking risks in contacting out services (S4). By reducing risks, government officials in various levels use resources to establish community organizations or encourage former civil servants to bid for service contracts.

In Beijing, the Municipal Government financially supports 51 hub organizations that help liaise local NGOs, give advice to new organizations and offer training to their staff members. These hubs commission small-scale projects to NGOs without needing to go through a bidding mechanism (B1). In Shanghai, local governments tend to offer service contracts to familiar social and community organizations (S4). Some retired government officials also set up community organizations to obtain contracts and provide services for people living in their districts (S1). In Beijing, the Women Alliance helped set up an organization to deliver services. The organization later gained additional autonomy and then assumed a role in providing direct services and monitoring and assessing the services of contracted agencies (B3).

Contacting Procedures and Contracted Services

The central government of China publishes purchasing guidelines, and local officials decide the actual implementation of policies. The three cities have adopted different procedures to commission social services. In Beijing, government departments have to go through a bidding procedure if a service contract is more than RMB 500,000 (B1). By contrast, the departments can directly commission an agency to provide a service if the contract amount is under RMB 500,000. Some mass organizations can also offer small-scale contracts without going through an open bidding process. As a respondent (B1) pointed out, 'I spoke to the Women Alliance about our project. They studied it and believed that it was good. It is easy to obtain a service contract with ten or twenty thousand dollars'.

According to a respondent (B2), the Beijing Municipal Government will invite a third party to conduct a service bid:

> The third party will invite an expert team to assess submitted bids. In the first round of selection, they will assess whether the submitted proposals have met the basic criteria. In the second round, experts will study some proposals and then invite the organizations to explain the contents of their projects. After that, marks will be given and the outcomes of a bid announced in the form of a public notice.

In Shanghai, the municipal government can use two financial sources to purchase services. One is regular annual budget, and another is welfare lottery (S1). Different methods are being used by the district governments in Shanghai to buy welfare services. For example, Shanghai Pudong District provides subsidies to elderly homes on the bases of the number of beds. It also purchases NGOs' workers' work hours to implement ageing in place services (S1). Government agencies in Shanghai can use a regular purchase procedure if the project sum is under RMB 100,000. Accordingly, government departments will ask interested parties to submit proposals, and then contracts will be offered to the proposals with good ratings (S4).

If the amount of a project is over RMB 500,000, a formal bidding platform is required. The Shanghai Municipal Government will entrust the Shanghai Community Services Centre to complete a bidding procedure. Experts will be invited to assess the quality of submitted proposals (S2). Apart from a formal bidding mechanism, the Shanghai Municipal Government will give money to hub organizations, which will then fund NGOs to launch small-scale services in a district without having to go through an open bidding mechanism (S2). The hub organizations will develop their own performance indicators to assess the performance of contracted projects. These hub organizations are responsible for supporting organizational building through the provision of professional training for NGOs.

In Beijing, some government departments offer contracts to organizations that have demonstrated good performances on service provisions. Very often, government officials will approach senior managers of NGOs and ask them to design services to sort out social problems. Then, they will give feedback on the submitted proposals. A service contract will be offered following an agreement on the final proposal between the two parties (B3).

Instead of asking a third party to deal with the bidding procedure, the Guangzhou government will launch the commission procedure by itself. It will announce service bids on the government's procurement website, listing out the requirements of relevant services (G5). Then, social welfare experts will be invited to give comments on submitted bids before a contract is offered. A senior officer of an NGO criticized the need for better transparency in the bidding mechanism (G5). The officer stated that some organizations were very close to government officials, which were 'children of some Street Offices' and had advantages in obtaining contracts (G5).

Contract Period and Monitoring

Concerning the duration of a service contract, it is one year in Beijing and Shanghai but three years in Guangzhou (it will be extended to five years for new contracts). In both Beijing and Shanghai, the finance department is very powerful so that service contracts have to follow a 12-month financial year. Several respondents voiced out their concerns about the duration of service contracts in Beijing and Shanghai. As a respondent pointed out (B2, p16),

> In Beijing, the duration of a service contact is constrained by the length of a financial year. All incomes and expenses need to be completed in one year. If a contract is three years, the finance department needs to make a three-year budget plan. There is little breakthrough on this matter.

The three cities have procedures to monitor contracted agencies. The Beijing municipal government asks a third party to evaluate the outcomes of a contracted service. A project will undergo a mid-term assessment and a final assessment for a project (B2). Relevant experts will be involved in the assessment process (B1). As explained by a respondent (B1), the indicators for the mid-term and final assessments were extremely detailed, covering all important areas. The assessors would ask the contracted agencies to respond to some questions. Then, they will rate the performance of the agencies.

In Shanghai, the contracted NGOs will be informed of the performance indicators of a project after successfully obtaining a contract (S1).

The indicators will assess a contracted agency on the project, organizational and financial management. In addition, the social impact of its services will also be evaluated.

The Guangzhou City government has commissioned evaluation agencies to assess the performance of contracted services. Accordingly, the evaluation agencies will invite experts to give comments on the services. A respondent (4) had classified the service assessors into four groups: Guangzhou social workers association, service agencies, academics from higher education institutions and the NGOs which deliver services in one district but act as service assessors in another district (G4). Apart from the potential conflict of interest among the assessors, performance indicators varied from district to district. Some were very strict, but others were relatively lenient (G4). The respondent proposed that common indicators for similar projects were essential to the development of contracting welfare services. Table 7.1 summarizes the similarities and differences in contracting out welfare services in the three cities.

In summary, the three studied cities have a similar mechanism to assess the performances of contracted NGOs. Both Beijing and Shanghai municipal governments entrust another agency to complete the bidding procedure, whilst the Guangzhou government invites bids for service contracts. Although experts are involved in assessing submitted bids, concerns exist on the fairness and transparency of the bidding procedure. In particular, some NGOs are managed by former civil servants or were even set up by local governments. The close relationships between government agencies and their funded NGOs may give advantages for these agencies to obtain service contracts.

Discussion

Contracting out social services in China requires investigation in the context of China's administrative structure, the power relationships between different departments and the historical development of Chinese NGOs. These factors also shape the implementation of contracting out social services in different cities.

As illustrated above, multiple purchasers across the three cities are a special feature of China's contracting social services. In many countries, commissioning social services is handled by one single government department at the national or regional level. A coordinating body is

Table 7.1 Similarities and differences in contracting out social services in the three studied cities

	Beijing	*Shanghai*	*Guangzhou*
Main purchaser at city level	a) City Civil Affairs Bureau b) Social Work Committee	a) City Civil Affairs Bureau b) Social Work Committee	Guangzhou Government
Other purchasers	Mass organizations such as Women Alliance, Disability Alliance, Community Youth Group and various local government levels	Mass organizations such as Women Alliance, Disability Alliance, Community Youth Group and various local government levels	Mass organizations such as Women Alliance, Disability Alliance, Community Youth Group and various local government levels
Contract period	1 year	1 year	3 years (current) 5 years (new contracts for integrated family services centres)
Contractors	a) Hub organizations b) NGOs funded by hub organizations	a) Registered non-governmental organizations b) NGOs funded by hub organizations	Registered NGOs
Contract Procedures	a) A formal bidding procedure is required for a contract with more than RMB 500,000 b) Local government departments directly commission NGOs for projects under RMB 500,000	a) A formal bidding procedure is required for a contract with more than RMB 500,000 b) No bidding procedure is required for a project under RMB 100,000	Service bids will be announced in the government's procurement website. The requirements on contracted services will be stated
Bidding organiser	Appoints a third party	The Shanghai Community Services Centre will be appointed to conduct bids for the local government The Shanghai Municipal Government also entrusts hub organizations to commission NGOs to launch small-scale projects	Guangzhou Government

(continued)

Table 7.1 (continued)

	Beijing	*Shanghai*	*Guangzhou*
Service Assessors	A third party will be appointed	Hub organizations will develop assessment criteria	Specific evaluation agencies will be appointed

occasionally tasked to oversee welfare contracts involving several government departments. In China, several services buyers exist at the city level, including the Civil Affairs Bureau, the Social Work Committee, the Women Alliance, the Disabled Alliance and the Communist Youth Group. As these organizations have the same status with political power, coordinating their work in contracting exercises is difficult (G4). In addition, other lower-level governments such as District Offices, Street Offices and even some Resident Associations have resources to purchase services. Given the little coordination among the multiple purchasers, resources may waste or inequalities may widen due to district differences in a city.

Multiple purchasers also imply that NGOs which obtained service contracts from different government agencies will find difficulty delivering services to meet their criteria because different service purchasers have their own performance indicators and evaluation procedures. Moreover, the managers of NGOs need a substantial amount of time to establish favourable work relationships with leaders of different government agencies for a better chance of obtaining service contracts.

As shown from the interview data, contracting out social services has been shaped by administrative structure and local politics. In Guangzhou, local leaders see commissioning social services as a key strategy for shifting the role of the public sector from a welfare provider to a service monitor. In fact, they have mobilized various departments to support this policy. Resulting from the support of local leaders, large amounts of service contracts were offered to NGOs with a contract period of three years. As a respondent (G4) emphasized, the leaders of the Civil Affairs Bureau of Guangzhou City were more realistic and human-oriented, who helped promote welfare development. These two features can rarely be found in Beijing and Shanghai where the sum of contracts is limited, and the contract period is constrained by the one-year rule of the Finance Bureau. As stressed by our respondents, the finance departments of the two cities are very powerful, thus creating an obstacle for other departments and official agencies to change this rigorous requirement (S1, p3). The respondent further exclaimed that the dominance of the Finance Bureau had suppressed the voices of community organizations (S1, p5): 'Being led by the Finance Bureau, contracting social services put much emphasis on statistics produced by contracted agencies. The voices of social organizations on contracting can hardly be heard'.

Local variations on commissioning social services are somewhat an outcome of the influences of other welfare systems and the historical welfare development of a city. For example, Guangzhou's welfare model has long been influenced by that of Hong Kong. According to some respondents of the study, Hong Kong social workers helped set up NGOs in Guangzhou and also offered supervision to their workers. In its early stage of welfare development, Guangzhou's welfare workers regularly visited Hong Kong to learn welfare practices. Hong Kong social work lecturers and practitioners also offered training courses to their counterparts in China. After visiting Hong Kong's welfare sectors, Guangzhou City's leaders organized a meeting to promote social services (G4). Guangzhou's policy on welfare contracting is similar to Hong Kong's model. In particular, contracted agencies are required to have trained social workers, and a longer contract is offered to NGOs. A respondent (G5, p 4) had pointed out the benefits of a three-year service contract for the integrated family centres:

> The Civil Affairs Bureau believes that service outcomes cannot be easily achieved for contracts less than three years. Also, the workforce of contracted agencies will be less stable if their service contract is only one year. Guangzhou has been launching the integrated family centres, it is hard for NGOs to facilitate the development of this service if contracted agencies change rapidly.

In Shanghai, a respondent believed that the city did not commission large-scale welfare projects due to the existence of many services and service units. As many services were already delivered by some organizations, space is limited for developing new ones. As a respondent (S3, p2) explained, the Pudong District in Shanghai adopts a big government approach. Consequently, the district government has many services, civil servants and government units. Therefore, little space exists for NGOs to expand their services. Thus, the extent and space of contracting out social services are partly shaped by a city's existing welfare arrangements. Moreover, shifting the role of direct welfare provisions from the public sector to NGOs in a short time is difficult because local governments have to protect the jobs of public workers and deal with resistances from state agencies.

Conclusion

On the basis of the experiences of China's three most developed cities, this paper has demonstrated some variations on contracting out social services, including the scale of contracted projects, contract period, commissioning procedure and monitoring arrangements. These differences are shaped by the power relationship among different government departments, local leaders' welfare strategies and a city's historical welfare development. Contracting social services in China may lead to waste and regional inequality as a result of multiple purchasers from different agencies and in different levels of governments. Therefore, China's central government has to address this issue by giving power to a city government to coordinate and plan for commissioning welfare services. In this way, wastes can be minimized, and the needs of different user groups in different regions can be equally met. This study investigates the practices of contracting out social services in three economically developed cities. Future studies can examine less developed regions and compare commissioning welfare in cities and rural areas. In this way, we can have a better grip on contracting welfare services in modern China.

References

Chan, C. K. (2018). Introduction: Contracting out social services in China. In J. Lei & C. K. Chan (Eds.), *China's social welfare revolution: Contracting out social services* (pp. 1–11). Routledge.

Duckett, J., & Carrillo, B. (2011). Introducing the local perspective. In J. Duckett & B. Carrillo (Eds.), *China's changing welfare mix* (pp. 18–36). Routledge.

Huang, X., & Kim, S. E. (2020). When top-down meets bottom-up: Local adoption of social policy reform in China. *Governance, 33*(2), 343–364.

Mok, K. H., & Wu, X. F. (2013). Dual decentralization in China's transitional economy: Welfare regionalism and policy implications for central–local relationship. *Policy and Society, 32*(1), 61–75.

Zhou, X. (2010). The institutional logic of collusion among local governments in China. *Modern China, 36*(1), 47–78.

Zhu, X., & Zhao, H. (2018). Recognition of innovation and diffusion of welfare policy: Alleviating urban poverty in Chinese cities during fiscal recentralization. *Governance, 31*(4), 721–739.

CHAPTER 8

Contracting Out Social Services and the Development of Non-governmental Organizations in China

Chak Kwan Chan and Xue Liu

Introduction

The Chinese welfare system has experienced several dramatic changes since the early 1980s. Before its open-door policy, China practiced socialist social policies, and the welfare of its citizens was mainly subsidized by work units in urban areas and communes in rural areas. However, these social and economic arrangements were criticized to be inefficient with low productivity, ranking China as one of the poorest

C. K. Chan (✉) · X. Liu
Asia-Pacific Institute of Ageing Studies, Lingnan University, Tuen Mun, Hong Kong SAR, China
e-mail: chakkwanchan@ln.edu.hk

C. K. Chan
Institute of Policy Studies, Lingnan University, Tuen Mun, Hong Kong SAR, China

K. H. Mok (ed.), *Cities and Social Governance Reforms*, Social Policy and Development Studies in East Asia,
https://doi.org/10.1007/978-981-16-9531-5_8

countries worldwide. Therefore, Chinese leaders launched economic reforms by introducing competition and market forces. As a result, China dismantled its socialist welfare system and introduced various types of insurance schemes on the basis of the contributions of workers in the labour market (Chan et al., 2008). Since the early 2010s, China has attempted to transform its role from a direct welfare provider to that of a monitor by asking various types of organizations to provide social services on behalf of the state. The roles of government officials are 'policymaking, supervision, investigation and assessment' (Hua, 2012). Government departments must focus on supervising the society and the market instead of organizing service provisions (Teets, 2012).

As a result of the Chinese government's new welfare approach, contracting out social services has become China's key welfare strategy (Chan, 2018). Various definitions exist on contracting out social services. Technically and procedurally, it is a process of selecting a provider (Woodin, 2006), negotiating the terms of a contract for services and products, and monitoring and assessing contract implementation (Bovaird et al., 2012). It is an open competition through a bidding mechanism (Domberger & Jensen, 1997), which involves the transfer of service provision from the public sector to external organizations (Jensen & Stonecash, 2005). The contract organizations can be non-profit or profit-making agencies, and several terms are used to name this activity, such as procurement, purchasing, outsourcing and commissioning (Schmid & Hasenfeld, 2008).

Two different views exist on the impact of contracting out social services on the state and society. The first argument believes that the contracting policy poses a threat to a government. This is because the state may be worried about contracting signals a loss of its authority and even sovereignty (Organisation for Economic Co-Operation and Development [OECD], 2010). Based on the second argument, the state can extend its control through a carefully designed contractual relationship with NGOs. Hasenfeld (2009) pointed out that contracting has reconstructed a new relationship between the state, contract agencies and users. The new relationship can allow the state to have more power to restrict NGOs' activities.

In China, contracting out remains a relatively new strategy. Thus, this chapter attempts to examine the impact of the policy on the development of NGOs on the basis of the existing literature and a research study conducted by a research team of one of the authors (Mok et al.,

2020). The chapter is divided into four sections. Section one examines the reasons for the state to commission services to NGOs and the section two critically analyses the impact of contracting out soical services in China. The final section proposes changes to address the existing problems on contracting social services.

Debates on Contracting Out Social Services

Various arguments exist about the benefits and problems of contracting out social services. Knapp et al. (2001) pointed out that contracting out policy in the UK helped the government to achieve social, political and economic objectives. Socially, it offers more choices to service users and improves their quality of life. Economically, it helps control government expenditure, achieving efficiency and equity. Politically, by reducing government's expenditure and promoting the well-being of service users, the policy helps win the support of the voters.

The state can use contracting to tackle the rigidities in the public sector and enhance public administration (OECD, 2010). A government can use contracting to achieve policy goals (Cornforth & Brown, 2013). It can adopt commissioning social policy to reduce costs, increase efficiency, improve quality, stimulate diversity and give more choices to service users (Blomqvist & Winblad, 2020). Contracting also can help fulfil social goals such as achieving social cohesion, improving services to satisfy citizens (Irish et al., 2009; Mok et al., 2020) and reforming the service delivery system (Zhao et al., 2016).

Contracting helps a government to produce innovative solutions, mobilizing social capital in a community. Given that NGOs are independent of the state and are more flexible, they can 'engage in experimentation' and introduce tailor-made innovative services to serve the community (Panet & Trebilcock, 2008). Shifting the delivery of public services from the state to community organizations can be seen as a decentralization policy. This move can enhance community participation, promote self-help ethics and help generate social capital to tackle local problems (Panet & Trebilcock, 2008).

Contracting is particularly useful for unstable societies. An OECD report (2010) pointed out that governments in fragile states contract NGOs to deliver services because their private sector is basic, physical infrastructure is impaired, the rule of law is minimal and qualified welfare workers are inadequate (OECD, 2010).

Apart from benefiting the state, outsourcing social services bring advantages to NGOs. With more financial support, NGOs can expand their services. For example, the UK's New Labour government's welfare contacts helped NGOs to expand services in crime prevention, drug action, victim support, children's fund, sure start, connections, new deal for communities, homelessness and hostel provision, new deals for young people, funding for transport services, digital hearing aids, different health services, veterans' services, skill forces and pilot schemes (Irish et al., 2009). Similarly, NGOs in France were offered to launch various services, such as children protection, adults in social difficulty, elderly homes, child day care, housekeeping services, home care services and family home help (Irish et al., 2009). In Australia, NGOs were involved in different services, including private hospital beds, arts and cultural services, community-based services (Irish et al., 2009), employment services and services for homelessness people, children and families, older people, disabled people and drug addicts (Goodwin & Phillips, 2015).

As a result of the expansion of the work of NGOs, more volunteers and users can be mobilized to address social and community problems. Particularly, service users can help shape and develop new services, making services more 'accessible', 'targeted' and 'responsive' (Ellins, 2012; Regmi & Mudyarabikwa, 2020). NGOs may also find that they have more opportunities to be involved in the policy-making process and shape future welfare measures.

Meanwhile, concerns exist about the contracting relationship with the state. One issue is 'a significant loss of independence' (Panet & Trebilcock, 2008, p. 28). Service contracting will lead NGOs to rely on the state, which will weaken their advocacy capacity and distort the original goals of their organizations. Depending on the public sector's contracts may compel NGOs to be a government agent for serving the political goals of the state (OECD, 2010). Contracting out may create more opportunities for corruption and lead to service inequality.

In addition, contracting requirements on finance, personnel and performance indicator lead to the development of professionalism and bureaucracy of NGOs. Due to public accountability, the state will request NGOs to fulfil performance indicators that have restricted their flexibility, which will foster bureaucratization (Panet & Trebilcock, 2008). Accountability and service performance facilitates the development of professionalization that increases the authority of senior managers and professional workers of NGOs but weakens the power of volunteers and low-level employees (Panet & Trebilcock, 2008).

Commissioning social services have benefited the civil society in terms of NGOs' expansion and their increasing influence on government policies and users' involvement in services. Meanwhile, some concerns exist on the autonomy of NGOs and the increasing bureaucratization caused by the state's stringent requirements. The following sections examine the impact of welfare contracting on the development of China's NGOs.

Contracting Out Welfare Services and Its Impact in China

In China, four types of not-for-profit organizations (NPOs) exist (International Center for Not-for-Profit Law, 2020):

a. Social Associations (社会团体): similar to membership associations
b. Social Service Organizations (社会服务机构): formerly named as Civil Non-Enterprise Units (民办非企)
c. Foundations (基金会)
d. Public Institutions (事业单位): social organizations that are established and financed by the state

The first three types are collectively categorized to be NPOs that quite differ from the last one, which is generally named 'government-organized non-governmental organization' (GONGO) (Cheng, 2020). NPOs are founded by individuals or companies that are registered under the Charity Law, with the aim of carrying out charitable activities to tackle social problems (Cheng, 2020). Meanwhile, GONGOs are quasi-governmental organizations created by the state to fulfil some social, political and educational duties (Cheng, 2020; International Centre for Not-for-Profit Law, 2020). The term NGOs used in this chapter mainly refers to the first three types of NPOs. In this section, previous studies and the data of an empirical study conducted in Beijing, Shanghai and Guangzhou are used to illustrate the impact of contracting on NGOs' development.

Benefits

Increasing Number of NGOs and Their Services

Contracting welfare services has contributed to the expansions of social services in China (Zhao et al., 2016). In the US, human service agencies jumped by three times from 1977 to 1997 as a result of an increase in government purchase services. In China, the central government has relaxed the registration procedure of NPOs in recent years. Moreover, welfare contracting has offered them a golden opportunity to bid social services. As a result of these favourable factors, the number of NGOs increased dramatically from 4,000 to 866,000 between 1988 and 2019 (Hui, 2019; Ministry of Civil Affairs of the PRC, 2020). The bar chart of the development of NGOs in recent 10 years indicates that the annual growth rate of social organizations increased from the lowest 3.4% in 2010 to the highest 10.8% in 2014, and then dropped to 6% in 2019, which fluctuated greatly (see Fig. 8.1). However, compared with the great fluctuations in annual growth, the cumulative number of NGOs

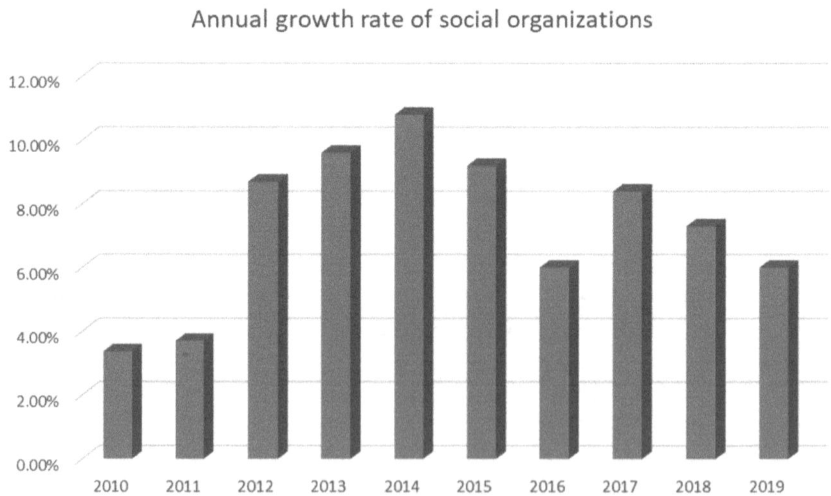

Fig. 8.1 Annual growth rate of social organizations (2010–2019) (*Source* Statistical bulletin on the development of civil affairs [China], http://www.mca.gov.cn/article/sj/tjgb/)

continued to increase in 2019, reaching 866,000 (Ministry of Civil Affairs of the PRC, 2020). In addition, over 800,000 workers were employed by these organizations in 2017 (Hui, 2019).

As a result of contracting, some NGOs, especially those from a disadvantaged background, are able to obtain more resources to run services (Zhao et al., 2016). Moreover, some NGOs can use their official contract agencies status to enlist support in their fundraising activities because the public may think that these organizations are more reliable (Zhao et al., 2016). As emphasized by Zhao et al. (2016, p. 2241), 'a government contract to some extent assures an NGO's service quality as well as its political safety'. NGOs are also engaging in various services. According to Wang and Zhao (2018), there exist more and different types of available services, including social security, social work services, services for the disabled, transportation, public culture, charity assistance, information services, law, agriculture and environmental protection, along with the continuous advancement of the pilot work of local governments (Liu et al., 2019; Wang & Zhao, 2018).

Although the number of NGOs has increased rapidly, welfare organizations in China face limitations, including small size, less management skills and specialists and government officials who are less capable of effectively launching a contracting procedure (Mok et al., 2020).

Innovation and Opportunities for Shaping Policies

Innovation is seen as a 'byproduct' of contracting out social services in the UK, the US, Canada and Australia (Phillips, 2020). According to Fürst and Holdaway (2015), indigenous environmental NGOs play a significant role in the policy innovation in China. In some regions, innovation is one of the criteria for obtaining a service contract. For example, the contract period for the integrated family centres in Guangzhou will be extended from three years to five years. Organizations bidding for new service contract must present a unique service of their projects (G3; G5). Therefore, the requirement will encourage more NGOs to design new service delivery methods to address community needs.

With greater interactions between NGOs and government agencies, some may help shape government policies. According to Teets (2012), some former civil servants established NGOs to obtain service contracts. Senior managers of these NGOs have a close relationship with state agencies and have more influence in local government policies.

Disadvantages

Limited Autonomy

Although NGOs have offered more resources and are involved in more services via contracting, their independence is weakened by the current contracting relationship in China. Particularly, some government officials did not recognize the rights and independence of NGOs but treated them as their subordinates, asking them to fulfil duties outside of their contracts (Chan & Lei, 2017; Wu & Chan, 2012; Zhao et al., 2016). A social work manager in Guangzhou said that the major obstacle was that local governments intervened in his services (G3).

According to Lei and Chan (2018), government officials regarded NGOs as foot soldiers, being asked to fulfil duties that were normally performed by civil servants. For example, one NGO took two months to complete some administrative work for the Office of Birth Planning. Welfare workers of NGOs were disappointed with the officials who failed to follow the contents of the service contracts by placing an additional burden on NGOs. Meanwhile, senior managers of NGOs found it hard to turn down the requests for fear of reducing chances on acquiring government contracts (Lei & Chan, 2018). Similar frustrations were expressed by welfare workers in other studies (Mok et al., 2020; Zhao et al., 2016). Therefore, NGOs in Beijing preferred a contracting system that can clearly define the duties and rights of both parties. Through this, they can act in accordance with the contents of a service contract with few uncertainties.

Hasenfeld (2009) highlighted the use of audits to impose state's expectations on NGOs. On the basis of the experience of the US, federal and local governments became more rigorous regarding financial management and increased site inspections and the frequency of reviews to compel NGOs to modify the practices. In China, performance indicators are used to require NGOs to fulfil service contracts and achieve the policy objectives of the state (Lei & Chan, 2018; Mok et al., 2020). The issue is further elaborated in the section below.

Although NGOs in China have operational autonomy, they are unable to launch projects to safeguard the rights of some disadvantaged groups because social actions taken by user groups are perceived as a threat to social stability and to the rule of the authorities. Some NGOs must drop politically sensitive services to obtain contracts (Zhao et al., 2016). As Zhao et al. (2016) pointed out, NGOs' operational autonomy is allowed but their activities are indirectly shaped by the Chinese government.

Unfair Tender Mechanism

Given that contracting services remain a relatively new measure in China, not all NGOs are unfairly treated in the current bidding process. Particularly, semi-official NGOs have an advantage compared with small and grass-roots NGOs. In Beijing, Zhao et al. (2016) reported that service contracts were awarded mostly to governmental or quasi-governmental NGOs and only a few to non-profit-making organizations. Moreover, the amount of funding for general NGOs was mostly under RMB 100,000 compared with government affiliated NGOs' RMB 150,000 to one million. In addition, government officials will tend to work with organizations that already have a good reputation or organizations whose managers they have close relationships with. As pointed out by a respondent in Beijing, government departments ask organizations that they could trust to deliver new services (B3). Therefore, receiving a service contract is difficult for new organizations (S4).

Government-funded NGOs also have conflict of interests under the existing contract arrangements. Hub organizations are officially funded agencies and are allowed to bid for service contracts. These organizations are also entrusted by the Beijing municipal government to administrate contracting and evaluate the performance of contracted NGOs (Zhao et al., 2016). Moreover, NGOs are required to submit their contract applications to the hub NGOs, and senior managers of some of these hub organizations are members of the application review committee (Zhao et al., 2016). As a consequence, the outcome of a contract bid is determined by an organization's relationship with hub organizations and local officials instead of the service capacity of an organization (Ni & Zhan, 2017; Zhao et al., 2016). In Shanghai, a respondent noticed that many district services were commissioned to community organizations founded by retired civil servants (S4). The tender mechanism is in favour of state-funded NGOs and social organizations that are closely linked with official agencies. Zhao et al., (2016, p. 2243) criticized that 'both the procedural and distributive fairness of contract funding allocation is questionable'. Different practices exist in evaluating contract services. In Guangzhou, the city government will commission NGOs to perform contract performance evaluations (G5). The impact of the service performance assessment on NGOs varies by region.

Risks of Service Delivery

NGOs encounter financial risks and face tremendous pressures whilst implementing a service contract. Oftentimes, local governments do not pay sufficient money for NGOs to implement activities. Moreover, some officials will ask contracted agencies to perform extra work not included in the original agreement (Lei & Chan, 2018). Consequently, NGOs must acquire extra resources to complete a service contract (Lei & Chan, 2018; Mok et al., 2020).

Moreover, NGOs face uncertainties in receiving contract cost. Zhao et al. (2016) reported that senior managers of NGOs were unable to receive money to implement projects following the successful bids for contract. They were asked to submit receipts and then claim the expenses only after project completion. This practice particularly affects small NGOs given their limited resources.

The performance assessment also places extreme pressures on contract NGOs. In Guangzhou, Chan and Lei (2017) reported that NGOs encountered several difficulties in meeting the requirements of local governments. Firstly, managers of NGOs had to prepare numerous documents to show their achievements. Secondly, they were not informed of the details of all performance indicators. Thus, many workers were overloaded, which affected the service quality. The respondents of NGOs criticized that the performance indicators greatly emphasized the statistics but neglected the personal development and long-term impact of services on users (Chan & Lei, 2017).

Contracting Relationships Between State and NGOs

Contracting out social services has created specific relationships between China's local governments and NGOs. Firstly, local officials have treated NGOs as semi-official agencies, asking them to perform tasks that were not stated in the service contracts (Chan & Lei, 2017). NGOs are in a subordinate position given that they rely on government's contracts to survive so that they must follow the instructions of local bureaucrats. NGOs' subordination to local governments is enhanced by their financial uncertainties because some government officials do not transfer the required money to pay for their existing work in time and the amount of income that they finally receive depends on the outcome of a performance assessment. Taking the local government to court is difficult for them under China's existing legal system. Therefore, the implementation of contracting social services is an extension of local government's power to the operation of NGOs (Chan & Lei, 2017; Mok et al., 2020).

Secondly, some local governments help establish NGOs or maintain a close relationship with NGOs operated by former government officials. Sometimes, local governments will actively approach NGOs, asking them to provide special services to address particular social problems. Therefore, informal contacts and negotiations are usual channels for obtaining service contracts. This contracting out process can ensure local governments that public services will be delivered through reliable NGOs with low risks. The relationship has become an important element in China's commissioning welfare services. Importantly, the existence of government-established NGOs implies that contracted agencies are actually semi-official bodies. These bodies not only help deliver some services but also commission projects to other NGOs. Therefore, China's contracting out policy does not mean that all contracted agencies are NGOs. Given that contracting out social services is a new approach in China and the number of NGOs is relatively small, the emergence of semi-official NGOs is a response of local governments to fulfil central government's welfare reform goal.

Conclusion

Different views exist on the impact of state's contracting services to the development of NGOs. On the basis of the case of China, this chapter illustrates that contracting has brought more resources to NGOs, increasing their numbers dramatically. NGOs are now involved in providing various services to meet the needs of different user groups. However, the bidding mechanism fails to offer an equal opportunity to non-profit-making organizations as government-established NGOs are granted power to bid services, assess bid applications and even evaluate the service performance of other NGOs. Local government departments have transferred some of their welfare delivery functions from the traditional bureaucratic system to semi-government welfare agencies. This means that governments have not fully shifted their role of direct welfare provisions to the community. Moreover, contracting and its monitoring system are being used by the state to manage the activities of NGOs. Through this, the expansion of the third sector and the involvement of the public in social services are under the state's control minimizing their threats to its authority. China's experiences unveiled that the state can adopt contracting welfare services to enlist community support and resources but will not challenge the power of the ruling party. The reason is because the dependence of NGOs on the state has driven welfare workers and volunteers to engage in service-oriented instead of rights-oriented activities.

References

Blomqvist, P., & Winblad, U. (2020). Contracting out welfare services: How are private contractors held accountable? *Public Management Review*, 1–22.https://doi.org/10.1080/14719037.2020.1817530

Bovaird, T., Dickinson, H., & Allen, K. (2012). Commissioning across government: Review of evidence. *Third Sector Research Centre Research Report 86*. University of Birmingham.

Chan, C. K. (2018). Introduction: Contracting out social services in China. In J. Lei & C. K. Chan (Eds.), *China's social welfare revolution: Contracting out social services* (pp. 1–11). Routledge.

Chan, C. K., & Lei, J. (2017). Contracting social services in China: The case of the integrated family services centres in Guangzhou. *International Social Work, 60*(6), 1343–1357.

Chan, C. K., Ngok, K., & Phillips, D. (2008). *Social policy in China: Development and well-being*. Policy Press.

Cheng, V. (2020). What exactly is a GONGO? *Centre for Asian Philanthropy and Society*. Retrieved from https://caps.org/insights/what-exactly-is-a-gongo/

Cornforth, C., & Brown, W. A. (Eds.). (2013). *Nonprofit governance: Innovative perspectives and approaches*. Routledge.

Domberger, S., & Jensen, P. (1997). Contracting out by the public sector: Theory, evidence, prospects. *Oxford Review of Economic Policy, 13*(4), 67–78.

Ellins, J. (2012). Public and user involvement in commissioning. In J. Glasby (Ed.), *Commissioning for health and Well-being* (pp. 189–208). Policy Press.

Fürst, K., & Holdaway, J. (2015). Environment and health in China: The role of environmental NGOs in policy innovation. In A. Fulda (Ed.), *Civil society contributions to policy innovation in the PR China* (pp. 33–76). Palgrave Macmillan.

Goodwin, S., & Phillips, R. (2015). The marketisation of human services and the expansion of the not-for-profit sector. In G. Meagher & S. Goodwin (Eds.), *Markets, rights and power in Australian social policy* (pp. 97–113). Sydney University Press.

Hasenfeld, Y. (Ed.). (2009). *Human services as complex organizations*. Sage Publications.

Hua, X. (2012, March 20). Number of NGOs in China grows to nearly 500,000. *China Daily*. Retrieved from http://www.chinadaily.com.cn/china/2012-03/20/content_14875389.htm

Hui, F. (2019). *Measuring China's nonprofit sector*. The Asia Foundation. Retrieved from https://asiafoundation.org/2019/05/22/measuring-chinas-nonprofit-sector/

International Center for Not-for-Profit Law. (2020). *Nonprofit law in China*. Council on Foundations. Retrieved from https://www.cof.org/sites/default/files/China-201905.pdf

Irish, L. E., Salamon, L. M., & Simon, K. W. (2009). *Outsourcing social services to CSOs: Lessons from abroad*. World Bank.

Jensen, P., & Stonecash, R. (2005). Incentives and the efficiency of public sector-outsourcing contracts. *Journal of Economic Surveys, 19*(5), 767–787.

Knapp, M., Hardy, B., & Forder, J. (2001). Commissioning for quality: Ten years of social care markets in England. *Journal of Social Policy, 30*(2), 283–306.

Lei, J., & Chan, C. K. (Eds.). (2018). *China's social welfare revolution: Contracting out social services*. Routledge.

Liu, J., Shi, B., Xue, J., & Wang, Q. (2019). Improving the green public procurement performance of Chinese local governments: From the perspective of officials' knowledge. *Journal of Purchasing and Supply Management, 25*(3), 100501.

Ministry of Civil Affairs of the PRC. (2020). *Statistical bulletin on the development of civil affairs (China)*. Ministry of Civil Affairs of the People's Republic of China. Retrieved from http://www.mca.gov.cn/article/sj/tjgb/

Mok, K. H., Chan, C. K., & Wen, Z. (2020). State-NGOs relationship in the context of China contracting out social services. *Social Policy & Administration, 55*(4), 687–701. https://doi.org/10.1111/spol.12651

Ni, N., & Zhan, X. (2017). Embedded government control and nonprofit revenue growth. *Public Administration Review, 77*(5), 730–742.

Organisation for Economic Co-operation and Development [OECD]. (2010). *Contracting out government functions and services in post-conflict and fragile situations*. OECD.

Panet, P., & Trebilcock, M. (2008). Contracting out social services. *Canadian Public Administration, 41*(1), 21–50.

Phillips, S. D. (2020). A changing management context: The US, UK, Canada and Australia. In H. K. Anheier & S. Toepler (Eds.), *The Routledge companion to nonprofit management* (pp. 11–27). Abingdon.

Regmi, K., & Mudyarabikwa, O. (2020). A systematic review of the factors-barriers and enablers-affecting the implementation of clinical commissioning policy to reduce health inequalities in the National Health Service (NHS), UK. *Public Health, 186*, 271–282.

Schmid, H., & Hasenfeld, Y. (2008). Contracting out social services. *Encyclopedia of Social Work*, 454–457.

Teets, J. C. (2012). Reforming service delivery in China: The emergence of a social innovation model. *Journal of Chinese Political Science, 17*(1), 15–32.

Wang, J. H., & Zhao, Y. L. (2018). The Chinese government's purchasing service policy: Evolution, characteristics and optimization. *Tribune of Study, 4*, 55–60.

Woodin, J. (2006). Health care commissioning and contracting. In K. Walshe & J. Smith (Eds.), *Healthcare management* (pp. 201–223). Open University Press.

Wu, F., & Chan, K. M. (2012). Graduated control and beyond: The evolving government-NGO relations. *China Perspectives, 2012*(3), 9–17.

Zhao, R., Wu, Z., & Tao, C. (2016). Understanding service contracting and its impact on NGO development in China. *International Journal of Voluntary and Nonprofit Organizations, 27*(5), 2229–2251.

CHAPTER 9

Cities and Social Integration: Reimagining China–Africa Relations in the Greater Bay Area

Obert Hodzi and Padmore Adusei Amoah

Introduction

Student mobility is influencing the transformation of higher education. According to UNESCO (2020), the number of international students worldwide increased from 2 million in 2000 to about 5.3 million in

O. Hodzi
Department of Politics, University of Liverpool, Liverpool, UK
e-mail: O.Hodzi@liverpool.ac.uk

P. A. Amoah (✉)
School of Graduate Studies, Lingnan University, Tuen Mun, Hong Kong SAR, China
e-mail: pamoah@ln.edu.hk

Institute of Policy Studies, Lingnan University, Tuen Mun, Hong Kong SAR, China

Department of Applied Pychology, Lingnan University, Tuen Mun, Hong Kong SAR, China

K. H. Mok (ed.), *Cities and Social Governance Reforms*, Social Policy and Development Studies in East Asia, https://doi.org/10.1007/978-981-16-9531-5_9

2017—compelling governments and other state and non-state agencies to intensify their higher education internationalization efforts (Altbach & Knight, 2007; Mihut et al., 2017). Most of these international students are from China, India, France, Saudi Arabia, Nigeria, and South Korea, and for many universities that host them, the students represent a critical component of the education sector's revenue and a reservoir of potential skilled workforce. To remain dominant and sustain their status in the global competition for external students, internationalization of education has become a marketing strategy that underpins the now entrenched neoliberal governance approaches at higher education institutions (Knight & de Wit, 2018; Lynch, 2006; McCaig et al., 2018; Mok, 2000; Nixon et al., 2018). Internationalization in higher education is, therefore, a means for universities to remain competitive and attractive to international students—thus maximizing their income and sustainability potentials. In advanced economies such as the UK, the US, and Hong Kong, international students are also a vital source of human resource. The human resources they provide are particularly critical in special economic and development zones such as the Bay Areas, which aim to attract and retain global talents (Douglass et al., 2011; Xie et al., 2020).

Over the years, the importance of international students to national socio-economic development has led to the creation of various funding schemes, the exchange of materials and resources, the opening of international campus branches, and an intensified collaboration between governments, universities, and markets to drive change (Altbach & Knight, 2007; Altbach et al., 2009; Chen, 2016; Knight & de Wit, 2018).

Additionally, as non-Western powers like China emerge, states are regarding higher education as a source of 'soft power' to achieve their geopolitical objectives. Nye (1990) defines soft power as the ability of a country to shape preferences of other countries through the attractiveness of its culture, values, political, social, and economic advancement so that the targeted country desires the outcomes the soft power country wants to have. Due to their cosmopolitan nature, universities are a bastion of multiculturalism and a tool for dispensing a country's culture, values, and norms beyond its citizens. Previously, this was limited to the developed West but now, even emerging powers in the Global South, including China, consider internationalization of higher education as a diplomatic strategy (Bodomo, 2015; Fijałkowski, 2011; Hodzi, 2019; Knight & de Wit, 2018; Yang, 2010). Even for Africa, the exploits of African economic and educational migrants have been described as a form of soft power (Bodomo, 2015), although African universities are still finding their footing in the global higher education space (Altbach et al., 2009).

Given the above opportunities, universities in China (used in this chapter mostly in reference to mainland China), including the special administrative regions such as Hong Kong and Macau, have made efforts to position themselves as key players in the global higher education industry. For the Chinese government, the ultimate goal is to make the mainland highly competitive as a destination for international students (Mok & Chan, 2008). Therefore, the country has initiated numerous policies and strategies to restructure education and governance systems to meet internal needs and be globally competitive (Chen, 2016; Mok & Chan, 2008; Zha, 2012). Popular among such policies are those relating to quality assurance of academic practices; international benchmarking of teaching and research; transformation of selected universities into world-class institutions; diversification of funding sources; promotion of international partnerships, and the creation of opportunities for international branch campuses in China as well as development of English language programmes (Chen, 2016; Mok & Chan, 2008; Mok & Lo, 2007; Zha, 2012). Cooperation between mainland China universities and institutions in Hong Kong such as the Chinese University of Hong Kong-Shenzhen has enabled strategic leveraging of competencies and resources; hence attracting more international students and academics. In Hong Kong, the institutionalization of the Ph.D. Fellowship Scheme in addition to other university-level scholarships offered to international students has increased the number of African students in the city with most of them coming from Ghana and Nigeria (University Grants Committee [UGC], 2021).

The operationalization of these policies has attracted African students to further their education in China through various forms of partnerships and avenues, as we discuss in the next section (Chan & Wu, 2019). As noted by several authors (Bodomo, 2011; King, 2014; Niu, 2013), China's educational internationalization has been particularly notable in its partnership with African nations since the turn of the century. Indeed, the statement that "the Chinese government attaches high symbolic value to the scholarships offered to Africa, and it has a long history of using educational aid as a means to reinforce ties with African countries" (Haugen, 2013b, p. 315) is unassailable. The result, as noted by Li (2018), is that the growth rate of African students in the past decade is highest among all international student arrivals in China.

However, internationalization does not only concern the process of attracting international students, researchers, and faculty. Universities and governments interested in establishing long-term relationships with such students must do more to ensure their well-being and strategically integrate such students into host societies. Extant research has variously discussed characteristics and issues of integration of African migrants in Chinese societies, including Hong Kong (Amoah et al., 2020; Bodomo & Ma, 2010; Castillo, 2015; Chow-Quesada & Tesfaye, 2020). An attempt to discuss some of these issues in the context of the Guangdong-Hong Kong-Macau Greater Bay Area (GBA) is yet to be done. This chapter offers a first attempt to research African students and graduates in Chinese societies in the context of the GBA. Based on existing literature, this chapter critically reflects on the social, economic, geopolitical perspectives of African students and graduates in Chinese societies. It particularly focuses on the factors that shape the social integration of African students (during and after their studies) in these societies, especially the GBA. The chapter proposes measures to promote the well-being and social integration of these Africans in the GBA as part of the broader Sino-African relations. The rest of the chapter is in four parts. The first part discusses trends in African students in Chinese societies, focusing mainly on mainland China. The second part presents issues of social integration of African students in Chinese societies. The third part focuses on the dynamics of social integration of African students who have graduated from universities in the GBA in terms of economic and geopolitical conditions. The final part reflects on measures to ensure the integration of African students and graduates in the GBA societies.

African Students in Chinese Societies: Trends, Social Integration, and Implications for the GBA

The initiation of the Forum on China-Africa Cooperation (FOCAC) in 2000 as a multi-purpose vehicle for engaging with Africa on all development fronts, including higher education, institutionalized China's education aid to Africa (FOCAC, 2020; King, 2014; Niu, 2013). In particular, the 2018 FOCAC action plan streamlined China's educational cooperation with Africa, consolidating it into two main categories—education and human resources (Ministry of Foreign Affairs, 2018). China regards its educational cooperation with Africa as an integral part of its broader development assistance. For instance, in Nigeria, due to the lack of qualified Nigerian railway engineers, the China Civil Engineering Construction Corporation is constructing a university for transportation studies as part of its corporate social responsibility. Nigeria's president, Muhammadu Buhari, described the project as paving the 'way for the domestication of railway engineering and general transportation sciences in Nigeria, thereby bridging the technology and skills gap in the railway and ultimately transportation sector' (Xinhua, 2019). This approach is inspired by China's fundamental principles of equality, mutual benefit, win–win economic development, solidarity, mutual trust, mutual support, and support for its partner nations to explore their preferred development paths (Ministry of Foreign Affairs, 2018). This is what has been termed as 'overseas aid with [Chinese] its own (*sic*) characteristics' (King, 2014, p. 3). Accordingly, China's education engagement with African institutions and nations has taken the form of support for various countries to pursue their priority education programmes and projects. This is exhibited in the construction of the Science and Technology University in Malawi and the building and equipping of the Ethio-China Polytechnic College in Ethiopia (King, 2014; Reilly, 2015). In addition, other aspects of China's educational partnership with African countries are facilitated through multilateral agencies such as the United Nations, Food and Agriculture Organization. Such partnerships are meant to achieve complex educational goals such as girl-child education and provide technical skills in areas such as agriculture (Reilly, 2015).

The implication is that China's international education investment agenda in the context of its relations with Africa departs from the purely market-driven approach adopted by many Western nations (Altbach & Knight, 2007; King, 2014; Lynch, 2006). Through bilateral and multilateral agreements and forums such as FOCAC, heads of states initiate, negotiate, and oversee the implementation of the internationalization process. However, this approach also means that universities and other education entities (mostly in mainland China) merely follow what political leaders decide at the state level—which may give an impression of a state-led higher education internationalization process. Thus, one could argue that the soft power dimension of China's educational engagement, such as the language and cultural services offered by its Confucius Institutes through various institutional partnerships (Reilly, 2015), does not differ from those of other high-income nations and emerging powers. Indeed, there is a running commentary on China's soft power engagement with Africa within and outside China (Chan & Wu, 2019). The result is that the process is geared towards achieving political and diplomatic objectives instead of an economic-led strategy. However, in Hong Kong, the scholarships and engagement with higher education institutions in Africa are based on the institutions' needs rather than part of a broad foreign policy agenda. Notwithstanding, China's involvement in African education has played a significant role in the past decade as regards internationalization of higher education (Altbach & Knight, 2007; Haugen, 2013b).

Trends in African Students to China

Following the background to the China-Africa educational partnership above, we now examine the status and trends of African students studying in China's higher education system. This, as argued by Helms and Rumbley (2017), is critical to an inquiry on whether higher education internationalization policies are essential to attaining academic, political, social, and cultural goals globally. On the surface, based on the increase of students from African countries studying at universities in China, China's internationalization process seems to be successful (Li, 2018). Pronouncements made at the 2018 FOCAC summit, such as increased scholarships, tailored study programs, and human resource capacity-building initiatives announced by China, indicate that the trend is likely to continue (Ministry of Foreign Affairs, 2018). According to the Ministry of Education (2019) official statistics, the annual number of students from Africa in China is third to those from Asia and Europe. The number of African students in China has increased dramatically in recent years, and it has surpassed the number of students from North and South America put together since 2013, reaching around 62,000 in 2016 (Fig. 9.1) (Ministry of Education, 2019). As of 2018, 81,562 Africans were studying in China, more than a 40-fold increase in 15 years, from just 1793 in 2003 (Lau, 2020; Li, 2018). Given that the growth rate of African students in China has remained highest among all other international students since 2008 (Fig. 9.2) (Ministry of Education, 2019), it is expected that African students will remain the second most populous in China, second only to students from Asia.

Moreover, while there is a notion that African students in China are motivated by financial incentives (scholarship incentives mainly) (Li, 2018), current trends depict a different situation (Haugen, 2013b). From 1976 to 1988, all African students in China were on scholarships. This trend changed from 1989 when two students started studying in China

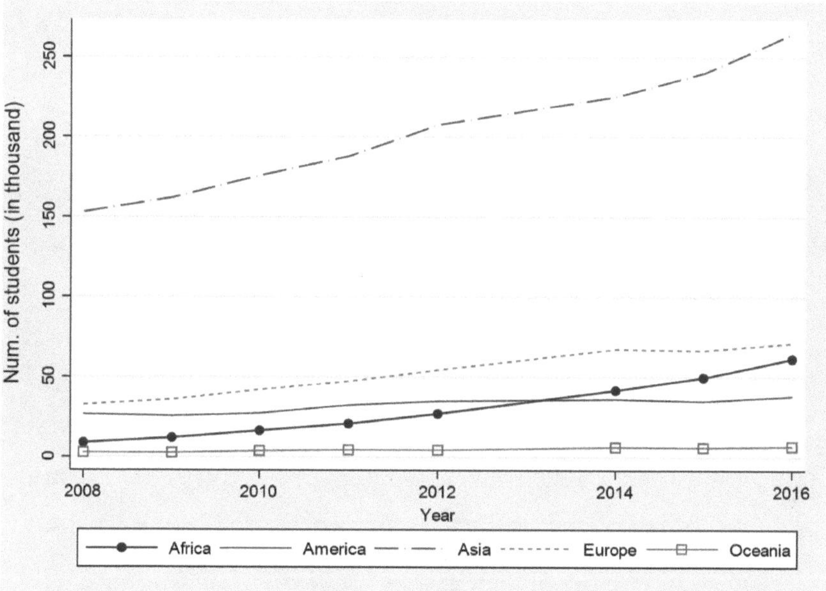

Fig. 9.1 Number of inward international students 2008–2016 (*Source* Ministry of Education [2019], China)

on a self-funding basis. The proportion of self-funded students rose each year until 1994, the number of those without scholarships exceeding those with scholarships for the first time (Li, 2018). Since 2006, the number of self-funded African students in China has always exceeded their compatriots with financial aid; this came about as a result of the 2006 FOCAC summit when new forms of educational exchanges and partnerships, as well as a more flexible visa application process, were introduced (King, 2014; Li, 2018). Consequently, there were as many as 41,322 self-funded students as against 8,470 students on scholarships as of 2015 (Li, 2018).

The proportion of overall international students on scholarships in China as of 2016 was approximately 11%, rising from about 5% in 2007, as shown in Fig. 9.3 (Ministry of Education, 2019). Therefore, one could argue that China has been able to ground its higher education internationalization agenda in Africa in the institutional realities of the most crucial partners, universities, and colleges (Helms & Rumbley, 2017).

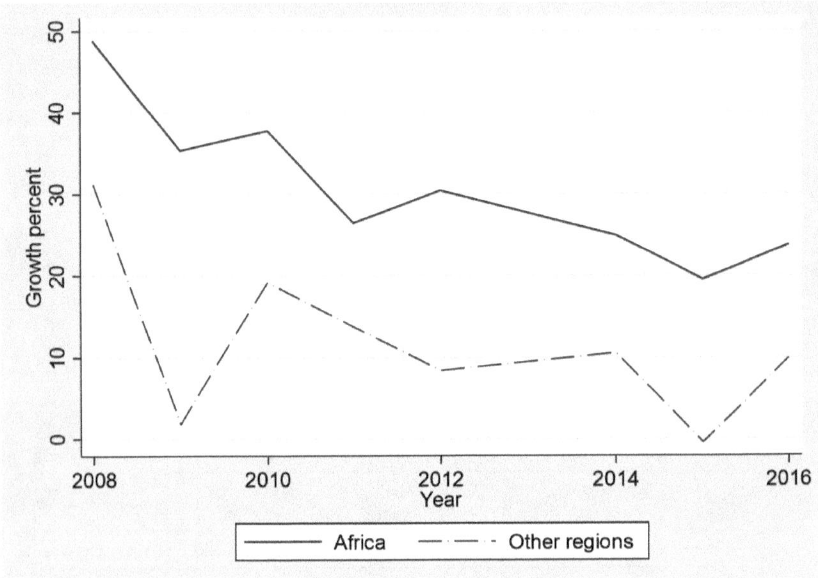

Fig. 9.2 Growth rate of inward international students, Africa and other regions (*Source* Ministry of Education [2019], China)

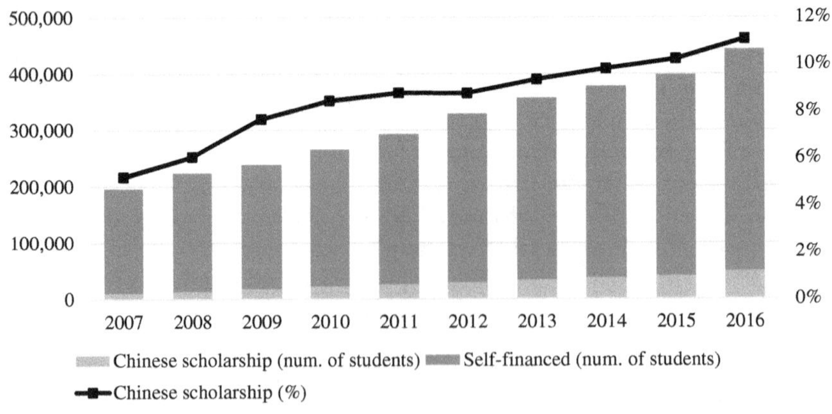

Fig. 9.3 Funding sources of international students in China including Africans (*Source* Ministry of Education [2019], China)

Notwithstanding, it must be emphasized that the success in drawing educational institutions in the China-Africa educational partnership is attributable to the prevailing attitude of the Chinese government towards international cooperation in the field of education. China has strategically used higher education institutions to achieve the desired soft power and internationalization outcomes (Mok, 2000, 2014; Mok & Chan, 2008; Mok & Ong, 2014).

While the policy aspect of the engagement is intriguing, the nature, conditions, and prospects of the students involved in the multifaceted arrangements between China and the African nations require further investigation. African students in China are far from homogenous, at least from a financial point of view and from the perspective of their pre-schooling circumstances.

Integration of African Students in Chinese Societies: Implications for the Greater Bay Area

Migration is an important factor in sourcing talent and workforce for the development of the GBA (2019). The governments in various GBA regions such as Hong Kong, Macau, and Guangdong as well as the central Chinese government have proactively been implementing policies to attract and retain talents, particularly in regions such as Hong Kong (Anshan, 2018; Chen, 2016; Li, 2018; Mok & Chan, 2008; UGC, 2020; Zha, 2012). In Hong Kong, various forms of scholarships such as studentships and Ph.D. fellowships administered at the government and university levels are available to attract international students at undergraduate and postgraduate levels to the region, including students from the African continent (UGC, 2020, 2021). Research indicates that some African students aspire to live or engage in economic activities in various Chinese societies on graduation, which is, at the core, consistent with the aim of the GBA (Bredeloup, 2014; Tsui & Tang, 2015). Because of its unique history as a former British colony, with English being widely spoken, Hong Kong is seen as a gateway to both mainland China and the West. In addition, it presents the benefits of studying in a Chinese context at Western standards of education.

Based on a study in Guangzhou, Bredeloup (2014) argued that African students in the city were pursuing globalization from below. The majority have over the years "envisaged tertiary education in China...as a springboard to profit from their new competencies and find a place (temporarily or permanently) in the host country.... More migrants from sub-Saharan Africa have come to perceive enrolment in Chinese universities as a disguised means to stay in China and to penetrate the import–export sector" (Bredeloup, 2014, p. 48). Li (2018, p. 22) adds that "African students become the bridge between Africa and China". In a broader sense, the vision and activities of the students correspond with the goal of the GBA of "going global" together...' (GBA, 2019, p. 5). However, there are challenges regarding the extent to which these students and other African economic migrants are able to integrate into the societies they find themselves (Mensah, 2019). Pre-COVID-19 pandemic literature indicates that issues of cultural incompatibilities, challenges in access to health and related social services, and general perceptions of life in Chinese societies affect the integration of African students and migrants. Such challenges put some dent in the GBA's internationalization plans as discussed below.

Culture and Integration of African Students in the GBA

A major challenge that most African migrants (including students) in Greater China and the GBA face relates to cultural differences, which often complicates their adaptation (Anshan, 2018; Li, 2018). In particular, differences in how people relate to each other in everyday settings and language barriers in casual communication and professional interactions have been reported severally (Bodomo, 2011; Mensah, 2019). Many African students in the GBA and other Chinese societies often report feeling alienated because of the divergence of culture (Burgess & Xed, 2016). These cultural differences heighten perceived discrimination and prejudices against the Africans due to race and health conditions (e.g. passing on COVID-19 and HIV infections) (Bodomo, 2020; Burgess & Xed, 2016). In places such as Hong Kong, related evidence suggests that Africans struggle to form lasting social relationships with the locals due to socio-cultural differences (Amoah et al., 2020). Universities in mainland China, including those that fall within the GBA, have adopted measures such as compulsory Chinese language courses and introduction to contemporary China (Wu & Chan, 2019) to reduce language barriers between international and local students, as well as ease the integration of international students into the community. This is consistent with the soft power dimension of promoting international education (Chan & Wu,

2019; Reilly, 2015; Wu & Chan, 2019). However, the effectiveness of such measures requires further investigations.

Access to Health and Other Social Services

Access and use of social services in the GBA among Africans, especially those relating to healthcare, are a topical issue in existing literature (Bodomo, 2020; Lin et al., 2015). In general, challenges in accessing key services in places such as Guangzhou include financial barriers, legal issues (e.g. pertaining to migration status), language barriers, and cultural differences (Bodomo, 2020; Hall et al., 2014; Lin et al., 2015). However, the situation among African students in the GBA is often different given that many students have scholarships and university services that provide them with essential services. In places such as Macau and Hong Kong, the public health system, in addition to university services (e.g. basic insurance packages), makes it easier for students to access most services. Notwithstanding, matters beyond finances, such as a language barrier, knowledge of the health system, and other cultural perceptions and attitudes towards certain health conditions, affect how these students seek needed services. This means that health and other social service providers and organizations in GBA cities must be culturally competent to address the needs of African migrants, particularly students (Lin et al., 2015).

Given the challenges in access to some vital services, religious groups are vital to the lives of Africans in the GBA cities such as Guanzhou as it provides a place for social support (Haugen, 2013a). This situation is similar to conditions of perceptions of African students in other Chinese societies such as Beijing. During the COVID-19 pandemic, these social networks and communities have been critical to Africans in GBA cities to gain access to preventive and curative measures to improve their health and well-being (Bodomo et al., 2020). Therefore, measures to promote the integration of African students in the GBA societies must be developed based on an understanding of these social dynamics to yield positive results.

Perception of Life and Environmental Conditions in Host Cities

The extent of social integration among African students in Chinese societies also relates to their perception of opportunities for social mobility and conditions in the regions or cities they find themselves (Akhtar et al., 2015). Studies show that when students perceive good or preferable career opportunities, they lean towards remaining in the city after graduation (Ferdjani, 2012). Perceived post-graduation economic advancement encourages students to learn the local language and do more to integrate into society (Ferdjani, 2012). However, in places such as Hong Kong, the difficulty of African students to bring their families with them due to the high cost of living weighs much on their decision to remain in the city post-graduation (Tsui & Tang, 2015). This affects their willingness to pursue opportunities for integration, and it implies that retention of such talents depends on family-friendly policies. Moreover, it has also been found that prior knowledge of cultural characteristics and nature of the physical environment (such as the weather) are useful to African students' adaptation to the Chinese societies they study (Akhtar et al., 2015). Thus, a thorough orientation must be provided to potential African students in the GBA to ensure that they are able to conenct with the local societies during the study.

Due to the challenges discussed above, some African students in Hong Kong hesitate to stay in the city after completing their studies (Tsui & Tang, 2015). Unfortunately, these challenges are likely to exacerbate in the post-pandemic era for students who remain in places like Guangzhou, as some immigration flexibilities may be tightened (Castillo & Amoah, 2020). Therefore, the enactment of the GBA provides an opportune moment to address these current and prospective challenges in the lives of African students in the region. After all, the social governance reforms within the context of the GBA and international students must go beyond a mere attraction of the students to the region to include measures that promote their socio-cultural inclusion and adaptation—i.e. more people-to-people engagements within and outside campuses and cities.

One way of addressing the challenges faced by African students regarding integration in the GBA societies is to understand the different categories of these students across cities. For instance, in her study, which included African students in Guangzhou, Haugen (2013b) provided a typology of students that can serve as a starting point for understanding the nature of the students, their challenges in integrating into the societies and their aspirations. In that study, various kinds of students were identified in terms of funding arrangements (four kinds), their schooling journey (four kinds), and the places of origin before commencing their studies, as shown in Table 9.1. Thus, while various policies encourage

Table 9.1 Typologies of African students in China

Type of student	*Place of abode before joining a Chinese University/College*	*Source of funding*
Scholarship students	Home country	Chinese government agencies, large corporate employers
Self-funding students	Home country Third country	Personal or family savings
Traders turned students	China	Profit generated from the students' own businesses
Family firm trainees	Home country Third country	Profit generated from family members' businesses in China

Source Haugen (2013b, p. 324)

African students to seek higher education in China, attention must be given to the varying current and prospective well-being of the students involved, given their heterogeneity. More importantly, this call is essential to the sustainability of the China-Africa education collaboration as the experiences of the students during and after their studies are critical to others embarking on similar journeys. As Haugen (2013b) demonstrates, negative experiences of African students can hurt the ambition of China to increase its soft power in Africa through educational engagements.

Social Integration of Africans in China and the GBA: Economic Perspectives and Geopolitical Implications

This section looks at social integration and social mobility issues of African students in Chinese societies post-graduation from economic and geopolitical perspectives. The social integration of Africans in China and the GBA is often overshadowed by state-level relations between China and African countries. The impression is that because African countries and China have cordial diplomatic relations, the same applies to Africans and the Chinese people. However, on several occasions, this equating of state-to-state relations with people-to-people relations has proved problematic in dealing with social integration challenges faced by Africans in China and its autonomous and special administrative regions. For instance, discriminatory treatment of Africans in China over perceived non-observance of COVID-19 regulations brought to the fore the fallacy of dealing with social integration issues at the diplomatic level (Burke et al., 2020). Partly, this is because most African embassies in China and regions such as Hong Kong and Macau do not have up-to-date registers of their citizens in the region. In addition, due to limitations of resources and expertise, few of the embassies can provide consul services to their citizens based in China. Furthermore, with some Africans overstaying their visas, most have failed to transition from student to working visa status legally, their social integration and the ability of their governments to support them is limited. According to Cisse (2021), China's lack of immigration support services results in "many migrants falling out of legal status… and then having to rely on informal or illicit networks to remain in the country". The implication is that even though there might be cordial Africa-China relations, Africans in Chinese societies have a precarious existence and straddle the legal-illegal divide.

Due to the above challenges, the ability of African students to bridge relations between China and Africa in a manner that enables both African countries and China to achieve their respective geopolitical objectives is limited. In many respects, the success is only limited to government-funded and professional students seconded to China by their respective governments, who are guaranteed of returning to their countries to continue in their government jobs (Hodzi, 2020). The rest of the students who are privately funded or are on other non-state scholarships, education in China, Hong Kong, and Macau is a tool for their social mobility and move to a third destination, mostly in West Europe and North America where the path to attaining permanent residence and citizenship is clear. Few remain in the region with formal jobs or as entrepreneurs. This means that the economic implications of African students failing to return to their home countries at the completion of their studies are difficult to decipher, especially in cases where they are self-funded or were supported through non-state scholarships at no cost to their governments. More research on the economic cost of these non-returning students on the government of China is imperative.

African students and other Africans residing in the GBA are, in most cases, not politically organized (Bodomo, 2012), apart from community social groups and associations organized around national and ethnic identity (Bodomo, 2020). There seem to be no pressure groups or civil society organizations representing Africans in the GBA's local governments. This lack of political organization means that their issues and grievances remain hidden and hardly a subject of discussion at FOCAC or other bilateral engagements between China and African countries. Furthermore, except for Ghana, few African countries have a dedicated diaspora desk in their foreign offices; hence, Africans in China lack platforms to engage their governments. The implication is that the social integration of Africans in the GBA remains a pipe dream to the extent that there are no official platforms in which the issues are discussed and resolved. Africans in the GBA, including students, remain on the fringes of their host societies and risk becoming illegal residents soon after completing their studies due to lack of formal employment opportunities, clear paths to residence, and unresolved but persistent integrations issues.

Conclusion

The pathway for African students and graduates to integrate into the GBA is fraught with challenges mainly emanating from cultural, language, and socio-economic differences between the host societies and the Africans as well as conditions of political arrangements. Partly, this is because the mobility of African students to mainland China, Hong Kong, and Macau is a recent phenomenon. In Macau, unlike in Hong Kong and China, there is little data on African students in the region, although the presence of African migrants is documented in the city (Bodomo, 2012). Nonetheless, while the governments of these territories and African countries seem to be geared towards encouraging more people-to-people exchange, the precarity faced by African students after graduating presents significant challenges for the GBA.

State-to-state relations between China and African countries play a significant role in the relations between Africans and Chinese. To deal with the myriad of challenges discussed in this paper, there is a need for more focused deliberation and implementation plans aimed at addressing the precarity of Africans in China and its territories. For instance, a platform can be created under the auspices of FOCAC to facilitate the social integration and social mobility of African students and graduates in Chinese societies such as the GBA. This should include clarity of immigrations rules, support services, and recognition of foreign-born residents in China. In addition, African governments should play a significant role in enhancing consular services available to their citizens studying, working, and living in China, and engaging with the Chinese government to address matters of concern.

Notably, current debates about China–Africa relations must be extended from the macro-level to the micro-level to examine the well-being, career, and social mobilities of the students involved in the China-Africa educational partnerships against the backdrop of the rising student numbers not only in China but other GBA cities such as Hong Kong. After all, creating social cohesion cannot be a task of educational institutions and regional governments alone. Support through central government collaborations can, where necessary, offer needed support to promote and design effective measures for African students' social integration. In the context of the GBA, this is even critical, given that the fundamental blocks and international profile of the region are still being developed.

In addition, as higher education institutions recruit more African students, they should begin to pay attention to the integration of these students beyond their campuses. The social integration of African students in the GBA must begin with a reformed orientation to ensure that newly arriving students will gain familiarity with services and facilities to support their lives, including those outside university campuses. Thus, the orientation of African and even other international students in the GBA must include information and workshops on the social services, community characteristics, and other socio-cultural practices beyond the walls of their educational institutions. This will encourage new students to initiate the process of integrating into their new societies with ease. Graduating students can also be offered support through workshops and seminars on the economic landscape of their study regions, particularly in places where there are already pathways for international students to settle post-graduation, such as Hong Kong.

Acknowledgement We would like to acknowledge the contribution of Dr. Jin Jiang of Department of Sociology, Hong Kong Baptist University, who helped to retrieve and analyse data on international higher education statistics in mainland China.

Conflict of Interest The authors declare no conflict of interest.

References

Akhtar, N., Pratt, C. B., & Bo, S. (2015). Factors in the cross-cultural adaptation of African students in Chinese universities. *Journal of Research in International Education, 14*(2), 98–113. https://doi.org/10.1177/1475240915592107

Altbach, P. G., & Knight, J. (2007). The internationalization of higher education: Motivations and realities. *Journal of Studies in International Education, 11*(3–4), 290–305. https://doi.org/10.1177/1028315307303542

Altbach, P. G., Reisberg, L., & Rumbley, L. E. (2009). Trends in global higher education: Tracking an academic revolution. Paper presented at *the UNESCO 2009 World Conference on Higher Education*, 5–8 July, 2009.

Amoah, P. A., Koduah, A. O., Anaduaka, U. S., Addae, E. A., Gwenzi, G. D., & Amankwaa, A. (2020). Psychological well-being in diaspora space: A study of African economic migrants in Hong Kong. *Asian Ethnicity, 21*(4), 542–559. https://doi.org/10.1080/14631369.2020.1775485

Anshan, L. (2018). African students in China: Research, reality, and reflection. *African Studies Quarterly, 17*(4), 5–44.

Bodomo, A. (2011). African students in China. A case study of newly arrived students on FOCAC funds at Chongqing University. Paper presented at *the Comparative Education Research Centre (CERC) Seminar*, University of Hong Kong.

Bodomo, A. (2012). *Africans in China: A sociocultural study and its implications for Africa–China relations*. Cambria Press.

Bodomo, A. (2015). African soft power in China. *African East-Asian Affairs: The China Monitor* (1–2). https://doi.org/10.7552/0-1-2-160

Bodomo, A. (2020). Historical and contemporary perspectives on inequalities and well-being of Africans in China. *Asian Ethnicity, 21*(4), 542–559. https://doi.org/10.1080/14631369.2020.1761246

Bodomo, A., Liem, A., Lin, L., & Hall, B. J. (2020). How African migrants in China cope with barriers to health care. *The Lancet Public Health, 5*(4), e192. https://doi.org/10.1016/S2468-2667(20)30048-7

Bodomo, A. B., & Ma, G. (2010). From Guangzhou to Yiwu: Emerging facets of the African Diaspora in China. *International Journal of African Renaissance Studies—Multi-, Inter- and Transdisciplinarity, 5*(2), 283–289. https://doi.org/10.1080/18186874.2010.534854

Bredeloup, S. (2014). West African students turned entrepreneurs in Asian trading posts: A new facet of globalization. *Urban Anthropology and Studies of Cultural Systems and World Economic Development, 43*(1/2/3), 17–56.

Burgess, L. M., & Xed. (2016). Conversations with African students in China. *Transition: An International Review, 119*, 80–91. https://doi.org/10.2979/transition.119.1.10

Burke, J., Akinwotu, E., & Lily, K. (2020, April 27). China fails to stop racism against Africans over Covid-19. *The Guardian*. Retrieved September 1, 2021, from https://www.theguardian.com/world/2020/apr/27/china-fails-to-stop-racism-against-africans-over-covid-19

Castillo, R. (2015). 'Homing' Guangzhou: Emplacement, belonging and precarity among Africans in China. *International Journal of Cultural Studies, 19*(3), 287–306. https://doi.org/10.1177/1367877915573767

Castillo, R., & Amoah, P. A. (2020). Africans in post-COVID-19 pandemic China: Is there a future for China's 'new minority'? *Asian Ethnicity, 21*(4), 560–565. https://doi.org/10.1080/14631369.2020.1773760

Chan, W.-K., & Wu, X. (2019). Promoting governance model through international higher education: Examining international student mobility in China between 2003 and 2016. *Higher Education Policy, 33*(3), 511–530. https://doi.org/10.1057/s41307-019-00158-w

Chen, Q. (2016). *Globalization and transnational academic mobility: The experiences of Chinese Academic returnees*. Springer.

Chow-Quesada, S. M. E., & Tesfaye, F. (2020). (Re)mediating 'blackness' in Hong Kong Chinese medium newspapers: Representations of African cultures in relation to Hong Kong. *Asian Ethnicity, 21*(4), 384–406. https://doi.org/10.1080/14631369.2020.1763776

Cisse, D. (2021, July 21). As migration and trade increase between China and Africa, traders at both ends often face precarity. Retrieved September 1, 2021, from https://www.migrationpolicy.org/article/migration-trade-china-africa-traders-face-precarity

Douglass, J., Edelstein, R., & Hoareau, C. (2011). A global talent magnet: How a San Francisco/Bay Area global higher education hub could advance California's comparative advantage in attracting international talent and further build US economic competitiveness. *UC Berkeley Research and Occasional Papers Series*. California: Center for Studies in Higher Education, University of California.

Ferdjani, H. (2012). *African students in China: An exploration of increasing numbers and their motivations in Beijing* [Research report].

Fijałkowski, Ł. (2011). China's 'soft power' in Africa? *Journal of Contemporary African Studies, 29*(2), 223–232. https://doi.org/10.1080/02589001.2011.555197

FOCAC. (2020). *About forum on China-Africa cooperation*. Retrieved February 18, 2020, from https://www.focac.org/eng/ltjj_3/ltjz/

GBA. (2019). *Outline development plan for the Guangdong-Hong Kong-Macau Greater Bay Area. Beijing: Guangdong-Hong Kong-Macau Greater Bay Area (GBA)*. Central Government of China.

Hall, B. J., Chen, W., Latkin, C., Ling, L., & Tucker, J. D. (2014). Africans in south China face social and health barriers. *Lancet (London, England), 383*(9925), 1291–1292. https://doi.org/10.1016/S0140-6736(14)60637-1

Haugen, H. Ø. (2013a). African Pentecostal migrants in China: Marginalization and the alternative geography of a mission theology. *African Studies Review, 56*(1), 81–102. https://doi.org/10.1017/asr.2013.7

Haugen, H. Ø. (2013b). China's recruitment of African university students: Policy efficacy and unintended outcomes. *Globalisation, Societies and Education, 11*(3), 315–334. https://doi.org/10.1080/14767724.2012.750492

Helms, R. M., & Rumbley, L. E. (2017). Global: National policies for internationalization—Do they work? In G. Mihut, P. G. Altbach, & H. de Wit (Eds.), *Understanding higher education internationalization: Insights from key global publications*. Sense Publishers.

Hodzi, O. (2019). *The end of China's non-intervention policy in Africa*: Palgrave Macmillan.

Hodzi, O. (2020). Bridging the asymmetries? African students' mobility to China. *Asian Ethnicity, 21*(4), 566–584. https://doi.org/10.1080/14631369.2020.1776097

King, K. (2014). China's higher education engagement with Africa: A different partnership and cooperation model? In G. Carbonnier, M. Carton, & K. King (Eds.), *Education, learning, training: Critical issues for development* (pp. 149–173). Martinus Nijhoff Publishers.

Knight, J., & de Wit, H. (2018). Internationalization of higher education: Past and future. *International Higher Education, 95*, 2–4. https://doi.org/10.6017/ihe.2018.95.10715

Lau, J. (2020). *Racism a 'barrier' for African students in China*. Retrieved February 18, 2020, from https://www.timeshighereducation.com/news/racism-barrier-african-students-china#survey-answer

Li, A. (2018). African students in China: Research, reality, and reflection. *African Studies Quarterly, 17*(4), 5–44.

Lin, L., Brown, K. B., Yu, F., Yang, J., Wang, J., Schrock, J. M., Bodomo, A. B., Yang, L., Yang, B., Nehl, E. J., Tucker, J. D., & Wong, F. Y. (2015). Health care experiences and perceived barriers to health care access: A qualitative study among African migrants in Guangzhou, Guangdong Province, China. *Journal of Immigrant and Minority Health, 17*(5), 1509–1517. https://doi.org/10.1007/s10903-014-0114-8

Lynch, K. (2006). Neo-liberalism and marketisation: The implications for higher education. *European Educational Research Journal, 5*(1), 1–17. https://doi.org/10.2304/eerj.2006.5.1.1

McCaig, C., Bowl, M., & Hughes, J. (2018). Conceptualising equality, equity and differentiation in marketised higher education: Fractures and fault lines in the neoliberal imaginary. In M. Bowl, C. McCaig, & J. Hughes (Eds.),

Equality and differentiation in marketised higher education: A new level playing field? (pp. 195–210). Springer International Publishing.

Mensah, I. K. (2019). Predictors of electronic government services adoption: The African students' perspective in China. *International Journal of Public Administration, 42*(12), 997–1009. https://doi.org/10.1080/01900692.2019.1572621

Mihut, G., Altbach, P. G., & de Wit, H. (Eds.). (2017). *Understanding higher education internationalization: Insights from key global publications.* Sense Publishers.

Ministry of Education. (2019). *Statistics for international students in China (2008–2016).* Ministry of Education, The People's Republic of China.

Ministry of Foreign Affairs. (2018). *Forum on China-Africa cooperation Beijing action plan (2019–2021).* Retrieved February 18, 2020 from https://www.fmprc.gov.cn/mfa_eng/zxxx_662805/t1593683.shtml

Mok, K. H. (2000). Marketizing higher education in post-Mao China. *International Journal of Educational Development, 20*(2), 109–126. https://doi.org/10.1016/S0738-0593(99)00062-0

Mok, K. H. (Ed.). (2014). *Internationalization of higher education in East Asia : Trends of Student Mobility and Impact on Education Governance.* Routledge.

Mok, K. H., & Chan, Y. (2008). International benchmarking with the best universities: Policy and practice in Mainland China and Taiwan. *Higher Education Policy, 21*(4), 469–486. https://doi.org/10.1057/hep.2008.21

Mok, K. H., & Lo, W. Y. (2007). The impacts of neo-liberalism on China's higher education. *Journal for Critical Education Policy Studies, 5*(1), 316–348.

Mok, K. H., & Ong, K. C. (2014). Transforming from "economic power" to "soft power": Transnationalization and internationalization of higher education in China. In Q. Li, & C. Gerstl-Pepin (Eds.), *Survival of the fittest: The shifting contours of higher education in China and the United States* (pp. 133–155). Springer Berlin Heidelberg.

Niu, C. (2013). China's educational cooperation with Africa: Toward new strategic partnerships. *Asian Education and Development Studies, 3*(1), 31–45. https://doi.org/10.1108/AEDS-09-2013-0057

Nixon, E., Scullion, R., & Hearn, R. (2018). Her majesty the student: Marketised higher education and the narcissistic (dis)satisfactions of the student-consumer. *Studies in Higher Education, 43*(6), 927–943. https://doi.org/10.1080/03075079.2016.1196353

Nye, J. S. (1990). Soft power. *Foreign Policy, 80*, 153–171. https://doi.org/10.2307/1148580

Reilly, J. (2015). *The role of China as an education aid donor* (Document code: ED/EFA/MRT/2015/PI/44). United Nations Educational, Scientific and Cultural Organization.

Tsui, C.-P. G., & Tang, H.-H. H. (2015). African university students in China's Hong Kong: Motivations and aspirations. *The Journal of Pan African Studies, 7*(10), 109–125.

UGC. (2020). *Non-local student enrolment (Headcount) of UGC-funded programmes by university, level of study, mode of study and broad academic programme category, 2019/20*. University Grant Committee (UGC).

UGC. (2021). *University Grants Committee (UGC): Annual report*.

UNESCO. (2020). *Outbound internationally mobile students by host region*. Retrieved February 14, 2020, from http://data.uis.unesco.org/Index.aspx?queryid=172

Wu, X., & Chan, W. K. (2019). Integrating international student mobility in the belt and road initiative: From state-dominated to state-steering? [Integrating international student mobility]. *Higher Education Evaluation and Development, 13*(1), 33–47. https://doi.org/10.1108/HEED-03-2019-0010

Xie, A., Postiglione, G. A., & Huang, Q. (2020). The Greater Bay Area (GBA) development strategy and its relevance to higher education. *ECNU Review of Education, 4*(1), 210–221. https://doi.org/10.1177/2096531120964466

Xinhua. (2019, December 3). Chinese firm to support Nigeria in building first transportation university. *Xinhuanet*. Retrieved from http://www.xinhuanet.com/english/201912/03/c_138602801.htm

Yang, R. (2010). Soft power and higher education: An examination of China's Confucius Institutes. *Globalisation, Societies and Education, 8*(2), 235–245. https://doi.org/10.1080/14767721003779746

Zha, Q. (2012). Understanding China's move to mass higher education from a policy perspective. In R. Hayhoe, J. Li, J. Lin, & Q. Zha (Eds.), *Portraits of 21st century Chinese universities: In the move to mass higher education* (pp. 20–57). Springer, Netherlands.

CHAPTER 10

Managing the Global COVID-19 Crisis: China's Strategies and Greater Bay Area Residents' Responses

Francis Arthur-Holmes and Ka Ho Mok

Introduction

As the world faces an unprecedented global health crisis after the outbreak of the COVID-19 pandemic, many countries have encountered tremendous political, health, financial, economic, and educational challenges. The COVID-19 pandemic which emerged in Wuhan, the People's

F. Arthur-Holmes (✉) · K. H. Mok
Department of Sociology and Social Policy, Lingnan University, Hong Kong, China
e-mail: francisarthurholmes@ln.hk; frarthur88@gmail.com

K. H. Mok
e-mail: kahomok@ln.edu.hk

K. H. Mok
Institute of Policy Studies, Lingnan University, Hong Kong, China

K. H. Mok (ed.), *Cities and Social Governance Reforms*, Social Policy and Development Studies in East Asia,
https://doi.org/10.1007/978-981-16-9531-5_10

Republic of China brought panic to the world in terms of its ramifications and spread. At the beginning, major world leaders in the West did not realize how severe COVID-19 pandemic was, hence many governments in Europe as well as the US did not take such a health crisis very seriously by introducing health preventive measures effective enough to combat this global disease. Later, tougher public health measures were adopted only when the crisis had gone beyond their national control. In contrast, most of the leaders in East Asia adopted relatively stringent public health policies to manage the COVID-19 because of their previous painstaking experiences when handling the widespread of SARS in 2003 (An & Tang, 2020; Suling, 2020).

This chapter sets out against the context of the deepening global health crisis which resulted from the outbreak of COVID-19 pandemic in early 2020 to critically examine the crisis management strategy of China. More specifically, the chapter discusses how the Chinese government has painstakingly turned the unprecedented global health crisis into development opportunities. This chapter not only reviews how the Chinese government has made attempts to reach out to the global communities by offering international aids through public health and COVID-19 pandemic-related materials to assert its global leadership by strengthening "soft security" via promotion of public health.

Drawing from a survey examining how Greater Bay Area (GBA) residents assess the Chinese government's strategies to reach out to different parts of the world offering medical and health support, this chapter reviews China's unique crisis management at the domestic and global levels. Our analysis offers insights into how China has turned the global crisis into development opportunity through diplomatic activism and increased international public health aids and soft power during the COVID-19 crisis. To understand the position of China in terms of international relations and crisis management, we examine how the authoritarian approach adopted by the Chinese government in combating the global health crisis impacts its geo-political leadership.

China's Authoritarian Approach in Crisis Management of COVID-19 Pandemic

When reviewing literature on different regime types in managing major natural or national crises, three prominent types, namely democratic, hybrid and authoritarian regimes, were identified (Greer et al., 2020).

After the foundation of the People's Republic of China since 1949, the Chinese government has accumulated very rich and diverse experiences in managing several natural disasters and national crises like the severe famine in the early 1950s, devastating crisis caused by the earthquake in Sichuan in 2008 (Chan, 2008; der Hilst, 2008; Shieh & Deng, 2011) and military rivalries across national borders during the wars between the US for North Korea and Vietnam after the Second World War (Hook & Spanier, 2012; Tellis & Tanner, 2012). International experts attempt to analyze national governments' approach in crisis management of major natural or human-made crises by adopting the three different governing approaches: democratic, hybrid and authoritarian regimes. In the light of these three regimes, some researchers conceive the governance in China as an authoritarian regime when handling challenging natural and human-made disasters. When managing major crises, authoritarian and hybrid-authoritarian regimes tend to adopt drastic measures that affect administrative activities (Greer et al., 2020). For instance, the "internal and external flow of information of both China and Russia inhibited crucial information, but only China chose and implemented really effective action" during the outbreak of COVID-19 (ibid., p. 1414). Viewing China from the authoritarian spectrum, we argue that China's government employed different pathways of producing economic growth and prosperity as well as managing crisis.

During the outbreak of COVID-19, the highly centralized system of administration in the country influenced the flow of information and a host of policies. Similarly, when analyzing how the Chinese government has succeeded in managing socio-economic changes against the condensed development context, it can be argued that China is an adaptive entrepreneurial state, adopting a pragmatic instrumental approach to ride over competing demands from multiple fronts for promoting economic growth balanced with a considerable degree of social cohesion (Mok, 2017; Mok & Kang, 2020). However, some observers and political commentators have questioned the way the Chinese authorities had handled the COVID-19 outbreak from its initial stage. As mentioned in various media platforms, information on the deadly virus was kept from the international community until its transmission was increasing at an alarming rate (Wong et al., 2020).

From the international community, the Chinese government was not too fast and concerned about what the outside world would think about the country. Despite these blame games, China's management of

COVID-19 and its anti-COVID-19 experiences were as a result of the way the government responded and handled it. Like any political (authoritarian) leaders, the political legitimacy becomes a priority for Chinese government rather than implementing flexible social mobility measures while keeping COVID-19 under control. However, some scholars may disagree with such an argument on the grounds that the intensity of the transmission of the virus requires herculean measures that will subsequently hinder people's movement and social relations. For example, Givens and Mistur contend that "politics play an important role in countries' reactions to COVID-19" which has the tendency to influence variety of policy decisions (Givens & Mistur, 2020, p. 2). Central to the US and China's trade relations, China's goal to become global leader or superpower might have affected Chinese authorities' early assessment of COVID-19 and its implications on bilateral or multilateral relations.

Embedded within the principles of authoritarian regimes, the Chinese government's rigorous and aggressive anti-COVID-19 measures including lockdowns, building temporary hospitals in few days, ban on consumption of wild animals, conducting massive testing and tracing helped to contain the rapid spread of the virus. Yet, despite the aggressive response by the Chinese government which is viewed as timely to many observers and public health experts, it would be difficult to recommend for other countries to adopt because of different regimes. In support of this, Kuperferschmidt and Cohen (2020) commended China's strictest control measures of COVID-19 pandemic and how it changed its rapidly spreading course but warned it might not work in other countries. The lockdowns in China restricted the people's movement and affected their work, yet affected persons received less or no welfare support from the government. Attributing the success of China in managing the COVID-19 crisis not because of regime types, Sharma (2021) argued that China has a high level of state capacity, combined with a competent executive leadership and a robust public health system with universal access to affordable care has distinguished the country as a leader overcoming the unprecedented global health crisis.

Evidently, the anti-COVID-19 measures in China thwarted hundreds of thousands of cases and mortalities in the country. However, most people felt away from their society, and social networks, especially friends and relatives as the government tried to control foreign transmissions. Among other things, the lockdown measures created disruptions in educational landscape. Commercial activities also experienced new trading medium which was mostly through online trading and shopping. As things stand now, border controls have limited student mobility and got people, particularly migrants stranded in China. However, despite these anti-pandemic experiences, Chinese government has demonstrated a strong leadership during this crisis when compared to other states, particularly in the West. Sun Xi (2020a) in Asia Times post asserted that "from the chaotic panic at the beginning to the comprehensive response and systematic recovery recently (in March), China has demonstrated remarkable resilience, adaptability, resourcefulness and self-reliance".

Promoting Diplomatic Activism: China's International Public Health Aids

According to Sun Xi (2020b), "COVID-19 is not only a serious public health issue but also a complex economic, social and political problem which needs systematic responses". Undoubtedly, China had experienced economic and financial downturn but its exemplary way of combating COVID-19 and position in the global value chain placed them in a befitting situation to provide public health aids to countries, particularly those in Africa, Southeast Asia and Latin America with poor healthcare systems and inadequate knowledge of infectious diseases. Governments in Africa, Southeast Asia and South America struggle to address the public health and economic problem resulted from COVID-19. For instance, COVID-19 has placed additional burden on primary healthcare systems and aggravated the existing challenges in the sectors in low-and middle-income countries (Arthur-Holmes et al., 2020). However, the Chinese government willingly intervened to provide a wide range of international public health aids to countries in these regions. These public health aids include personal protective equipment (PPE), test kits, medical supplies and face masks. While countries including the US and those in Europe were struggling from upsurges in confirmed COVID-19 cases and mortalities, China exhibited multifaceted COVID-19 diplomacy across Africa, Southeast Asia, Latin America and Caribbean (Bone & Cinotto, 2020; Sanborn, 2020).

In the context of the ongoing pandemic, China has turned the crisis into opportunities to strengthen its diplomatic relations with the developing world. Supporting this, Sanborn mentioned that "while the United States abandoned a global leadership role in fighting this pandemic, many governments in Latin America turned to China for assistance" (Sanborn,

2020, p. 2). China's response to assist countries struggling with the management of COVID-19 in Latin America was "timely, strategic and significant" (ibid., p. 2). Conceptually, China's drive to respond quickly to the call of Latin American and Caribbean governments for COVID-19 assistance cannot be observed as an opportunity to battle the US for economic power in the sub-region but rather as humanitarian action in a period of global crisis. However, in terms of China and the US trade relations, China acted more proactively during this global health crisis as a donor by supplying large quantities of medical resources to almost all Latin American countries which have diplomatic relations with China. According to Table 10.1, China reached to the developing countries for offering a wide range of international health aids. For example, Venezuelan government received 300 tons of medical supplies worth over USD 41 million from the Chinese government to respond to the pandemic (as of 6 June 2020) (See Table 10.1). Also, the Chilean government obtained COVID-19 medical aid estimated at USD 12.6 million. In a study conducted in Latin America, 531 Chinese medical-related donations were given to 33 Latin American and the Caribbean (LAC) countries between mid-February and June 2020 which amounted to USD 128 million (Telias & Urdiñez, 2020). Despite these China's medical donations and aid to the Latin American countries, Michael Strott as a Latin American editor for *Financial Times* mentioned that "Beijing's 'mask diplomacy' will boost trade and investment in traditional American zone of influence" (Stott, 2020).

Early in the pandemic, African nations also requested for COVID-19 aid and medical donations from the Chinese government. In response, the Chinese government offered bilateral assistance to African countries in order to control the spread of the pandemic (Bone & Cinotto, 2020). But while the Chinese government provided medical assistance to African states through sending of experienced medical experts and donation of PPE, face masks and testing kits, some Chinese private firms also offered donations (Bone & Cinotto, 2020; Mwangi, 2020; Nyabiage, 2020). For instance, the Chinese government reached out to Africa during the early spread of COVID-19 in the region by sending 5.4 million face masks, over a million test kits and thousands of protective suits which were distributed to all the African countries (as of early March) (Mwangi, 2020). African countries, including Ethiopia, Nigeria, Burkina Faso, Sudan, Democratic Republic of Congo, Djibouti, Algeria, Zimbabwe and Cote d'Ivoire, have received scores of medical experts

Table 10.1 Details of China's COVID-19 assistance to reaching to Latin American and Caribbean Countries

Date	*Recipient*	*COVID-19 assistance information*
06 June 2020	Chile	Medical aid estimated at USD 12.6 million (Sanborn, 2020)
06 June 2020	Peru	Medical aid worth US$7.5 million (Sanborn, 2020)
06 June 2020	Venezuela	Receive 300 tons of medical worth over USD 41 million (Sanborn, 2020)
23 July 2020	Latin American and Caribbean countries	Special video conference of foreign ministers with Chinese State Counsellor on COVID-19. Share COVID-19 experience and send medical experts (Sanborn, 2020)
10 April 2020	Argentina	Received medical supplies and information regarding COVID-19 prevention and control (Xinhua, 2020)
07 May 2020	Colombia	The Chinese government delivered US$1.5 million worth of medical supplies. They involved 30,000 nucleic acid tests and 680,000 masks, glasses, gloves, protective suits, infrared thermometers and respirators (Gamba, 2020)
March 2020	Mexico, Brazil, Costa Rica, Panama, Peru, Bolivia, El Salvador and Cuba	Received medical supplies (Gamba, 2020)

Source Compilation of open-source information of China's COVID-19 assistance by the authors. *NB* The table only provides some evidence of China's aid but not a complete list of all the supports

from China to fight the COVID-19 pandemic (ibid.). Critically assessing China's COVID-19 assistance to Africa, Nyabiage (2020) argued that China has been providing African countries with medical experts before the pandemic. From the perspective of Chinese private firms, Jack Ma's foundation donated millions of medical supplies to 54 African states (that is 200,000 medical masks, 20,000 test kits and 1000 medical-use protective suits and face shields to each African country) (Nyabiage & Choi, 2020). In light of the above mentioned assistance, some African leaders and institutions have commended China's assistance as a "demonstration of global solidarity", particularly in difficult times (Huaxia, 2020a) although there are skepticisms concerning humanitarian aid in Africa.

As part of China's strategy to promoting diplomatic activism during the crisis, the government also offered COVID-19 assistance and medical aid to the Association of Southeast Asian Nations (ASEAN). However, compared to other regions, particularly Africa and Latin America, China's aid to Southeast Asian countries has received less recognition (Fook, 2020). Probably, because China has a strong relationship with the ASEAN (Idrus, 2020), observers and scholars have ignored China's government COVID-19 assistance in the region. Therefore, it is of essence to highlight Chinese government's contribution to COVID-19 responses in the ASEAN. As pointed by Fook (2020), the ASEAN received two forms of China's assistance: material aid (such as medical supplies and equipment) and sharing of experience and experts in combating the pandemic in different aspects which include prevention and control, testing, diagnosis, treatment and training of medical personnel. But there were variations in China's assistance received by countries in Southeast Asia. As shown in Table 10.2, many Southeast Asian countries received different medical supplies and assistance from Chinese government with surgical masks being the commonest. On 3 February 2020, the Philippines obtained 200,000 surgical masks and medical information and findings on COVID-19 pandemic (Parrocha, 2020). China supplied Malaysia with 100,008 nucleic acid diagnostic testing kits, 500,000 surgical masks, 100,000 N95 masks, 50,000 sets of PPE and 200 ventilators to control the transmission of the pandemic (Jaipragas, 2020). Despite China's COVID-19 aids in these regions, it could be viewed as a strategy to change Beijing's narratives on the COVID-19 outbreak and the global perception concerning China's bilateral relations and international aid. Importantly, not every reaction to China's international public health aid received positive comments as some commentators, scholars and economists questioned China's motives behind their COVID-19 assistance in the global South. For instance, in the context of Malaysia, Jaipragas (2020) stressed that China's motivation to supply medical materials and share COVID-19 knowledge and experiences with other nations has been part of its so-called 'mask diplomacy'. Receiving less regional recognition of China's contributions in Southeast Asia could demonstrate the tensions/pressures that countries in Southeast Asia currently experience, especially when the US government has tried to play up the

Table 10.2 Details of Chinese government COVID-19 assistance to some Southeast Asian countries

Date	*Recipient*	*COVID-19 assistance information*
24 April 2020	Myanmar	12 medics from China's Yunnan Province and more than RMB 4 million worth of laboratory equipment and medical supplies. The Chinese team had a 14-day mission and shared its experience, trained medics as well as donating the needed supplies to the country (Lwin, 2020)
12 December 2020	Myanmar	China's Hubei provincial government donated medical supplies worth 2 million yuan. 30,000 PPEs, 30,000 isolation gowns, 42,000 N95 masks and 150,000 surgical masks (Huaxia, 2020b)
28 March 2020	Malaysia	Supply 100,008 nucleic acid diagnostic testing kits, 100,000 N95 masks, 500,000 surgical masks, 50,000 sets of personal protective equipment and 200 ventilators (Jaipragas, 2020)
29 June 2020	Thailand	The Chinese Embassy in Bangkok, on behalf of China, donated 1.3 million surgical face masks, 70,000 N95 face masks, 150,000 COVID-19 test kits and 70,000 PPE suits etc. (Huaxia, 2020c)
30 September 2020	Vietnam	300,000 medical masks and 20,000 protective masks (Kiet, 2020)
3 February 2020	Philippines	200,000 surgical masks; Sharing of medical information and findings on COVID-19 (Parrocha, 2020)
29 March 2020	Philippines	Bank of China donated 500,000 disposable medical masks to the Department of Health (DOH) of the Philippines (Huaxia, 2020d)
27 August 2020	Timor-Leste	40,000 protective masks to the Ministry of the Interior (Government of Timor-Leste, 2020)
08 June 2020	Cambodia	Donation of about 16 tons of medical supplies in late April. Another batch of medical supplies in early June (Heng & Ang, 2020)

Source Compilation of open-source information of China's COVID-19 assistance to ASEAN by authors. Some were compiled by Fook (2020) and the others by the authors. *NB* The table only provides some evidence of China's aid but this cannot be seen as a complete list of all the supports provided to Southeast Asian countries

geo-political card in the region to contain the rise of China (Wrobel, 2019).

In addition to the developing world, China also reached out to Europe by sending medical aid and experts to assist fighting against the COVID-19 pandemic. For example, China sent medical supplies and doctors with

COVID-19 experiences to help Italy, especially when its health system was under severe pressure to handle the COVID-19 outbreak (Gamba, 2020; Wood, 2020). Before China's decision to send their third batch of medical experts from the eastern China's Fujian Province to Italy in March 2020, the government had already sent 22 medical experts along with more than 20 tons of medical supplies to help Italy tackle the pandemic (Huaxia, 2020e). The Chinese government also sent medical experts and protective equipment to Iran and France, respectively (Gamba, 2020). As reported by the Vice-Minister of Foreign Affairs of China, Ma Zhaoxu, the Chinese government through its institutions had offered material assistance to more than 150 countries and 4 international organizations to tackle the global COVID-19 pandemic (as of 31 May 2020). Vice-Minister Ma also mentioned that the country had sent medical experts to 27 countries and held over 180 videoconferences with experts from over 170 countries and international bodies (Jin, 2020). The COVID-19 statistics from Vice-Minister Ma shows that China had exported anti-epidemic materials to over 200 countries in addition to the export of 70.6 billion face masks and 340 million pieces of protective clothing from 1 March to 31 May 2020 (ibid.). In a speech delivered at the 73rd World Health Assembly in 2020, President Xi unveiled a range of measures that China will adopt to deal with the COVID-19 on a world scale, including $ 2 billion international aid, working with the UN to provide any vaccine as a global public good and make China a global humanitarian crisis response hub (Cited in Idrus, 2020). These figures clearly demonstrate that China has turned the global COVID-19 crisis into development opportunity preserving global and regional public health security. Yet, there are some controversies surrounding China's health diplomacy in Europe. For example, there was pushback from Italian civil society about China's "generosity" that the supplies were not "aid" or donations but rather in the forms of "purchase contracts" by the Italian government.

GBA Residents Supporting the Government's International Aids Efforts

To understand how citizens in China assess their local governments' crisis management capabilities, particularly against the present global health crisis, the Joint Research Centre by Lingnan University and South China University of Technology conducted a study entitled "GBA mainland residents' evaluation of COVID-19 measures" in April 2020. The survey shows that mainland residents in the GBA believe their local governments to be more effective in measures of epidemic prevention compared to the Hong Kong and Macau governments. Such perceptions and assessments did influence their attitudes toward the Chinese government's efforts to send out international aids' teams to the developing world for combating the COVID-19 crisis through offering anti-COVID-19 pandemic-related materials. The research team adopted an online survey platform to examine citizens in the GBA in Guangdong province of China. The online questionnaire was conducted in early April, and successfully surveyed 1040 mainland residents aged 18 or above living in the nine mainland cities of GBA (including Guangzhou, Shenzhen, Foshan, Dongguan, Zhuhai, Zhongshan, Huizhou, Jiangmen and Zhaoqing). With 10 being "very good" and 0 representing "no idea", the survey invited respondents to give scores to medical staff, their local governments, and the Hong Kong and Macau governments on their performance of epidemic prevention.

The results show that medical staff received the highest score of 9.41. As for the governments in the GBA, Hong Kong and Macau, mainland governments had the best score for COVID-19 crisis management with an average of 8.61, with Zhuhai getting the highest score (8.88) followed by Dongguan (8.81). Regarding Hong Kong and Macau, the government of Macau scored 8.36, and Hong Kong scored 7.14 (see Fig. 10.1).

Amidst the deep crisis of COVID-19 pandemic, the Chinese citizens show strong support to the Chinese government's efforts for reaching out to the regional and global communities for offering help in combating the global health crisis. About the epidemic situation, the survey shows that 80.67% of respondents agreed that the mainland China should provide Hong Kong with protective materials, such as face masks, to help the city fight the epidemic. This is perhaps because the epidemic situation has become stable in the mainland while Hong Kong continues to face greater challenges, especially shortage of protective materials. In addition, 63.46% of respondents believed that Hong Kong and Macau citizens diagnosed with COVID-19 in the mainland should be entitled to the same free medical services that are available in their local cities. Obviously, GBA mainland residents' evaluation of epidemic prevention in Hong Kong was not negative, as the scores were only slightly inferior to that of the mainland and Macau. However, GBA mainland residents' overall impression of Hong Kong requires special attention.

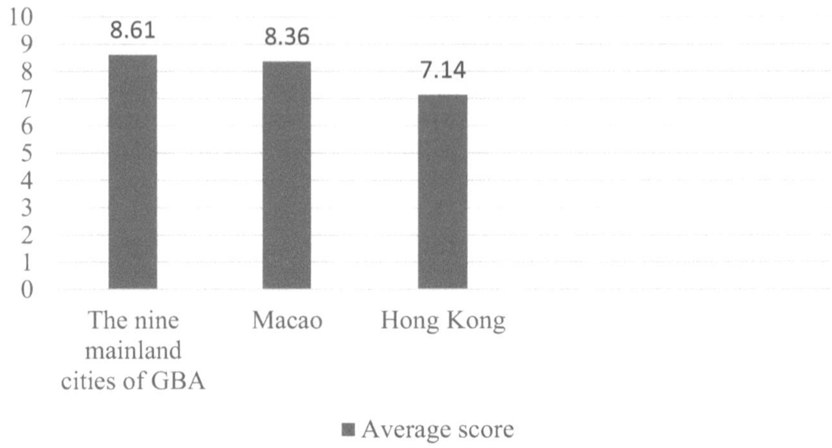

Fig. 10.1 Evaluation of governments' COVID-19 crisis management by Chinese citizens in the GBA (*Source* The authors)

Most interesting of all, with the epidemic situation in mainland China where it became stable but in different parts of the world which faced greater challenges, especially the comparative shortage of protective materials, this study indicates that more than 67% of the respondents supported their government to provide other countries with public health materials through its international aids projects by offering protective materials such as facial masks to the developing world to fight the pandemic (Mok & Huang, 2020). Such findings clearly provide a strong mandate for the Chinese government to engage in international aids and public health diplomacy though some Western liberal economies criticize China for recycling the neo-colonization projects through its Globalizing China Project.

Moving beyond the developing world, the Chinese government also reached out to Italy for offering health preventive support. In Italy and Spain, for example, the citizens relied on the responsive measures of the government to control its spread and reduce mortalities as well as health complications. At the forefront, nationalism in the UK and other countries in Europe emerged to stop the global health crisis. Yet, despite the attempt to rearrange the "global order" by placing national interests over

Table 10.3 Responses from recipient countries toward China's international health aids

Date	*Recipient*	*Response*
03 Feb 2020	Philippines	Acknowledge the Chinese government support to better understand and contain the virus (Parrocha, 2020)
24 April 2020	Myanmar	Myanmar Health and Sports Minister Dr. Myint Htwe, thanked the Chinese assistance team for supporting the country to fight COVID-19 pandemic (Lwin, 2020)
29 June 2020	Thailand	Thai Prime Minister Prayut Chan-o-Cha recommended the Chinese government for the assistance and assured that long-standing relationship with China will continue in all aspects including social, cultural, and economic ties (Huaxia, 2020c)
30 Sept. 2020	Vietnam	Acting Minister of Health Nguyen Thanh Long showed gratitude for China's aid and "hoped both sides will increase the sharing of experience in combating COVID-19, as well as healthcare cooperation to benefit their peoples" (Kiet, 2020)
27 Aug 2020	Timor-Leste	Vice Minister of Interior, António Armindo, thanked the Chinese government's donation through his ambassador and how such assistance will help the country in the fight against COVID-19 (Government of Timor-Leste, 2020)
04 June 2020	Cambodia	Cambodia's Health Minister Mam Bunheng thanked the Chinese government for donating medical supplies to the country emphasising that items will help strengthen measures of prevention, control, and response to the COVID-19 (Huaxia, 2020f)
15 May 2020	Venezuela	Venezuelan President Nicolas Maduro expressed gratitude for Chinese government COVID-19 aid (CGTN, 2020)
10 April 2020	Argentina	Argentina's President Alberto Fernandez showed appreciation to China for its strong support. China has showed "strong leadership and the ability to innovate during its COVID-19 fight" (Xinhua, 2020)

Source Compilation of open-source information of China's COVID-19 assistance by the authors

anything else, they failed (Mok et al., 2020). Though the COVID-19 initially impacted the developed countries, its impact on the developing world cannot be ignored. The COVID-19 pandemic has inexorably resulted in economic and financial recession (Yap, 2020). Moreover, it has exposed the healthcare capacities and leadership in the global South

(Arthur-Holmes et al., 2020). Greer et al. (2020) also mentioned that "states are being put to tests (of which many economies) have not recently seen" (p. 1413).

In the developing countries, the responsive measures toward the control of COVID-19 pandemic, particularly the lockdown policies implemented by various governments have culminated in job reduction, liquidity shortages and trade challenges (United Nations Conference on Trade and Development [UNCTAD], 2020). As shown in Table 10.3, countries after receiving COVID-19 aid expressed gratitude to the Chinese government for offering medical supplies and sharing medical expertise to tackle the pandemic. Given how the Chinese government responded to the outbreak of COVID-19, the government was commended for its quick response and managing strategies. Despite the criticisms of some Western liberal democracies for China's efforts to assert its global influences through the colonization projects, other research has indicated that those developing countries warmly receive China's soft security projects. Many African countries have benefited from China's aid, particularly when they have repeatedly received consistent public health support from the international aids sent by China (Castillo & Amoah, 2020; Hanauer & Morris, 2013, 2014). A critical review of the responses of countries which have received aids and help from China during the COVID-19 crisis shows positive feedback from recipient countries.

NB The table only provides some positive feedback of countries which received COVID-19 support from China but it cannot be seen as a complete list of recipients' responses.

Reimagining China's Soft Power Through International Health Aids Project

While China has been blamed for its role in the outbreak of COVID-19, the Chinese government responses toward COVID-19 in the global South were aligned with its foreign policies and as a result, showed evidence of China's soft power. To understand how the perception of China in the world changed in the recent decade, we briefly revisit the narrative of President Xi Jinping and his vision for the country. After coming into power in 2013, he pursued a different path of development devoid of conflicts, called "peaceful development" (Lee, 2016). In the literature, Nye (1990) used the concept of public diplomacy to explain soft power and how it could be achieved. As debated in academic and political discourses, China's soft power is borne out of the goal to improve its international image and diplomatic relations. Yet, many people (including scholars, politicians, observers and international relations experts) doubted the vision of China under the leadership of Xi Jinping and also questioned if the Chinese government was following "revisionist" path associated with imperialist policies or adopting neoliberal institutionalism (Lee, 2016).

By drawing on neoliberal institutionalism, soft power is crucial for international cooperation and interdependence between nations. In other words, soft power could be achieved if there is absence of military, economic and technological hard power (Nye, 1990). Soft power is basically about making others do what you want without being under duress or coercion but rather through attraction (Nye, 2004). According to Nye (2004), culture, political values and foreign policy are the three major resources of soft power that in a way promotes good governance and strengthens international and regional cooperation. Yan (2007) also asserted that "in building soft power, a nation's capacity to use its material resources, both overseas and at home, is more important than the number of resources available to it" (cited in Lee, 2016, p. 105). However, while the concept of soft power is contested, "the core of soft power in political power is represented by a nation's international attractiveness and its international and domestic mobilizing forces" (Yan, 2007, cited in Lee, 2016, p. 105). Undoubtedly, China's soft power has increased through its international public health aid project during the COVID-19 pandemic. Though some observers and politicians have stressed that China used the pandemic as a chance to secure global economic power and improve its international image, the Chinese government offered assistance without persuasion but rather with a genuine intention to offer support to tackle this global health crisis that has far-reaching ramifications.

China's prominent role in promoting public health diplomacy during global and regional health crises has consolidated its global leadership. Consequently, this has strengthened China's "soft security" than "hard security", paving a pathway for its Globalizing China Project. According to Tambo and colleagues, China's health diplomacy "emphasizes the importance of health financing in establishing health development commitment and investment in improving the gains and opportunities, importantly efficiency and value health priorities and planning" (Tambo et al., 2016, p. 116). The China-African Health Development Initiatives also show that the joint efforts and joint investments have brought positive outcomes to the public health and well-being to sub-Saharan African countries. More specifically, China's health diplomacy clearly shows "innovative evidence of operational joint solutions and strategies are critical in advancing healthcare delivery, and further enhancing universal health care, and Sustainable Development Goals to attain global health improvements and economic prosperity" (ibid., p. 119). Like its Ebola international aids project, China was the first of Africa's partners to get the coronavirus outbreak under control. According to Eric Olander, the Managing Editor of ***The China-Africa Project***, compared to Europeans and Americans, China is in a unique position in Africa because of having a large migrant population working and living in the continent with a relatively established business community (Chimbelu, 2020).

Our above discussions have indicated how the Chinese government reached out to different parts of Africa to offer coronavirus crisis-related aid and support with an estimated US 280 million. Although the China-Africa relations have experienced some difficult times, the level of private engagement linked to COVID-19 relief also shows growing trends in 2020. Against this broader political economy context with China's diplomatic activism, political scientists and international relations experts have begun to argue the importance of rethinking the "global borders" and new global governance in managing the post-COVID-19 world (Chimbelu, 2020). A group of experts therefore argue:

> The COVID-19 crisis has caused us to reconceive international and sub-national borders where new 'borders' are being drawn; and the need to anticipate a steady stream of crises similar to the COVID-19 pandemic arising from climate change and related challenges, and develop new national and international governance strategies for fostering population and community resilience. (Brousselle et al., 2020, p. 369)

Meanwhile, some political commentators call for rethinking and reimagining governance strategies, we should forge cooperation across not only the state, market, community and wider society but also engage with sub-national and international governance for better management of post-COVID-19 related consequences (Brousselle et al., 2020). Some other political scientists and sociologists also compare how liberal democracies and authoritarian regimes have managed the COVID-19 crisis, looking for the best practices in managing the post-COVID-19 society. Comparative studies have shown that despite China being regarded as an authoritarian state, the government has effectively and successfully managed the COVID-19 crisis (Alon et al., 2020). Further, China is also known as the first country across the globe to resume economic activities and production. When the world is still facing deepened health crisis and challenges to get back to normal operation, China stood out as a giant economy in the world beginning with steady economic growth by the end of 2020 (Mok, 2021).

Contrary to Nye's arguments on the concept of soft power, the Chinese notion of soft power involves "influences" which rest on economic and technological power (Lee, 2016). But Nye contends that "soft power is not a merely influence" (Nye, 2008, p. 95). Given this ideology, Nye did not consider economic and technological power as soft power but rather as part of hard power. Using this conceptualization, China's comparative advantage in terms of economic and technological power, which has translated in providing humanitarian and public health aid to countries during COVID-19 pandemic, cannot be considered as a soft power. However, not only Chinese scholars but also some Western scholars will agree that the Chinese government has redefined and extended its soft power in a more concrete form through the COVID-19 managing strategies and its engagement with countries hard-hit by the pandemic through public health emergency response by donations (such as medical equipment), sending medical experts, sharing anti-COVID-19 experience and providing other services. Some politicians, commentators and observers, particularly those in the West have tried to downplay the China's soft power in various media platforms by politicizing the country's "sincere and substantial assistance, alleging politics of generosity, mask diplomacy and propaganda" (Fengyuan, 2020). In addition, Mulakala and Ji (2020) summed up how China is perceived on the global stage during the COVID-19 pandemic.

> ...China's humanitarian response as an attempt to whitewash its internal missteps or "cover-up" during the early days of the crisis by portraying itself as a country that is handling the crisis well at home while being an international benefactor abroad.

By critically reflecting on China's international public health aid project, we argue that Chinese government has a common goal to improve the public health emergency response systems of nations that are having challenges to combat the pandemic. It is worth noting that China's assistance to countries in need during the COVID-19 crisis is entrenched in its culture as it projects Chinese culture to the world. This could also be noticed when China hosted the 2008 Olympics with a theme of "One world, One dream". During this COVID-19 pandemic, China has showcased that aspect of Chinese culture that does not discriminate but live in unison through offering support to non-Chinese citizens during crises. Since culture is an essential aspect of soft power (Nye, 2008), the Chinese government has promoted its Confucian cultural values by offering support to the outside world during the COVID-19 crisis.

Conclusion: Asserting Soft Security for Geo-Political Leadership

From the foregoing discussions, it is clearly shown how tactical the Chinese government has dedicated the efforts to asserting its global leadership through offering international aids on humanitarian ground. To achieve the national strategic goal to stage the country as a global leader, the Chinese government has also proactively engaged in internationalization and transnationalization of higher education to assert the "soft power" (Mok, 2021), painstakingly promoting Chinese culture and language to establish its global presence through Confucian Institutes in the last two decades (Lo & Pan, 2014, 2018). This chapter adds to the established literature when examining how China has tried to assert its global leadership by strengthening its "soft power" through raising scientific research and global engagements in research collaborations. This chapter clearly demonstrates how China has also stepped up its international aid to the developing world through public health and well-being promotion. If we contextualize the major findings presented in this chapter against the ***Globalizing China Project***, we would appreciate the significance of China's efforts in strengthening "soft security" through its consistent efforts in reaching out to offer international aids in terms of public health support. Putting China's efforts in asserting ***soft security*** and ***soft power*** together (see Mok, 2021), all these initiatives and efforts have clearly demonstrated China's unique approach adopted for promoting diplomatic activism to becoming a superpower (Cabestan, 2020a, 2020b).

Our discussions and analysis have clearly demonstrated how the Chinese government has turned the COVID-19 pandemic into international engagement for managing global health crisis. Riding over the global health crisis, the Chinese government has successfully turned the COVID-19 pandemic into development opportunity not only by adopting an authoritarian approach in managing the present health crisis domestically but also proactively reaching out to the international community by offering international aids and public health-related supports in combating the pandemic. This chapter has shown how the authoritarian regime commonly conceived by political scientists in the West has tactically maneuvered through the global crisis by actively promoting diplomatic activism through strengthening "soft security" and "soft power" performing as a global creditor to asserting its geo-political leadership.

This chapter also reveals how China being an adaptive entrepreneurial state as Mok (2017) conceived, has not only responded adaptively to changing external environments but also introduced domestic social policy and welfare reforms to balance the competing demands for economic growth and social expenditure for social harmony. Besides, the unique adaptive state with entrepreneurial approach under the authoritarian regime is proven very effective in China for management of natural and national crisis, for example the COVID-19 pandemic. The authoritarian regime with proactive and entrepreneurial approach to reach out to the international community by promoting diplomatic activism through public health support to the countries in need of international aids also helps China gain international recognition. In closing this chapter, the COVID-19 pandemic fundamentally disrupts the global order, however the extent to which superpowers rebalance the geo-political influences asserting for their global leadership seems to have become an increasingly important research topic. Future research must go beyond the conventional hard security approach to examine the changing geo-politics between China and Western democracies from the soft security and soft power perspectives.

References

Alon, I., Farrell, M., & Li, S. M. (2020). Regime type and COVID-19 responses. *FIIB Business Review*, *9*(3), 152–160. https://doi.org/10.1177/2319714520928884

An, B. Y., & Tang, S. Y. (2020). Lessons from COVID-19 responses in East Asia: Institutional infrastructure and enduring policy instruments. *The American Review of Public Administration, 50*(6–7), 790–800.

Arthur-Holmes, F., Akaadom, M. K. A., Agyemang-Duah, W., Abrefa Busia, K., & Peprah, P. (2020). Healthcare concerns of older adults during the COVID-19 outbreak in low-and middle-income countries: Lessons for health policy and social work. *Journal of Gerontological Social Work, 63*(6–7), 717–723.

Bone, R. M., & Cinotto, F. (2020, November 2). China's multifaceted Covid-19 diplomacy across Africa. *The Diplomat*. https://thediplomat.com/2020/11/chinas-multifaceted-covid-19-diplomacy-across-africa/

Brousselle, A., Brunet-Jailly, E., Kennedy, C., Phillips, S. D., Quigley, K., & Roberts, A. (2020). Beyond COVID-19: Five commentaries on reimagining governance for future crises and resilience. *Canadian Public Administration, 63*(3), 369–408.

Cabestan, J.-P. (2020a). *What is China's security engagement with Africa?* Paper presented at the Cities & Governance Seminar Series, 8 December 2020, Lingnan University, Hong Kong.

Cabestan, J.-P. (2020b). Social governance in China under Xi Jinping: Big brother is watching you! In A. S. Ding & J. P. Panda (Eds.), *Chinese politics and foreign policy under Xi Jinping* (pp. 62–84). Routledge.

Castillo, R., & Amoah, P. (2020). Africans in post-COVID-19 pandemic China: Is there a future for China's 'new minority'? *Asian Ethnicity, 21*(4), 560–565.

CGTN. (2020, May 15). Venezuelan president expresses gratitude for Covid-19 aid in Chinese. *CGTN*. https://news.cgtn.com/news/2020-05-15/Venezuelan-President-expresses-gratitude-for-COVID-19-aid-in-Chinese-QvAA1pz46A/index.html

Chan, E. Y. (2008). The untold stories of the Sichuan earthquake. *The Lancet, 372*(9636), 359–362.

Chimbelu, C. (2020, June 8). COVID-19 pandemic to transform China-Africa relations. *DW News*. https://www.dw.com/en/covid-19-pandemic-to-transform-china-africa-relations/a-53724530

der Hilst, B. H. (2008). A geological and geophysical context for the Wenchuan earthquake of 12 May 2008, Sichuan, People's Republic of China. *GSA Today, 18*(7), 5.

Fengyuan, D. (2020, April 20). Three saying things to characterize China's role in the global pandemic fight. *CGTN*. https://news.cgtn.com/news/2020-04-20/Three-sayings-to-characterize-China-s-role-in-global-pandemic-fight-PGFh7IK5Ms/index.html

Fook, L. L. (2020). *China's Covid-19 assistance to Southeast Asia: Uninterrupted aid amid global uncertainties*. ISEAS Perspective, Issue 2020/58.

https://www.iseas.edu.sg/wp-content/uploads/2020/04/ISEAS_Perspective_2020_58.pdf

Gamba, L. (2020, June 10). China makes massive medical donations to Latin America. *Anadolu Agency*. https://www.aa.com.tr/en/americas/china-makes-massive-medical-donations-to-latin-america/1871366

Givens, J. W., & Mistur, E. (2020). The sincerest form of flattery: Nationalist emulation during the COVID-19 pandemic. *Journal of Chinese Political Science*, 1–22.

Government of Timor-Leste. (2020, August 27). Chinese government offers 40,000 protective masks to Ministry of Interior to prevent Covid-19. *Government Homepage, News*. http://timor-leste.gov.tl/?p=25640&n=1&lang=en

Greer, S. L., King, E. J., da Fonseca, E. M., & Peralta-Santos, A. (2020). The comparative politics of COVID-19: The need to understand government responses. *Global Public Health, 15*(9), 1413–1416.

Hanauer, L., & Morris, L. J. (2013). *Chinese engagement in Africa: Drivers, reactions, and implications for U.S. policy*. RAND Corporation. https://www.rand.org/pubs/research_reports/RR521.html

Hanauer, L., & Morris, L. J. (2014). *China in Africa: Implications of a deepening relationship*. RAND Corporation. Retrieved December 10, from https://www.rand.org/pubs/research_briefs/RB9760.html

Heng, K., & Ang, L. (2020, July 8). Who's helping Cambodia weather Covid-19? *The Diplomat*. https://thediplomat.com/2020/07/whos-helping-cambodia-weather-covid-19/

Hook, S. W., & Spanier, J. (2012). *American foreign policy since WWII 19th edition*. Cq Press.

Huaxia. (2020a, April 28). Interview: China's assistance to Africa in fighting COVID-19 proof of global solidarity, says Libyan official. *Xinhuanet*. www.xinhuanet.com/english/2020-04/28/c_139015048.htm

Huaxia. (2020b, December 12). China donates more medical supplies for Myanmar to fight Covid-19. *Xinhuanet*. http://www.xinhuanet.com/english/2020-12/12/c_139583676.htm

Huaxia. (2020c, June 29). China donates medical equipment to Thailand to stem Covid-19. *Xinhuanet*. http://www.xinhuanet.com/english/2020-06/29/c_139175892.htm

Huaxia. (2020d, March 29). Bank of China donates 500,000 face masks to Philippines to help fight Covid-19 spread. *Xinhuanet*. http://www.xinhuanet.com/english/2020-03/29/c_138928536.htm

Huaxia. (2020e, March 25). China sends third group of medical experts to Italy. *Xinhuanet*. http://www.xinhuanet.com/english/2020-03/25/c_138915898_3.htm

Huaxia. (2020f, June 4). China provides more medical supplies to Cambodia for Covid-19 fight. *Xinhuanet*. http://www.xinhuanet.com/english/2020-06/04/c_139114618.htm

Idrus, P. G. (2020, May 29). China 'ready' to include ASEAN in $2b Covid-19 aid. *Anadolu Agency*. https://www.aa.com.tr/en/asia-pacific/china-ready-to-include-asean-in-2b-covid-19-aid/1857846

Jaipragas, B. (2020, March 28). Coronavirus: Malaysia receives much-needed medical supplies from China in biggest consignment yet. *South China Morning Post*. https://www.scmp.com/news/asia/southeast-asia/article/3077401/coronavirus-malaysia-receives-much-needed-medical-supplies

Jin, Z. (2020, June 7). China sent Covid-19 aid to 150 countries, four global bodies. *China Daily*. https://www.chinadaily.com.cn/a/202006/07/WS5edc819fa3108348172514e5.html

Kiet, A. (2020, September 30). US, China donates ventilators and masks to aid Vietnam's Covid-19 combat. *Hanoi Times*. http://hanoitimes.vn/us-china-donate-ventilators-and-masks-to-aid-vietnams-covid-19-combat-314369.html

Kupferschmidt, K., & Cohen, J. (2020). Can China's COVID-19 strategy work elsewhere? *Science, 367*(6482), 1061–1062.

Lee, P. S. (2016). The rise of China and its contest for discursive power. *Global Media and China, 1*(1–2), 102–120.

Lo, T. Y., & Pan, S. Y. (2014). Confucius Institutes and China's soft power: Practices and paradoxes. *Compare*. Published online on 30 May 2014.

Lo, T. Y., & Pan, S. Y. (2018). Reflecting on the research into China's soft power in international education with comparative perspective: The case of Confucius Institutes. *Annual Review of Comparative and International Education, 2017*, 49–57.

Lwin, N. (2020, April 24). In Myanmar, concerns that China's help on Covid-19 comes with strings attached. *Irrawaddy*. https://www.irrawaddy.com/opinion/analysis/myanmar-concerns-chinas-help-covid-19-comes-strings-attached.html

Mok, K. H. (2017). Wither the developmental state? Adaptive state entrepreneurship and social policy expansion in China. In T. Carroll, & D. Jarvis (Eds.), *Asia after developmental state: Disembedding autonomy*. Cambridge University Press.

Mok, K. H. (2021). *Globalizing China's social and governance reforms*. Routledge.

Mok, K. H., & Huang, G. H. (2020). *Greater Bay area mainland residents' evaluation of COVID-19 prevention and city impression of Hong Kong and Macau*. Published online in April 2020. https://scholars.ln.edu.hk/en/publications/greater-bay-area-mainland-residents-evaluation-of-covid-19-preven

Mok, K. H., & Kang, Y. Y. (2020). Social cohesion and welfare reforms—The Chinese approach. In A. Croissant et al. (Eds.), *Social cohesion in Asia*. Routledge.

Mok, K. H., Ku, Y. W., & Yuda, T. K. (2020). Managing the COVID-19 pandemic crisis and changing welfare regimes. *Journal of Asian Public Policy*, (2021), 1–12, published online on 17 December 2020.

Mulakala, A., & Ji, H. B. (2020, April 29). Covid-19 and China's soft power ambitions. *The Asia Foundation*. https://asiafoundation.org/2020/04/29/covid-19-and-chinas-soft-power-ambitions/

Mwangi, N. (2020, June 18). China's aid to Africa in fighting Covid-19. *CGTN Africa*. https://africa.cgtn.com/2020/06/18/chinas-aid-to-africa-in-fighting-covid-19/

Nyabiage, J. (2020, May 17). Coronavirus: China's aid effort in Africa is nothing new, observers say. *South China Morning Post*. https://www.scmp.com/news/china/diplomacy/article/3084750/coronavirus-chinas-aid-effort-africa-nothing-new-observers-say

Nyabiage, J., & Choi, M. (2020, March 17). Alibaba's founder Jack Ma donates millions of face masks, test kits to each of the 54 countries in Africa to combat coronavirus outbreak. *South China Morning Post*. https://www.scmp.com/business/companies/article/3075538/alibaba-founder-jack-ma-donates-millions-face-masks-test-kits

Nye, J. S. (1990). *Bound to lead: The changing nature of American power*. Basic Books.

Nye, J. S. (2002). *The paradox of American power: Why the world's only superpower can't go it alone*. Oxford University Press.

Nye, J. S. (2004). *Soft power: The means to success in world politics*. Public affairs.

Nye, J. S. (2008). Public diplomacy and soft power. *The Annals of the American Academy of Political and Social Science, 616*(1), 94–109.

Parrocha, A. (2020, February 3). China donates 200K surgical masks to PH. *Philippines News Agency*. https://www.pna.gov.ph/articles/1092714

Sanborn, C. (2020). *Latin America and China in times of Covid-19*. Latin American Program—Kissinger Institute. https://www.wilsoncenter.org/sites/default/files/media/uploads/documents/FINAL%20Updated%20Sanborn%20Article.pdf

Sharma, S. (2021). *Prosperity with inequality: A comparative political economy of the United States, China and India*. Paper presented to the Webinar Series on China and India Studies Series, 2 February 2021, Lingnan University, Hong Kong.

Shieh, S., & Deng, G. (2011). An emerging civil society: The impact of the 2008 Sichuan earthquake on grass-roots associations in China. *The China Journal, 65*, 181–194.

Stott, M. (2020). China cleans up in Latin America as US flounder over coronavirus. *Finance Times*. https://www.ft.com/content/741e72ed-e1db-4609-b389-969318f170e8

Suling, L. (2020, January 31). Commentary: SARS was scary, but the experience was invaluable in shaping our Wuhan virus response. *CNA Digital News*. https://www.channelnewsasia.com/news/commentary/wuhan-virus-singapore-cases-response-sars-2003-quarantine-12360244

Tambo, E., Ugwu, C. E., Guan, Y. Y., Wei, D., Xiao, N., & Zhou, X. N. (2016). China-Africa health development initiatives: Benefits and implications for shaping innovative and evidence-informed national health policies and programs in Sub-saharan African countries. *International Journal of Maternal and Child Health and AIDS, 5*(2), 119–133.

Tellis, A. J., & Tanner, T. (Eds.). (2012). *China's military challenge*. National Bureau of Asian Research.

Telias, D., & Urdinez, F. (2020). *China's foreign aid determinants: Lessons from a novel dataset of the mask diplomacy during the COVID-19 pandemic*. https://www.researchgate.net/profile/Francisco_Urdinez/publication/344035590_China's_Foreign_Aid_Determinants_Lessons_from_a_Novel_Dataset_of_the_Mask_Diplomacy_During_the_COVID-19_Pandemic/links/5f4e9485299bf13a3196ea83/Chinas-Foreign-Aid-Determinants-Lessons-from-a-Novel-Dataset-of-the-Mask-Diplomacy-During-the-COVID-19-Pandemic.pdf

United Nations Conference on Trade and Development (UNCTAD). (2020). *UN calls for $2.5 trillion coronavirus crisis package for developing countries*. https://unctad.org/en/pages/newsdetails.aspx?OriginalVersionID=2315

Wong, E., Barnes, J. E., & Kanno-Youngs, Z. (2020, August 19). Local officials in China hid coronavirus dangers From Beijing, U.S. agencies find. *New York Times*. https://www.nytimes.com/2020/08/19/world/asia/china-coronavirus-beijing-trump.html

Wood, J. (2020, March 16). China is sending medical experts and supplies to help Italy fight coronavirus. *World Economic Forum*. https://www.weforum.org/agenda/2020/03/coronavirus-covid-19-italy-china-supplies/

Wrobel, R. M. (2019). Chinese geopolitics in Southeast Asia: A new pattern of economic power within ASEAN? *Asiatische Studien-Études Asiatiques, 73*(1), 149–191.

Xi, S. (2020a, March 10). China's painful gains from Covid-19 crisis. *Asia Times*. https://asiatimes.com/2020/03/chinas-painful-gains-from-covid-19-crisis/

Xi, S. (2020b, September 19). How China was able to vanquish Covid-19 so quickly. *Bangkok Post*. https://www.bangkokpost.com/opinion/opinion/1988127/how-china-was-able-to-vanquish-covid-so-quickly

Xinhua. (2020, April 10). Xi says China ready to continue helping Argentina with COVID-19 prevention, aid. *China Daily*. https://www.chinadaily.com.cn/a/202004/10/WS5e904264a3105d50a3d15625.html

Yan, X. (2007, May 22). The core of soft power is political power. *Global Times*. http://news.xinhuanet.com/world/2007-05/23/content_6139900.htm. (in Chinese).

Yap, O. F. (2020). A new normal or business-as-usual? Lessons for COVID-19 from financial crises in East and Southeast Asia. *The European Journal of Development Research, 32*(5), 1504–1534.

CHAPTER 11

Cities, Higher Education and GBA Development from Comparative Perspectives

Ka Ho Mok

Introduction

Based upon the above empirical findings and critical analysis, this chapter aims to offer a critical review of how the rapid urbanization taking place in the GBA has affected social integration. What are the major policy issues and challenges for governance given the increasing mobility in the GBA? Drawing from the experiences of other Bay economies overseas like New York Bay, Tokyo Bay and Florida Bay, this chapter offers comparative and international perspectives in understanding policy issues and challenges for governance when managing the rise of cities and its related integration problems. More importantly, this concluding chapter discusses the role of higher education in future GBA development by referring to other successful Bay economies in terms of the contributions of universities to urban development. This chapter also acknowledges the limitations of the present research and points to future research agenda.

K. H. Mok (✉)
Institute of Policy Studies, Lingnan University, Hong Kong, China
e-mail: kahomok@ln.edu.hk

K. H. Mok (ed.), *Cities and Social Governance Reforms*, Social Policy and Development Studies in East Asia,
https://doi.org/10.1007/978-981-16-9531-5_11

GBA Development from Comparative Perspectives

This volume begins by presenting the policy background and evolution of the Greater Bay Area (GBA) Development Blueprint. Given that much research related to GBA has focused on economic development or megacity development with emphasis on infrastructure and spatial management, our above discussions have highlighted the social, psychological and even broader political economy perspectives when analysing GBA development challenges and opportunities. After the GBA Development Plan was rolled out, unfortunately, the development process has been disrupted by the outbreak of the COVID-19 pandemic since December 2019 and early 2020. Owing to the closure of borders between Hong Kong and the GBA area, including the Hong Kong–Macao border, many good development ideas have been put on hold. Nonetheless, one major area of collaboration driving GBA development that was only partially delayed is inter-university cooperation among universities across Hong Kong, Macao and different cities in the Bay area. Although face-to-face interactions and exchanges are disrupted, different forms of research activities have been organised through online platforms like webinar series, conferences and research symposia. Collaborative projects under the Alliance of Universities in Guangdong–Hong Kong–Macao continue to operate during the COVID-19 pandemic.

Institutional cooperation has taken place in the GBA well before the promulgation of the GBA Development Blueprint in 2018. As early as 2005, Hong Kong Baptist University established the United International College in Zhuhai in collaboration with Beijing Normal University, offering international higher education to address the growing diversity of learning needs. In 2009, with the strong support of the central government, a piece of land with an area of 1092.6 km^2 on Hengqin Island, which originally belongs to Zhuhai City close to Macao, was approved as the location of the University of Macau. In 2014, in collaboration with Shenzhen University, the Chinese University of Hong Kong (Shenzhen) was established. In 2019, the Hong Kong University of Science and Technology also reached an agreement with Guangzhou University to set up a campus in Nansha, Guangdong. Other universities based in Hong Kong have also rolled out plans either to establish their branch campuses or joint institutes in strengthening cooperation with institutions in the GBA. City University of Hong Kong has reached an agreement with Dongguan City to establish a City University of Hong Kong campus in the city.

Similarly, Hong Kong Polytechnic University collaborated with Foshan City government for setting up a branch campus in the city, whereas Lingnan University reached agreements of cooperation with Shenzhen University and Open University (Shenzhen) for developing joint academic programmes, setting up a Joint Research Institute and Joint Institute for Advanced Studies offering Ph.D. programmes and research collaboration (Mok, 2021a; Sharma, 2021).

However, one major distinction of GBA from other Bay economies in China could be captured by the 'Three I's', as Xie et al. (2021) highlighted. The Triple 'I' helix strategy has been promoted by the Chinese government to turn the GBA into an area that promotes ***Integration***, ***Innovation*** and ***Internationalization***. Seeing the strengths of the two Special Administrative Regions (SARs) of Hong Kong and Macao, the Chinese government considers that the GBA Development Blueprint not only generates economic benefits but also *social and cultural integration*. Under the 'One Country, Two Systems' framework, the Chinese government expects that people from the two SARs could integrate well with residents in the GBA. In his speech presented during the 19th National Congress of the Communist Party of China, President Xi stated that 'We will give priority to the development of Guangdong–Hong Kong–Macao Greater Bay Area, cooperation between Guangdong, Hong Kong and Macao, and regional cooperation in the pan-Pearl River Delta, thus fully advancing mutually beneficial cooperation between the mainland and the two regions' (cited in Xie, et al., p. 212). He strongly believed such a regional development would offer great opportunity for Hong Kong and Macau to further integrate with the mainland, bringing prosperity to the country and the international community (Xie et al., 2021).

In addition, the Chinese government considers that the deeper collaboration between the two SARs and the nine cities in the GBA would promote innovation-centric entrepreneurship, such entrepreneurship could enhance the country's successful transformation from a manufactory-oriented economy to a high-technology-oriented economy through the promotion of innovation-centric research, which turns into business and commercial opportunities. Given the competitive edge of universities in Hong Kong, the Chinese government strongly believes that the deep collaboration between universities from Hong Kong and Macau with those in the GBA will forge productive synergy across the border, especially when the GBA is considered China's most developed region with leading industries in the areas of manufacturing, financial services and technological innovation (Chen, 2018). Hence, governments in Mainland China believe that the deep collaboration between the two SARs with cities in Guangdong would create a new momentum as a new engine that drives China's growth towards an *innovation-centric economy* (Deloitte, 2018).

Recognizing the strategic importance of positioning the country in the global stage, President Xi Jinping calls for active participation in and promotion of economic globalization. Having experienced different forms of 'containment' resulting from new geo-politics, the rivalry between world powers has put China into a challenging position for future development. With strong conviction to energize China's development project, Chinese leaders are consistent in their governance approach, highlighting the importance of remaining open to the world and repeatedly calling for international cooperation and collaboration. Seeing *internationalization* as top priority, the Chinese government believes the GBA Development Plan serves as a vehicle to promote the deep structural adjustment of China's economy. It is also a roadmap for opening the country to the outside world through its coastal location. As Xie et al. have rightly argued: 'as the most open region to the outside world, the Greater Bay Area has an advantage in global economic positioning. As expected, it will play a key role in the Belt and Road Initiative and shoulder the responsibility of piloting more reforms to help China internationalize its economy' (2021, p. 213).

The Rise of Megacity: Implications for Shenzhen and Hong Kong

When Shenzhen celebrated its 40th anniversary after being established as China's first special economic zone on 2 October 2020, President Xi unveiled a new list of reforms which would give the city considerably more autonomy to achieve the national strategic development goals via Shenzhen. From a tiny fishing village in the 1950s, Shenzhen has demonstrated the power of Chinese economic reforms to become the country's leading hub for innovation and technology, with its GDP edging ahead of Hong Kong's at RMB 2.7 trillion in 2019. With 4.10% of GDP spent on R&D in 2018, among the highest in the world, Shenzhen has successfully groomed world-leading companies like Huawei and Ping An in Brand Finance's 2020 top 10 most valuable brands (The Hong Kong General Chamber of Commerce [HKGCC], 2020). In view of Hong

Kong's social and economic uncertainties in 2019 and 2020 partially resulting from the social unrest that emerged in 2019, the Chinese government began to attach far more weight to Shenzhen, making the city the engine for GBA development. Chapter 4 analysed the findings generated from two major surveys related to how Hong Kong people evaluate the rise of Shenzhen and its impact on Hong Kong's regional and global competitiveness. Our above discussion also reported how Shenzhen people evaluate the competitiveness of Shenzhen and their willingness to continue to stay in the city for future development. Critical reflections on these surveys clearly show potential conflicts between the two cities, especially when the central government has planned to offer Shenzhen more flexible policy environment to strengthen its leading role in China's national development.

Specifically, President Xi Jinping's speech in Shenzhen on 14 October 2020 stated China's commitment to promote the building of an open world economy through its steadfast and complete opening-up. Positioning Shenzhen as a world-class innovation powerhouse and model of economic reform for the nation, the Chinese government would enable the city to undertake new ventures in 40 areas including financial markets, the business environment, technology and innovation and international cooperation. To achieve such strategic goals, Shenzhen will be turned into an important engine to drive development of the GBA and promote the integration of Hong Kong and Macau. President Xi also sees that the GBA would provide a great platform for attracting more young people from Hong Kong and Macau to study, work and live in the mainland (HKGCC, 2020, p. 12). In view of the rise of Shenzhen, commentators may worry about the role of Hong Kong being 'eclipsed' or gradually 'marginalised'. As Zhu has rightly argued, the rise of Shenzhen would inevitably create conflict between Hong Kong and Shenzhen (see Chapter 4). Nonetheless, other commentators and business analysts think that Hong Kong would remain competitive in the context of GBA development. The Chinese government's 'policy shift' may support Shenzhen as the driver for GBA growth and development; nonetheless, Hong Kong's strategic role in supporting not only the GBA regional development but also contributing to the nation's global development goal through the 'Belt and Road Initiatives' would not be undermined owing to its position as an international finance and trade centre, its international connectivity and internationally trusted public administration and legal systems (Li & Kwok, 2019). Hence, we should not underestimate Hong

Kong's 'connectivity' not only with international businesses but also with leading universities and research institutions across different parts of the globe (Mok, 2021a; Xu et al., 2019).

The call for GBA development, with weight being attached to the collaboration between universities, industries and business, has been identified by the Chinese government as a major driver of Bay development projects. The world-leading research conducted by universities in Hong Kong as revealed by the most recent international peer reviews, that is, Research Assessment Exercise (RAE 2020), undertaken by the University Grants Committee (UGC) in Hong Kong released in May 2021 clearly demonstrated Hong Kong's strengths in research and innovation generation. According to the RAE 2020 results, the overall research performance of the eight publicly funded universities in Hong Kong is commended by international review panels as 'world leading' and 'internationally excellent'. Approximately 70% of research outputs and projects were rated 3* (internationally excellent) and 4* (world leading) in the RAE 2020, showing significant improvements from a similar RAE conducted in 2014 (University Grants Committee [UGC], 2021). The success of Hong Kong universities would undoubtedly facilitate development of innovation-centric entrepreneurship through strengthening the role of the inter-university–industries-business cooperation/collaboration. Table 11.1 highlights the number of world-leading universities located in different bay areas.

Compared with other bay areas like New York Bay, Boston Bay, California Bay and Tokyo Bay, which only have 2–4 Top 100 universities, the GBA in South China has 5 Top 100 universities as revealed by the 2021 QS World University Rankings. Referring to THE Rankings 2019, a similar league table is presented, clearly showing the competitive edge

Table 11.1 Number of world-leading universities located in different bay areas

Bay areas	Times higher rankings (2019)	QS world rankings (2020)
New York Bay	Top 100: 4	Top 100: 4
Boston Bay	Top 100: 3	Top 100: 3
California Bay	Top 100: 3	Top 100: 2
Tokyo Bay	Top 100: 1	Top 100: 2
Greater Bay	Top 100: 3	Top 100: 5

Source The rankings and QS world university rankings, 2019 and 2020

of the GBA in terms of leading universities with international reputation. Collaboration across 170 higher education institutions with a student population of more than 2 million in the GBA, coupled with resources allocated for research and innovation enhancement by the central and local governments in the GBA to promote inter-university and international research cooperation/collaboration between Hong Kong, Macao and Guangdong will bring positive impact to the GBA development (Xie et al., 2021; Xu et al., 2019). The inter-city cooperation will utilize the strengths of each city to energize economic and social developments of the GBA, and competitive edge of the bay economies could be maximized with better policy coordination across the GBA cities. The distinct feature of the three I's—*Integration, Innovation* and *Internationalization*—could be well presented through the deep cooperation across the cities in the Bay area (Xie et al., 2021). Business analysts also believe that with the Chinese government's stringent measures in combatting the COVID-19 pandemic, the country would revive its economy through the 'dual circulation' model. This model encouraged greater self-sufficiency in technology and increased domestic consumption, and the enhanced Hong Kong–Shenzhen cooperation in co-directing and co-driving the GBA development would continue to strengthen the role of Hong Kong in the national, regional and global development (HKGCC, 2020).

In a study on major bay economies in Boston, New York, California and Tokyo, Mok (2021b) found that the role of universities, particularly a cluster of successful universities with high-quality research and strong capacity of knowledge transfer, is fundamental for GBA development. The discussion in Mok's recent book, which critically examines of the role of the universities in Bay economies from comparative perspectives, has clearly shown that the success of leading university clusters in other major Bay areas requires an open and inclusive environment. Xie et al. (2021) argued that faculty and students working in these leading universities need a working environment conducive for creativity and innovation production. Hence, greater institutional autonomy and professional autonomy are crucial for attracting talents from all over the world to collaborate with other higher education hubs to turn brilliant research ideas into positive impacts to the wider society and human betterment (Xie et al., 2021). In particular, policies of collaborations leading to integration of knowledge networks require a higher degree of institutional autonomy and within-institutional professional autonomy, especially when the university systems across Hong Kong, Macao and Guangdong vary. Universities based in Hong Kong, being independent legal entities, have long enjoyed a high degree of institutional autonomy in making their own development plans and decisions, whereas institutions in Macao and the mainland may operate differently as they need to seek approvals from different levels when conceiving their development plans (Postiglione, 2015; Xie et al., 2021). How these different university systems work closely in harmony when their management and governance styles differ requires careful policy coordination to prevent implementation deficit from happening during the processes of collaboration.

Concluding Remarks: Urbanism and Social Psychological Well-Being for GBA Future

International and comparative studies related to megacity development, happiness and satisfaction with community, family and friends are used as measures of well-being against the context of urbanization. In examining new migrants' adaptability after migrating to a megacity for study, work and residence, Palisi and Canning (2010) have clearly shown the close relationship between urbanism and citizens' social-psychological well-being. Social scientists have conducted research on the impact of megacities on human well-being and happiness. Some recent research has revealed that the core characteristics of urban life, particularly in terms of size and density, contribute to urban unhappiness and other urban problems (Okulicz-Kozaryn & Mazelis, 2016). International research has also suggested that without appropriate social and psychological support, deterioration of primary relationships would adversely affect social-psychological well-being of new migrants (Lewis & Lyon, 2010). Our discussions in Chapters 3 and 4 regarding young people or working adults in Hong Kong have clearly revealed that, when assessing development challenges and opportunities, the key concerns are not economic incentives but social and cultural integration matters and quality of life or preferred lifestyle in urban settings.

According to a recent research conducted by Zhu et al. (2021) regarding young working adults in Hong Kong assessing the development opportunity in the GBA in 2020, many young people aged 18 to 35 indicated their preference for an urban and cosmopolitan lifestyle. Respondents' major concerns when conceiving migration to work and stay in the GBA are closely related to children's education, accessibility to the Internet and free flow of communication, and social networks and support (Zhu et al., 2021). This study points out that young working adults in Hong Kong perceive a 'psychological distance', which may deter them from moving beyond the border across to the GBA for development. As different successful Bay economies are competing for leading talents, governments in the GBA must work closely to co-create an environment that offers these talents the preferred lifestyle, that is, cosmopolitanism and urbanism (Douglas, 2021; Nelson, 2021; Mok, 2021b). Other research highlights that the importance of resilient and equitable urbanism by design positively contributes to the collaborative process to reimagine the California Bay Area development (Mendler, 2019). Most recently in August 2021, an opinion survey was conducted among Hong Kong citizens with particular reference to examine their attitude towards the GBA development. The survey was conducted by Our Hong Kong Foundation, one of the think tanks in the city. Among the respondents, 79% considered venturing in the GBA would offer great business opportunity if professional qualifications and working experiences being recognized, while 66% of the respondents showed interests to reside in the GBA if living costs are reasonable. In addition, 58% of the respondents believed the GBA would provide diverse opportunities for future developments (Our Hong Kong Foundation, 2021).

Through critical reflections on cities, Kotkin (2016) highlights the importance of the human dimension with the rise of cities, raising the question, *what is a city for*? In his book entitled *The Human City: Urbanism for the Rest of Us*, Kotkin points out the problems with megacities and urges for serious consideration of the importance of everyday life when most urban dwellers are living inside the 'glamour zone'. Echoing Kotkin, the critical analysis of the rise of cities in the GBA discussed in this book has provided further evidence showing the importance of social and cultural integration for future GBA development. In conclusion, we should take social and socio-psychological factors into consideration when developing appropriate policies in attracting young talents to work in the GBA. The future success of GBA development should not be measured in terms of economic growth and technological/ innovation advancement alone. Creating megacities in the GBA should take the social, cultural and humanistic aspects into serious consideration. After all, the future success of the GBA depends upon how residents assess the quality of life and their well-being when working and living in the Bay area while enjoying their preferred lifestyles.[1]

[1] The author wants to thank Dr Doyoung Oh (2022) for sharing his research article about universities and cities, part of the analysis of this chapter draws from the insight of Oh's work.

Future Research Agenda

Future research regarding GBA development could focus on how city governments in the GBA work together for policy frameworks appropriate for the different expectations and preferences of lifestyles across the nine cities in Guangdong and two SARs of Hong Kong and Macao. As the Chinese government has long been valuing the fine balance between social changes and social stability as a response to the rapid changes generated from urbanization processes (Holbig & Gilley, 2011; Mok & Kang, 2020), the rise of megacities in the GBA with increased human mobility across the region inevitably creates different forms of urban problems. More research related to public management and urban governance should be conducted with reference to how governments in the GBA can develop policies that promote social harmony in addressing rapid social changes against the context of urbanization. When the borders across Guangdong–Hong Kong–Macao are completely reopened after the COVID-19 pandemic is well under control, more policy research evaluating the GBA's prosperity, the nation's rejuvenation and people's well-being and happiness should be developed.

References

Chen, G. (2018). *Guangdong-Hong Kong-Macao Bay area development report*. People's University Press.

Deloitte. (2018). *From the world factory to the world-class bay area*. http://www.199it.com/archives/766251.html

Douglas, J. (2021). Knowledge-based economic areas and flagship universities: A look at the new growth ecosystems in the U.S. and California. In K. H. Mok (Eds.), *Higher education, innovation and entrepreneurship from comparative perspectives: Reengineering China through the Greater Bay economy and development*. Springer.

Guo, S. P. (Ed.). (2021). *Guangdong-Hong Kong-Macao Greater Bay area*. World Scientific.

HKGCC. (2020). Shenzhen celebrates 40 years. *Bulletin*. Hong Kong General Chamber of Commerce.

Holbig, H., & Gilley, B. (2011). *In search of legitimacy in post-revolutionary China: Bringing ideology and governance back in* (GIGA Working Paper, No. 127).

Kotkin, J. (2016). *The human city: Urbanism for the rest of Us*. B2 Books.

Lewis, S., & Lyon, L. (2010). The quality of community and the quality of life. *Sociological Spectrum, 6*(4), 397–410.

Li, C. L., & Kwok, M. T. (2019). Unpacking the plan for the Guangdong-Hong Kong-Macau Greater Bay area: A mechanism for reform. *China and the World, 2*(2), 1950010.

Mendler, S. (2019). *Resilient and equitable urbanism by design: Insights from the collaborative process to reimagine the SF Bay Area.* Doctoral Dissertation, University of South California.

Mok, K. H. (2021a). *Seizing the COVID-19 crisis as new development opportunity: China's three-pronged approach managing the new geo-politics in international higher education* [Unpublished paper].

Mok, K. H. (Ed.). (2021b). *Higher education, innovation and entrepreneurship from comparative perspectives: Reengineering China through the Greater Bay Economy and Development*. Springer.

Mok, K. H., & Kang, Y. Y. (2020). Social cohesion and welfare reforms: The Chinese approach. In A. Croissant & P. Walkenhorst (Eds.), *Social cohesion in Asia: Historical origins, contemporary shapes and future dynamics*. Routledge.

Nelson, A. (2021). Higher education and human capital and in the "New York Bay Area": Historical lessons from the City University of New York. In K. H. Mok (Eds.), *Higher education, innovation and entrepreneurship from comparative perspectives: Reengineering China through the Greater Bay economy and development*. Springer.

Oh, D. Y. (2022). The university and East Asian cities: The variegated origins of urban universities in colonial Seoul and Singapore. *Journal of Urban History, 48*(2), 336–360.

Okulicz-Kozaryn, A., & Mazelis, J. M. (2016). Urbanism and happiness: A test of Wirth's theory of urban life, *Urban Studies*, published online on 10 May 2016.

Our Hong Kong Foundation. (2021). *Greater Bay area opportunities: Survey and analytical observations*. Our Hong Kong Foundation.

Palisi, B. J., & Canning, C. (2010). Urbanism and social psychological well-being: A test of three theories. *Sociological Spectrum, 6*(4), 361–378.

Postiglione, G. (2015). Research universities for national rejuvenation and global influence. *Higher Education, 70*, 235–250.

Sharma, Y. (2021, March 13). So many new universities: Where will the staff come from? *University World News.*

UGC. (2021). *Research assessment exercise 2020 report*. University Grants Committee.

Xie, A. L., Postiglione, G. A., & Huang, Q. (2021). The Greater Bay Area (GBA) development strategy and its relevance to higher education. *ECNU Review of Education, 4*(1), 210–221.

Xu, Z. Q., et al. (Eds.). (2019). *Higher education, regional innovation and economic growth: An analysis of the role of university in bay area development from comparative perspective*. Guangdong Higher Education Press.

Zhu, A., Mok, K. H., & Huang, G. H. (2021). Migrating to GBA cities in mainland China: Assessing a model of psychological distance among Hong Kong working adults. *Analyses of Social Issues and Public Policy*, published online on 28 January 2021.

Index

A

Africa, 163
Argentina, 165, 171
Association of Southeast Asian Nations (ASEAN), 166, 167
attitudes, 78, 96, 99, 100, 103, 105, 106, 112, 147, 169
autonomy, 18, 34, 113, 127, 130, 188, 191

B

Beijing, 2, 21, 53, 110–118, 127, 130, 131, 147, 164, 166
Beijing-Tianjin-Hebei Economic Zone, 18
Belt and Road Initiative, 2, 5, 8, 21, 188
bidding mechanism, 113–115, 124, 133
Boston Bay Area, 190

C

California Bay Area, 190
Cambodia, 167, 171
Caribbean, 163–165
challenges, 4–9, 14, 18, 22, 146–151, 159, 163, 169, 170, 172, 174–176, 185, 186, 192
China, 2, 3, 6, 7, 9–13, 20–22, 24, 31, 33, 46, 52, 53, 56, 75, 77–80, 83–85, 87–89, 96, 97, 109–113, 116, 119, 120, 123, 124, 127–133, 138–146, 149–152, 160–163, 165–177, 187–190
Closer Economic Partnership Arrangement (CEPA), 20, 27
collaboration, 191
comparative perspectives, 7, 191
competitiveness, 4, 9, 21, 23, 25, 34, 53, 54, 56, 68
contracting, 11, 110, 111, 113, 116, 116–120, 124–133

K. H. Mok (ed.), *Cities and Social Governance Reforms*, Social Policy and Development Studies in East Asia, https://doi.org/10.1007/978-981-16-9531-5

cooperation, 2, 13, 17–20, 22, 24, 26, 27, 34, 47, 51–53, 55, 58, 65, 66, 106, 140, 145, 171, 173, 186–191
COVID-19, 3, 10, 13, 95, 98–103, 105, 106, 146, 147, 150, 159–177, 186, 191, 194
crisis management, 160, 161, 168
cross-border governance, 27, 28
cross-border innovation ecosystem, 52, 53
cross-border mobility, 9, 27, 28

D
diplomatic activism, 13, 160, 166, 174, 177
Dongguan, 19, 23, 24, 100, 169, 186

E
East Asia, 160
economic development, 5, 21, 22, 26, 27, 56, 58, 64, 65, 138, 141, 186
expectations, 4, 130, 194
experiences, 2, 6, 11, 14, 79, 88, 111, 120, 134, 149, 160–163, 166, 168, 185, 193

F
Florida Bay Area, 7, 185
Forum on China-Africa Cooperation (FOCAC), 140–143, 151
Foshan, 19, 23, 24, 100, 169, 187
Foundations, 127
fragmented authoritarianism, 110
France, 126

G
Ghana, 139, 151
global governance, 13, 174
government-organized non-governmental organization (GONGO), 127
Greater Bay Area (GBA), 1–14, 17–28, 31–47, 53, 55, 56, 68, 74–80, 83–85, 87–89, 97, 100, 106, 140, 145–152, 160, 168–170, 185–194
Guangdong, 4, 5, 7, 10, 18, 19, 21–23, 25, 28, 33, 97–100, 140, 145, 169, 186–188, 191, 194
Guangzhou, 11, 19, 22–25, 27, 100, 110–112, 115–119, 127, 129–132, 145, 147, 148, 169
Guangzhou–Shenzhen–Hong Kong Express Rail Link, 26

H
health security, 99, 102, 103, 105, 168
health services, 96, 99, 100, 103, 105, 126
higher education, 12, 14, 34, 53, 116, 137–143, 149, 152, 176, 185, 186, 191
Hong Kong, 2–10, 18–28, 31–37, 41, 42, 45–47, 51–53, 55–68, 75, 77–80, 82, 83, 85, 87–89, 96–104, 106, 119, 138–140, 142, 145–148, 150–152, 169, 186–192, 194
Huizhou, 19, 23, 24, 100, 169
human capital, 34, 52, 53, 55, 66–68

I
impressions, 32, 100–103, 105, 106
infrastructure, 4, 20, 26, 125, 186
innovation, 1, 2, 4, 5, 7, 18, 24, 27, 28, 33, 34, 36, 52, 53, 55, 66, 67, 74, 129, 187–191, 193

institutional concerns, 32, 33, 36, 37, 39, 45
integration, 1, 4–6, 8, 10, 12, 14, 20, 26, 27, 83, 88, 106, 140, 146–149, 151, 152, 185, 187, 189, 191–193
internationalization, 12, 34, 138–143, 146, 187, 188
investment, 9, 19, 53, 74–78, 83, 85, 88, 89, 141, 164, 174
Italy, 168, 170

J
Jiangmen, 19, 23, 24, 100, 169
Jing-Jin-Ji Coordinated Development Initiative, 3

L
Latin America, 163, 166

M
Macao/Macau, 2, 4, 5, 7, 9, 10, 18–28, 74, 100, 106, 139, 140, 145, 147, 150, 151, 169, 186, 187, 189, 191, 192, 194
Malaysia, 21, 166, 167
Maritime Silk Road, 18, 22, 28
mass organizations, 111–113
mega-cities, 1, 4, 5
migrants, 9, 10, 96, 103, 106, 138, 140, 146, 147, 150, 151, 163, 192
migration, 4, 9, 31–34, 47, 53, 54, 74–79, 83–85, 88, 89, 147, 192
Myanmar, 167, 171

N
New York Bay Area, 2, 7, 185, 190
New York Metropolitan Area, 25, 27
Nigeria, 138–140, 164
non-for-profit organizations (NPOs), 127, 128
non-governmental organizations (NGOs), 11, 111–120, 124–134

O
One Country, Two Systems, 18, 21, 22, 97

P
partnership, 4, 139, 141, 142, 145
Pearl River Delta, 2, 17, 19–21, 26–28, 106, 187
Philippines, 21, 166, 167, 171
policy variations, 109–111
political economy, 4, 6, 8, 11, 18, 174, 186
positive self-esteem, 76, 77
premium human resources, 52–54, 56, 57, 66, 67
public health aids, 160, 163
Public Institutions, 127
public perceptions, 32

Q
quality of life, 4, 33, 46, 55–58, 64–68, 125, 192, 193

R
reforms, 2, 5, 7, 11, 124, 148, 177, 188
regime, 13, 160, 162, 177
regional development, 3, 4, 7, 8, 19, 187, 189
relative deprivation, 54, 66–68
risk-takers, 9, 75, 77, 79, 80, 85, 88, 89
risk tolerance, 75–78, 84, 88, 89

S

San Francisco Bay Area, 25–27
Shanghai, 2, 53, 110–119, 127, 131
Shenzhen, 3, 9, 19, 20, 23, 24, 27, 51–53, 55–68, 100, 139, 169, 186, 188, 189, 191
Silk Road Economic Belt, 22
Singapore, 3
Sino-African relations, 13, 140
Social Associations, 127
social cohesion, 2, 21
social development, 2, 26, 53
social governance, 5, 11, 27, 83, 148
social mobility, 9, 34, 74, 77, 88, 147, 149–151, 162
social policy, 6, 7, 10, 99, 100, 125, 177
Social Service Organizations, 127
social services, 11, 12, 96, 110–113, 116–120, 124–129, 132, 133, 146, 147, 152
Social Work Committee, 111, 112, 117, 118
soft power, 13, 34, 138, 141, 145, 146, 149, 160, 172, 173, 175–177
soft security, 13, 160, 172, 173, 177, 178
Southeast Asia, 163
Southern China, 1, 2, 4–7, 17, 28
South-South Cooperation, 13
Spain, 170

T

talents, 13, 138, 145, 148, 191, 193
technology, 2, 4, 7, 18, 19, 23, 24, 27, 28, 51, 55, 141, 187–189, 191
Thailand, 167, 171
Timor-Leste, 167, 171
Tokyo Bay Area, 7, 25–27, 185, 190

U

United Kingdom (UK), 21, 125, 126, 129, 138, 170
United States (US), 21, 130, 138, 160–164, 166
urban governance, 1, 5–7, 194
urbanization, 4, 5, 7, 14, 185, 192, 194

V

Venezuela, 164, 165, 171
Vietnam, 21, 161, 167, 171

W

welfare, 5, 6, 9–11, 27, 37, 45, 47, 54, 96, 99, 100, 105, 106, 110–116, 118–120, 123–130, 133, 162, 177
well-being, 4, 33, 36, 54, 56, 58, 64, 65, 105, 125, 140, 147, 149, 152, 174, 176, 192–194

Y

Yangtze River Delta, 3, 18
Yangtze River Economic Belt, 3

Z

Zhaoqing, 19, 22–24, 100, 169
Zhongshan, 19, 23, 24, 100, 169
Zhuhai, 19, 23, 24, 100, 169, 186

Kolibri 360 GmbH
Ferdinand-Jühlke-Straße 7
99095 Erfurt, Deutschland
produktsicherheit@kolibri360.de